THE NEW RATIONAL MANAGER

AN UPDATED EDITION FOR A NEW WORLD

CHARLES H. KEPNER

BENJAMIN B. TREGOE

Princeton Research Press
Princeton, New Jersey

For information address
Kepner-Tregoe, Inc.
17 Research Road, P.O. Box 704
Princeton, New Jersey 08542

Library of Congress Catalog Card Number: 97-65859
Benjamin B. Tregoe and Charles H. Kepner
The New Rational Manager: An Updated Edition for a New World
Updated Edition
Princeton, New Jersey
Kepner-Tregoe, Inc., Princeton, New Jersey

Jacket design: Fairbrother and Company
Book design: CAT Design

ACKNOWLEDGMENT

A great many people have contributed to the writing of this book, far too many to name. Thousands of individuals have used the procedures and concepts of Rational Management on the job, against real concerns and problems, and have then told us of their experiences. More than a thousand client organizations around the world have shared information with us, often of a highly proprietary nature, in an effort to learn more about Rational Process. Several thousand program leaders have also shared their insights with us. Our own colleagues and associates have been particularly helpful. We could not have written this book without them, for it largely reports the experiences of others in using and promoting these ideas. We wish to thank all of these people for the contributions they have made. They are the true authors of this book.

Contents

Case Histories

FOREWORD

Best-selling business and management books seem to have a life span only slightly longer than the average fruit fly. The book is released, often with fanfare and accolades. Shortly thereafter, often within a period of only a few months, the vultures begin to circle. An article is written noting that the author has missed several key points that invalidate the book's thesis. A study is released showing that the ideas promoted in the book do not, in practice, produce an organizational or even a personal "breakthrough." Finally, a new book with a different, but equally compelling thesis is published, and the old book is consigned to the dustbin labeled "management fads." It is for this reason that any stroll through the business section of a bookstore will reveal few titles with copyrights over two or three years old. A five-year-old work, in this context, is truly a classic.

So, we come to this updated edition of *The New Rational Manager*, a book, in its two iterations, now over thirty years old, still read each year by thousands of business people around the world. How has this text, ancient by business standards, escaped relegation to the category of "yesterday's news?" Surely, the subject of the original book, *The Rational Manager*, has a great deal to do with its success. Leaders, after all, had been making decisions for centuries, and there was a fairly high likelihood that they were going to continue to make decisions and solve problems for the next few centuries. Decision making and problem solving as business topics were certainly timeless.

Timeless topics do not, however, always produce timeless books, as the hundreds of books on motivation have painfully proven. What really distinguished *The Rational Manager* was the genesis of the ideas it contained. The book is not a collection of interesting theories that suddenly appeared in a Pentecostal moment to young Tregoe and Kepner on a gloriously sunny California day in 1957.

The real inspiration that drove these two was that they didn't know a lot about problem solving and decision making, and, to their surprise, it appeared nobody else did either. True to their roots in sociology and anthropology, they set out to see how people solved problems and made decisions, rather than to theorize about these activities. Their understanding of why some people were better problem solvers and decision makers than others led to a set of empirical and repeatable processes that were described in detail in their original 1965 book.

By the early 1980s, the Kepner-Tregoe processes for problem solving and decision making had become *the approach* to problem solving and decision making in business. Most impressively, the processes had proven to be universal. In less than fifteen years, the concepts had been used in nearly every commercial and industrial environment and had demonstrated their value in over forty countries and twenty languages.

In 1981, Kepner-Tregoe published *The New Rational Manager*. This revised version of the management classic took the originally articulated problem-solving and decision-making processes and put them into an updated context, using case examples acquired since the publication of the original book. *The New Rational Manager* also offered a slightly different explanation of the processes, based upon fifteen years of experience in helping people around the world understand how these concepts worked in various organizational settings.

This new edition encompasses some of what Kepner-Tregoe, Inc. has learned since the 1981 publication of *The New Rational Manager*. Like that work, it sets the problem-solving and decision-making processes firmly in the context in which they are used. The explanation of the concepts also takes advantage of learning how to more precisely describe these processes to people from diverse backgrounds and disciplines.

When I first met Ben Tregoe in the late 1970s, I, like so many others, was in awe of the contribution he and his colleague Chuck Kepner had made to the field of management.

Now, over twenty years later, my awe is undiminished as I find myself learning daily the amazing power these ideas hold to improve the quality and the effectiveness of talented people in organizations worldwide. Today, Ben Tregoe, through the non-profit Tregoe Educational Foundation, is working diligently to build these critical concepts into the primary and secondary educational experiences that our youth are receiving. The efforts of this foundation are designed to ensure that young people begin their careers and adult lives with a solid grounding in the problem-solving and decision-making processes that can be of such value to their development and success in life.

For the thousands of us who completed school and could diagram a sentence but were at a loss to tackle our first thorny business problem, this edition of *The New Rational Manager* will prove to be the same valuable business guide as its predecessors.

T. Quinn Spitzer, Jr.
Chairman and Chief Executive Officer
Kepner-Tregoe, Inc.

ONE

THE PREMISES OF RATIONAL MANAGEMENT

IN THIS CHAPTER

The Search for Organizational Effectiveness
Four Basic Patterns of Thinking
Basic Patterns of Thinking in the Organizational Context
The Rise, Fall, and Rise Again of Teamwork
Applying the Model: Needs of the Modern Organization
Rational Management

THE SEARCH FOR ORGANIZATIONAL EFFECTIVENESS

The organization is one of mankind's all-time great inventions. An organization is intended to operate as one unit, with all its parts in efficient coordination. But, too often, it does not. The parts operate at disparate levels of efficiency, or they overlap, or they work against one another's best interests—therefore against the best interests of the organization as a whole. There is misunderstanding and miscommunication, sometimes by accident and sometimes not. Things get done, progress is made. But not enough of the right things get done as well as they should. Progress, however it is defined, does not meet expectations.

The search has been on for many years to find ways of improving organizational effectiveness. Everyone agrees that there is room for improvement, that the organization as we know it is not perfect. Failure of the organization to perform as a functional unit limits full realization of its potential. What to do about it and how to improve the organization to make it more productive and efficient are subjects of great disagreement.

1

In 1965, we wrote *The Rational Manager*. In that book, we described the concepts and techniques we had developed for using information in problem solving, decision making, and planning for the future. During the period before and after 1965, we conducted week-long workshops for twenty or so executives at a time, offering intensive training in the use of these concepts and techniques. How the executives would apply what they had learned when they returned to their jobs was left largely up to them. Nearly everyone left the workshop determined to put the new ideas to work.

Not surprisingly, results were better in the organizations that promoted and encouraged the continuing use of these ideas. Where there was little or no encouragement to use the ideas, where there were few or no other people who also had been exposed to them, their use dwindled.

Organizations recognized these facts. "Show us how to use these ideas on a team basis" became a familiar refrain. Since the mid-1960s, we have learned a great deal about the ways in which our concepts and techniques can be shared by the members of an organization in a common approach to addressing the tasks of problem solving, decision making, and planning. We have learned how to help our clients establish the teamwork they have come to value at least as highly as discrete management skills. From these clients we have learned what works and what does not. This book, then, has grown out of the experience we and they have amassed since the writing of *The Rational Manager*—years of research, trial, error, and innovation based on what they have told us they want and need.

THE GROUP AND THE TEAM

When interacting in a common cause, people can become a cohesive group. Understanding one another as individuals, being consciously sensitive to one another, and knowing how to adapt to individual peculiarities are trademarks of a functioning group that will hold together. Common regard and the psychological benefits that group members derive from the association make group activity desirable and reasonable to achieve. Such a group, however, is not a team.

A team is built primarily on the technical capabilities of its members working in pursuit of specific goals, only secondarily on attraction among the members as individuals. The members of a team must be able to tolerate one another enough to work closely together. Beyond this, all the members must be committed to a common goal and the same set of procedures for achieving that goal.

An athletic team does not win a game because the members like to be together. It wins because it plays smart, knows how to play the game better than the opposition, avoids unnecessary errors, and pulls together as a coordinated unit. Camaraderie may grow out of mutual respect for one another's abilities, but this is usually the result, not the purpose, of the team. Most certainly, it is not the mechanism that makes the team succeed. The overall goal of a team is to win, and every member keeps this firmly in mind. But when you analyze *how* a game is won, you discover that it happens because all the players know what to do and how to coordinate their efforts.

BUILDING A MANAGEMENT TEAM

Consider now the successful management team, so fervently sought after. The members are specialists in all required areas of expertise, with unique contributions to make by virtue of unique experiences and knowledge. They are necessarily different sorts of people: the entrepreneur with an aggressive, driving nature and quick insights; the financial expert, with a measuring kind of intelligence and a finely developed ability to move patiently while being pushed; the sales and marketing executive, with unbounded enthusiasm and, sometimes, unbounded impatience; the director of research and development, able to control the balance between the feasible and the desirable; and the production manager, motivated chiefly by the realities of what it takes each day to get the product out the back door. All these men and women were hired because they were different and had different things to offer. They might not choose each other's company for a weekend trip, but, given common organizational goals to work toward and a method for coordinating their efforts, they could become an unbeatable management team.

What kind of method for coordinating their efforts? One consisting of simple, common, sensible guidelines and procedures expressed in a commonly understood language. These guidelines and procedures should bridge the differences within the team and its individual functions, and allow the team members to jointly carry out their responsibilities without inhibiting each other's contributions. They should also keep the team focused and prevent the addition of new tasks that are not essential.

Just as you would give the members of an athletic team routines and techniques that would help them coordinate their individual abilities to win the game, you should give a management team common guidelines and procedures for gathering, sharing, and using information to solve problems, make decisions, and safeguard the organization's future. Now let's extend the analogy a bit further. Sports rise above local language and culture. A Brazilian soccer player, for example, can play the game in any country. He can move from one team to another because the rules are international and transcultural. The skills of good team playing are transferable in sports, and so it is in management. A competent manager can be a member of many teams, contributing wherever there is a need for his or her skills and experience, and be an active partner in the coordinated activity that makes an organization thrive.

One of our clients, a large commodity-trading corporation with operations in twenty countries, faced a series of difficult decisions. Should the company continue to rent storage and handling facilities in the Port of Antwerp or move to some other location in Europe? If the company were to seek another location, where? Once a location had been agreed upon, how should the company operate it? Build new facilities? Rent existing ones? Form a joint venture with someone having such facilities? Once the type of operation was decided, what would be the best way to communicate and sell the recommendation to all the others involved? How would foreign exchange, time and cost of shipping, and sales and marketing considerations be integrated into this decision?

A task force of executives from five nations convened in Europe. They were from different organizational levels, with different kinds of expertise and different native tongues. Many of them had never worked together—some had never even met—but all of them were familiar with Kepner-Tregoe decision-making concepts. Although some of the managers had originally learned the concepts in French, German, or Italian, everyone was fluent enough in English to use that as the common language.

Over the next two days they worked their way through the entire set of decisions. "They knew where to start, what questions to ask, what to do," said the vice president for international operations. "They really did work as a team. With that approach to decision making, a term such as 'objectives' had only one, very specific meaning. Such a simple thing, you might think, but it meant that with a minimum of internal translation, each person was able to grasp what was going on all along the way, to ask and answer questions so that everybody understood what everybody else was saying. Which is not usual in such a situation, I can tell you. I have never attended a meeting that covered so much ground, in which so little time was wasted trying to figure out what people meant by what they said."

One does not have to go to Antwerp to find different backgrounds, points of view, or ways of speaking. Put sales, production, and finance people of any organization together in the same room, and you may see the same result. Knowing where to start, what questions to ask, and what to do is just as important, regardless of whether people all come from the same geographical area or even from the same building.

A team that functions efficiently can be put together, but it must be *managed* into being. If you wish to develop an organization to its full potential, many things must be done in addition to teaching and installing a common approach and a common language for addressing management concerns. Introducing the concepts presented in this book is only the first step toward realizing their benefits. Continual, routine, shared use of the concepts must be planned for and implemented by the organization if these benefits are to be achieved and maintained.

CASE HISTORY: INSTALLING RATIONAL PROCESS

After a number of highly successful years in office, an executive in one company of a medium-sized conglomerate was promoted to the position of president and chief executive officer of the entire organization. The organization was stale. This fact was denied by no one. Under tight control by the previous president and major stockholders, with decision making confined almost exclusively to the top level, rifts and cliques had developed. One company within the conglomerate was played off against another to the detriment of overall productivity. The notion of mutual responsibility was unknown. Major problems had been ignored or swept under the rug for years. Now our executive was in the top position, not an altogether enviable one.

He contacted Kepner-Tregoe and explained that he wanted to build a management team around the use of our approaches. Five years earlier he had attended one of our workshops. He had believed then and ever since that the shared use of the ideas could do much to build teamwork among his organization's managers. Now he was able to put that belief to the test. He wanted managers at all levels—in all companies within the organization—to learn and use the Kepner-Tregoe approaches individually and together. He felt that this experience would enable the managers to begin to see themselves as managers of a single organization, not as vassals of a collection of fiefdoms.

Under his leadership, the new president and his twenty-four senior executives were the first to learn and use the concepts. They analyzed nearly thirty situations in the first week, some of which had been avoided for years. Some were resolved; decisions were made to correct many more. Soon after, another group of managers went through the same procedure. They learned to use the concepts, put them to work identifying and analyzing situations of major concern, and planned for continuing their analyses to the point of resolution. Shortly thereafter, a final group of managers followed suit. In this way, over a period of two months, eighty-four managers learned to use common approaches for addressing and resolving management concerns. New systems and procedures were established to support continuing use of these approaches.

By his actions, the new president said these things loudly and clearly, and everyone in the organization heard them:

▷ This is one organization.

▷ By using common approaches to solving problems and making decisions, we can work together cooperatively as parts of one organization.

▷ Everyone will use these approaches, beginning with me.

▷ You can think. Your knowledge and experience are important. You are in a position to effectively use the new approaches you have learned.

▷ What you do with these approaches will have an important impact on the organization.

▷ You are all valuable members of the management team.

The climate of that organization changed rapidly. People learned to talk about problems that had never been discussed openly before. They learned how to communicate good ideas so others could understand why they were important. Through the use of systematic, commonly shared approaches, they solved more problems and made better decisions than they had before. Who knows how much of this conglomerate's subsequent success was due to the use of systematic, commonly shared approaches, and how much to the sense of participation and pride engendered by the overall set of changes? The question is academic. One element without the other could not have produced the same result.

The president in this example let his people know he believed they could think. He wanted them to express their ideas; he would listen to them, and he wanted them to listen to each other. He provided them with new conceptual tools so they could do a better job of working with available information. He led the way by using the new ideas himself. He established credibility for the new approaches by putting them to the test on real and important situations. He let people learn for themselves that the approaches worked in solving the kinds of concerns faced by the conglomerate and all its components.

▷ He made a *planned intervention* into his organization.

▷ He introduced the kinds of *major changes* he believed would do the most good.

▷ He introduced a *new idea* to his people: I value your ability to think, to come up with good ideas, to express those ideas individually and cooperatively.

▷ He introduced *a means by which thinking could be coordinated and channeled.* The *climate of cooperation and teamwork followed and was a result of the intervention.*

▷ Finally, he modified the systems and procedures of the organization to *provide support* for the continuing use of the new ideas.

The new president did not set out to build teamwork or group cohesiveness as desirable things that would somehow improve the operation of the company. He did not try to heal the scars of past infighting and conflict. He let teamwork, cohesiveness, and mutual respect grow out of the experience of working together with common guidelines and procedures. He made sure the results of that experience—problems accurately identified and resolved, decisions well formulated and successfully implemented—were recognized and rewarded.

CONDITIONS FOR WORKABLE CHANGE

For years, social scientists have said that humans resist change—and so they do. But they resist only those changes they do not understand, are suspicious of, or consider to be against their interests. Humans embrace change that seems good for them or good for the world they live in and care about.

A new idea or a new expectation, in itself, will seldom bring about change. On the other hand, change can be very attractive if it is the product of a new idea or expectation that appears to be in the best interests of the people who are expected to adopt it, if it is accompanied by the means for its fulfillment, and if it results in recognition and approval. To improve an organization, we must introduce good ideas, establish the means for making them work, and provide a visible payoff for the effort involved.

No organization can reach its full potential unless it promotes and enjoys the coordination of productive activities among its members. The more complex the activities of the organization, the more need there is for coordination if the organization is to flourish. No one knows it all anymore. Teamwork is an increasingly critical element in organizational success. Fortunately, teamwork can be achieved by creating and nurturing the conditions that produce it.

FOUR BASIC PATTERNS OF THINKING

A foundation for effective teamwork can be laid by teaching the people involved to consciously use the four basic patterns of thinking they already use unconsciously. These four basic patterns of thinking are reflected in the four kinds of questions managers ask every day:

What's going on?

Why did this happen?

Which course of action should we take?

What lies ahead?

What's going on? begs for *clarification*. It asks for a sorting out, a breaking down, a key to the map of current events, a means of achieving and maintaining control. It reflects the pattern of thinking that enables us to impose order where all has been disorder, uncertainty, or confusion. It enables us to establish priorities and decide when and how to take actions that make good sense and produce good results.

Why did this happen? indicates the need for *cause-and-effect* thinking, the second basic pattern. It is the pattern that enables us to move from observing the effect of a problem to understanding its cause so that we can take appropriate actions to correct the problem or lessen its effects.

Which course of action should we take? implies that some *choice* must be made. This third basic pattern of thinking enables us to decide on the course of action most likely to accomplish a particular goal.

What lies ahead? looks into the future. This fourth basic pattern of thinking enables us to assess the problem that *might* happen, the decision that *might* be necessary next month, next year, or in five years.

Four kinds of questions. Four basic patterns of thinking. Of course, people ask other questions and think in other patterns. Nevertheless, every productive activity that takes place within an organization is related to one of these four basic patterns.

In the Beginning: Thinking Patterns for Survival

The four basic patterns of thinking have not altered substantially since the emergence of the human race. The patterns are universal and applicable to any situation. Over millions of years, through natural selection, these neurological structures—the patterns of thinking, response, and behavior that promoted survival—tended to be preserved and passed on; patterns with low survival value dropped out. Humans became adaptive (problem solving) in their way of life. The elements that made possible those patterns of thinking became part of human nature.

The ability to ask and answer these four questions—"What's going on?" "Why did this happen?" "Which course of action should we take?" and "What lies ahead?"—made civilization possible. By accumulating answers to these questions, humans learned how to deal with complexity, how to discover why things are as they are, how to make good choices, and how to anticipate the future.

Survival was guaranteed by the ability to use these patterns, to think clearly, and to communicate with one another for a common purpose. To most people, "survival" implies a teetering on the edge of death and a need for constant individual effort to remain alive. In mankind's distant past, when survival concerned the individual alone, this may indeed have been true. But survival depended more often upon the actions of a group of individuals working together, perhaps as a hunting or food-gathering group. The group became a team by working together. Teamwork ensured a food supply for everyone. Teamwork ensured shelter, protection, and a basis for living in a brutally competitive world. There was a place for physical strength, but brains combined with strength counted for far more.

Pattern 1: Assessing and Clarifying

For our earliest ancestors, the most important of the four basic patterns of thinking was the one that enabled them to assess, clarify, sort out, and impose order on a confusing situation. Humans could separate a complex situation into its components, decide what had to be done, and determine when, how, and by whom it would be done. They could set priorities and delegate tasks. This was an integral part of human adaptability—the condition that permits us to change based on an assessment of "What's going on?" Animals adapt and change in response to external changes, but human adaptation is a chosen behavior resulting from such assessment. Twenty thousand years ago, the answers to "What's going on?" may have pointed to a slowly vanishing food source, a recurring flood, or an influx of animal pests. In response, humans took the steps necessary for survival. They moved to a new location, altered eating habits, adopted better hunting practices. In short, this fundamental pattern of thinking enabled humans to prevail in a variety of surroundings and against an array of profoundly adverse conditions.

PATTERN 2: RELATING CAUSE TO EFFECT

The second basic pattern of thinking—the one that permits us to relate an event to its outcome, a cause to its effect—gave early man the ability to assign meaning to what he observed. The earliest humans did not understand such natural events as birth, illness, and death, or the rising and setting of the sun. That understanding came much later, through the accumulation, contemplation, and communication of observations about their world. It was the refinement of cause-and-effect thinking that enabled humans to move beyond mere reaction to their environment, to make use of the environment instead of being forever at its mercy.

Small children constantly ask, "But *why*?" They are exhibiting this basic thinking pattern: the desire to know why things are as they are and why they happen as they do. This desire is so basic that even an inaccurate explanation of a puzzling fact is preferable to none at all. Early man was satisfied with an explanation of a universe that revolved around the activities of supernatural beings. It was far preferable to no explanation at all for such readily perceived phenomena as the changing nature of a star-filled sky. Even today we have relatively few answers to the gigantic puzzle of the universe, but the answers we do have are comforting.

The thinking pattern we use to relate cause to effect is as basic and natural as the pattern we use to assess and clarify complex situations. Both enable us to survive, flourish, and maintain a true measure of control over our environment.

PATTERN 3: MAKING CHOICES

The third basic pattern of thinking enables us to make reasoned choices. It is the pattern that permitted early man to decide whether to continue the hunt all night or wait until morning, hide in this cave or that tree, camp on this or that side of the river. Productive, coherent action—as opposed to simple reaction to the event of the moment—depends on a sound basis for choice. In a hostile environment populated with larger, stronger, and faster creatures, random action too often could have only one end for early man, and that sudden. The development of sophistication in the making of choices, along with goal setting and consideration of the consequences of one action as opposed to another, meant that humans could sometimes eat tigers instead of vice versa.

The choice-making pattern gives rise to three major activities:

▷ Determination of purpose (to what end the choice is being made).

▷ Consideration of available options (how best to fulfill the purpose).

▷ Assessment of the relative risks of available options (which action is likely to be safest or most productive).

When faced with a choice, we are likely to spend most of our time and thought on only one of these three activities. But whatever the balance, however complex the choice, these three factors determine the kinds of choices humans have always made and continue to make.

PATTERN 4: ANTICIPATING THE FUTURE

The fourth basic pattern of thinking enables us to look into the future to see the good and bad it may hold. This ability to imagine and construe the future, even a little way ahead and that imperfectly, gave our ancestors a tremendous advantage. It permitted them to anticipate the storm and the snake, the starvation of winter, the thirst of summer. Future-oriented thinking was made possible largely by the superior development of cause-and-effect thinking (the second basic pattern described above). Humans learned to apply their knowledge of cause-and-effect relationships: of what *had happened*, and why, to what *could happen* and what the future *might hold*. They learned to take actions in the present against the possible and probable negative events of the future.

Although preventive action is as old as the human race, the thinking pattern that produces this action is less successful than our other patterns. Unfortunately, the future carries less urgency than the present. Early man learned to keep some of the food of summer against the ravages of winter—but the supply was rarely adequate. The importance of the future tiger, the future fire, or future starvation was small compared with the immediacy of the tiger five yards away, the threat of fire visibly approaching, or the reality of imminent starvation. Even today we face the unfulfilled potential of this fourth basic pattern of thinking: the ability to plan ahead, to take action today against the negative events of tomorrow.

BASIC PATTERNS OF THINKING IN THE ORGANIZATIONAL CONTEXT

Kepner-Tregoe has developed four basic Rational Processes for using and sharing information about organizational concerns. These processes are systematic procedures for making the best possible use of the four patterns of thinking. This is why the Kepner-Tregoe processes are universally applicable, regardless of cultural setting or the content against which they are applied. Whether managers are Japanese, Canadian, or Brazilian, they are all equipped—as a result of common human experiences—with identical, unchangeable patterns of thinking. It is only the content that changes.

SITUATION APPRAISAL

The Rational Process based on the first thinking pattern is called *Situation Appraisal*. It deals with the question "What's going on?" and with assessing and clarifying situations, sorting things out, breaking down complex situations into manageable components, and maintaining control of events.

When a management situation occurs, the available information is usually a confusion of the relevant and the irrelevant, the important and the inconsequential. Before anything reasonable or productive can be done, the situation must be sorted out so that its components can be seen in perspective. Priorities must be set and actions delegated. There must be some means of keeping track of information as old situations are resolved and new ones take their place.

Situation Appraisal is designed to identify problems to be solved, decisions to be made, and future events to be analyzed and planned. Therefore, we must understand the Rational Processes applicable to these areas before studying the techniques and procedures of Situation Appraisal itself. For this reason, Situation Appraisal is presented in Chapter Seven, following the explanation of the three remaining Rational Processes: Problem Analysis, Decision Analysis, and Potential Problem and Potential Opportunity Analysis.

PROBLEM ANALYSIS

The second Rational Process, called *Problem Analysis*, is based on the cause-and-effect thinking pattern. It enables us to accurately identify, describe, analyze, and resolve a situation in which *something has gone wrong without explanation*. It gives us a methodical means to extract essential information from a troublesome situation and set aside irrelevant, confusing information.

Problem Analysis is explained in Chapter Two, and examples of its use are presented in Chapter Three.

DECISION ANALYSIS

The third Rational Process, based on the choice-making pattern of thinking, is called *Decision Analysis*. Using this process, we can stand back from a decision situation and evaluate its three components. We can analyze the reasons for making the decision and examine its purpose. We can analyze the available options for achieving that purpose. We can analyze the relative risks of each alternative. From this balanced picture of the situation, we can then make the wisest and safest choice—the one that has emerged after careful consideration of all the factors.

Decision Analysis is explained in Chapter Four, and examples of its use are presented in Chapter Five.

POTENTIAL PROBLEM (OPPORTUNITY) ANALYSIS

The fourth Rational Process is based on our concern with future events—with what *might* be and what *could* happen. We call it *Potential Problem and Potential Opportunity Analysis*. A potential problem exists when we can foresee possible trouble in a given situation. No one knows for sure that trouble will develop, but no one can guarantee that it will not. This process uses what we know or can safely assume in order to avoid possible negative consequences in the future. It is based on the idea that thinking and acting beforehand to prevent a problem are more efficient than solving a problem that has been allowed to develop. Likewise, Potential Opportunity Analysis involves looking ahead and anticipating situations that we may be able to turn to our advantage. This Rational Process enables an organization to take an active hand in shaping its future.

Chapter Six deals with the ways organizations have used Potential Problem Analysis to reduce the number and severity of their problems and Potential Opportunity Analysis to benefit from their opportunities.

THE RISE, FALL, AND RISE AGAIN OF TEAMWORK

All humans have the inherent capacity to think in terms of Situation Appraisal, Problem Analysis, Decision Analysis, and Potential Problem and Potential Opportunity Analysis. These processes are basic and natural. Unfortunately, they cannot be put to work automatically, used equally well by all humans, or shared. Why should this be so?

Every person has a personal, idiosyncratic way of understanding, handling, and communicating such things as cause-and-effect relationships and choice making. Some people develop better ways than others. Some may be only moderately skilled in, say, cause-and-effect thinking, but be exceptionally good at communicating their conclusions. (They may be more successful than others who are more skilled but less communicative.) The way a person thinks can be deduced only by observing that person's behavior and paying careful attention to his or her conclusions. What information was used and how it was used remains invisible. "I don't see how you could arrive at that" is our ordinary way of expressing the fact that thinking is an inside job.

So we have a twofold need, complicated by the fact that we are often unaware of even our own thinking patterns. The actual *level of skill in thinking*—about problems, decisions, and all other organizational concerns—*needs to be as high as it can be.* That level of skill rises when people have grasped the techniques of the Rational Processes and have learned to apply their basic thinking patterns to management concerns. That's the easy part. *It is more difficult for people to learn to think together.* How can we achieve teamwork in an activity as individual and internal as thinking?

Teamwork in the use of patterns of thinking does not just happen. As discussed earlier, it must be contrived, consciously planned, or unconsciously fostered through the closeness and visibility of the team members. A group may become a team of sorts simply by working together on a particular task for a long enough time. They may come to understand each other's roles in a common task. They may come to appreciate each other's ways of thinking and learn to accommodate individual idiosyncrasies in the way information is used. Although a workable set of effective and appropriate compromises may emerge from this context, this group is not yet the full-scale, multipurpose team that can truly share in the thinking process.

HUNTING AND GATHERING: MODELS OF SUPERIOR TEAMWORK

We can gain insight into what is useful in today's organizations by speculating on the achievement and consequences of teamwork exhibited by our earliest ancestors. Teamwork is perceived as a precious commodity today, and the earliest humans had it down pat.

For early man, available information was largely visual: tracks, signs, and indications could be mutually observed and pointed out. Hunting and food-gathering groups were small—probably fifteen to forty people of all ages. The young learned from the old through intimate contact and close observation. Old and young pooled their intellectual resources by talking about what they saw. They thought aloud—a characteristic typical of people who live together closely. In this way they acquired commonly understood meanings for their words. Their language became expressive of detail, of fine distinctions of form, color, texture, and of thoughts and feelings. They developed few abstract terms. The languages of hunting and gathering groups that survive today retain these characteristics, suggesting how life's business probably was conducted by early man. Although there is no difference between their mental processes and ours, early man's need for communication led to a language rich in concrete, literal words that were open to verification and that had explicit definitions within a shared reality.

With a common experience of their environment and a common set of terms to describe it, the members of a hunting team functioned more as a single coordinated body than any comparable modern group. There was no need for their leader to give orders and directions constantly. Everyone understood what was to be done, who could do it best, and how to mesh individual efforts into a concerted whole. Entire vocabularies were committed to sign language to preserve silence. Hundreds of words could be expressed by formalized gestures, instantly and commonly understood.

It is little wonder that hunting and gathering people were able to achieve such a high order of coordination and teamwork in their activities. It was as though they carried computers within themselves, all of which were commonly programmed with a single shared set of routines and instructions. With these computers so closely aligned, even a little information was sufficient to trigger a common understanding among all those who received it. They knew what the information meant and what was to be done with it. There was little ambiguity or uncertainty in the treatment of and response to an input. Success and survival depended upon everyone's getting the same message at the same time. Teamwork among humans probably reached its highest point of development immediately before the advent of agriculture. This teamwork was made possible by the possession of a common language to express and share a common way of thinking.

The domestication of plants and animals doomed the hunting life. No longer was it necessary for the members of a band to think and exist in so parallel a fashion. Now there was specialization of function. Groups became larger, and diverse social and political units appeared.

Now there was room for different beliefs and behavior. Gone was the economic uncertainty of hunting and gathering, but gone also was the closeness such a life imposed. The intense teamwork of the hunting group disappeared forever; the luxury of individual thought and individual interpretation of ideas had arrived.

APPLYING THE MODEL: NEEDS OF THE MODERN ORGANIZATION

No one in his right mind wants to go back to the days of hunting and gathering. But it would be tremendously valuable if we could recapture that ability to work together, with even a fraction of that efficiency, to deal better with modern problem situations. Now, through contrivance and planning, we can recapture that ability and channel it to meet the needs of the modern organization.

This is not to say that the organizational team will somehow represent a modern hunting group armed with ballpoint pens instead of bows and arrows. Hunters' ways of thinking were totally aligned, and their lives were totally aligned. What is required today is not total teamwork in all aspects of life; rather, it is a selective, functional teamwork that can be turned on when needed, limited to those activities where it will be most productive. What is required is teamwork that can be summoned to handle organizational problems yet leave team members free to act as individuals in all other respects.

When we need answers to specific questions, we need an approach that can be invoked and shared regardless of content. The "What's going on?" applies order to complexity and confusion. The "Why did this happen?" applies to any set of circumstances in which the cause-and-effect relationship is obscure. The "Which course of action should we take?" applies to any situation in which one course of action must be adopted over others. The "What lies ahead?" must be thoughtfully considered to protect and nurture the organization's future.

We need the kinds of accurate communication and common understanding that prevailed in the hunting bands. These must be modernized, selectively adapted to current conditions, and directed toward

THE NEW RATIONAL MANAGER

the critical functions of organizational activity where teamwork is most essential.

All of this can be done. It is exactly what was done by the new president mentioned earlier in this chapter. He brought into his organization a common language and common approaches for using the four basic patterns of thinking to produce order, resolve problems, make good choices, and protect against future threats. His people learned to share this language and use these approaches. Their acceptance of his new and different *modus operandi* came as a result of their own experience.

The new, common language they learned was not a long list of jargon that required a month to memorize. It consisted of down-to-earth words and phrases that conveyed an exact meaning to everyone exposed to that language. Such sentences as "I'm not sure you really understood what I meant" were heard less and less frequently. The new, common approaches worked when they were applied to actual situations within the organization. The individual payoff for adopting the new behavior was great; the organizational payoff was greater. The people of the organization soon were equipped to act as a team in the fullest sense of the word.

RATIONAL MANAGEMENT

Such results begin to occur only after planning and plain hard work. Rational management, which means *making full use of the thinking ability of the people in an organization,* is a continuing process. Use of the ideas—and their benefits—will eventually fade out if they are not continually used and reinforced.

Rational Management aims at major change and therefore demands major commitment. The four Rational Processes we will describe in the next several chapters constitute an explicit, logical system that can have a far-reaching impact within an organization. But this system cannot be introduced by halfheartedly sprinkling a few ideas and suggestions among a random mix of the organization's people in the hope that something good will happen. We must identify the people who have the greatest influence on the important issues facing the organization. They should be the first to learn and use the new ideas. We must identify the people who provide them with information. We must identify those who will implement the conclusions that come out of the use of the ideas. In short, it is imperative to pinpoint *all the people within an organization who make things happen*. The objective is to move the organization closer to its full potential. This can only be done by introducing teamwork based on the continuing *conscious* use of common approaches expressed in a simple, common language and directed toward resolution of an organization's important concerns.

TWO

PROBLEM ANALYSIS

IN THIS CHAPTER

The Conditions and Skills of Problem Solving
The Structure of a Problem
The Process of Problem Analysis

THE CONDITIONS AND SKILLS OF PROBLEM SOLVING

People like to solve problems. While people in organizations enjoy the rewards that go with success, they also enjoy the process that produces success. Regardless of their organizational level, they will not only accept but will also seek problem-solving opportunities as long as four conditions exist:

▷ They possess the skills needed to solve the problems that arise in their jobs.

▷ They experience success in using those skills.

▷ They are rewarded for successfully solving their problems.

▷ They do not fear failure.

The converse is equally true. People will avoid problem-solving situations when they are unsure of how to solve their problems, when they do not experience success after trying to solve a problem, when they feel that their efforts are not appreciated, and when they sense that they have less to lose either by doing nothing or by shifting responsibility. This chapter is concerned with the first condition: *the skills that make problem-solving behavior possible.* The other conditions for habitual, successful problem solving will be discussed in subsequent chapters.

Problem Analysis provides the skills needed *to explain any situation in which an expected level of performance is not being achieved and in which the cause of the unacceptable performance is unknown.* If "any situation" seems too strong a phrase, remember that we are concerned with *the way in which information is used to approach deviations in performance.* These deviations may appear in the performance of people or the performance of systems, policies, or equipment, that is, anything in the work environment that may deviate from expected performance with no known cause. As long as this structure applies, the techniques of Problem Analysis also apply.

In this chapter, we will explain and demonstrate Problem Analysis by examining a problem that occurred in a production plant owned by one of our clients. We have selected this problem as a case vehicle because it is concrete and easily understood, therefore ideal for introducing the techniques of Problem Analysis. In Chapter Three, we will describe the use of these techniques in a variety of industries, at differing organizational levels, and over a wide spectrum of problem situations.

CAUSE AND EFFECT

Problem solving requires cause-and-effect thinking, one of the four basic thinking patterns described in Chapter One. A problem is the visible effect of a cause that resides somewhere in the past. We must relate the effect we observe to its exact cause. Only then can we be sure of taking appropriate corrective action—action that can correct the problem and keep it from recurring.

Everyone has experienced the "solved" problem that turns out not to have been solved at all. A simple example is the car that stalls in traffic, goes into the shop for costly repair, and then stalls again on the way home. If the cause of the stalling is a worn-out distributor and the action taken is a readjustment of the carburetor, then the car will continue to stall. Superior problem solving is not the result of knowing all the things that can produce a particular effect and then choosing a corrective action directed at the most frequently observed cause. Yet this is the way most people approach problems on the job. Problem Analysis is a systematic problem-solving process. It does not reject the value of experience or of technical knowledge. Rather, it helps us to make the best use of that experience and knowledge. Our objectivity about a situation is often sacrificed under pressure. When a quick solution to a problem is required, it is too easy to rely on memories of what happened in the past, on the solution that was successful once before, or on the remedy that corrected an apparently similar problem. This is the most common approach to problem solving, and problem solving by extrapolation is a tough habit to break despite its relatively poor payoff in appropriate, lasting corrective actions. A chief purpose of this chapter and the next is to demonstrate that the habit can be broken. Through the experiences of people in our client organizations, we will show that the effort required to adopt a systematic approach to problem solving is small in light of the results that follow.

THE CRITERIA THAT DEFINE A PROBLEM

The following are typical examples of problems. They meet our definition of a problem because in each one an expected level of performance is not being achieved, and the cause of the unacceptable performance is unknown.

> "From the day we introduced the computer, we've had nothing but trouble in getting our inventories to balance. I just don't understand it."

> "Emory Jackson was referred to us as an outstanding engineer, but he certainly hasn't fulfilled expectations in this department."

> "Our Number Eleven paper machine never produces more than 80 percent of its design capacity, no matter what we try."

> "Some days we meet our schedules without any trouble. Other days we can't meet them at all. There just doesn't seem to be any good reason for the discrepancy."

> "The system worked well for months. Then, in the middle of the morning three weeks ago, it went dead. It's still dead, and we don't have the slightest idea of what happened."

Despite disparities in content, seriousness, and scope of these five examples, they all indicate a degree of performance failure, confusion or total lack of understanding about its cause, and the need to find a correct explanation.

There are other kinds of problem situations that do not meet our specific definition. For example:

"There is no way we can meet our deadline on the project with our present staff and no way we can get authorization to bring on anyone new. This is a serious problem. . . ."

This statement represents the need for one or more decisions. It does *not* represent a deviation between expected and actual performance that is of *unknown* cause. In this example, resolution will consist not of an explanation as to why the situation arose but of a choice. Those concerned must identify some course of action that can produce satisfactory results under less-than-optimal conditions.

Compromises will probably be identified. Objectives for meeting the goal may have to be reviewed, reshuffled, or altered. Any number of potential actions may be considered. But the cause of the difficulty is known all too well. Decision Analysis, which is presented in Chapters Four and Five, is useful for resolving this kind of dilemma. A decision requires answers to the following questions: "How?" "Which?" "To what purpose?" A problem always requires an answer to the question "Why?"

THE STRUCTURE OF A PROBLEM

A performance standard is achieved when all conditions required for acceptable performance are operating as they should. This is true for everything in the work environment: people, systems, departments, and pieces of equipment. If there is an alteration in one or more of these conditions—that is, if some kind of change occurs—then it is possible that performance will alter, too. That change may be for better or for worse. Sometimes conditions improve, positive changes occur, and things go better than expected. But an unexpected rise in performance seldom triggers the same urgent response as an unexpected decline. The more serious the effect of the decline, the more pressure there is to find the cause and do something about it.

We may visualize the structure of a problem as shown in Figure 1.

FIGURE 1

STRUCTURE OF A PROBLEM

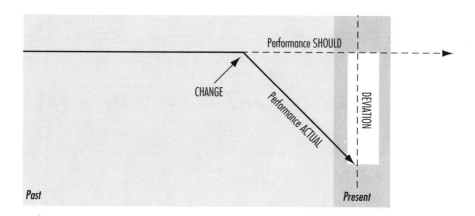

Performance SHOULD

CHANGE

Performance ACTUAL

DEVIATION

Past

Present

If performance once met the SHOULD and no longer does, then a change has occurred. At the outset of problem solving, we do not know exactly what that change consisted of or when it occurred.

The search for cause usually entails a search for a specific change that has caused a decline in performance. In some cases, however, a negative deviation in performance—a so-called Day One Deviation—has always existed. An example is an equipment unit that "was never any good *from the day it came on line….*" In this instance, using our terminology, ACTUAL has always been below SHOULD. This kind of problem can be visualized as shown in Figure 2.

FIGURE 2

STRUCTURE OF A DAY ONE DEVIATION

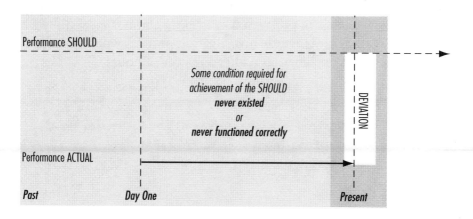

Performance SHOULD

Some condition required for achievement of the SHOULD never existed or never functioned correctly

DEVIATION

Performance ACTUAL

Past

Day One

Present

The Process of Problem Analysis

Both kinds of problems—a current deviation from formerly acceptable performance and a performance that has never met expectations—can be approached through the techniques of Problem Analysis.

The techniques of Problem Analysis are divided into these activities:

▷ State the problem.

▷ Specify the problem.

▷ Develop possible causes from knowledge and experience or distinctions and changes.

▷ Test possible causes against the specification.

▷ Determine the most probable cause.

▷ Verify assumptions, observe, experiment, or try a fix and monitor.

Case History: The Leaking Soybean Oil Filter

The history of our true case vehicle is a necessary prelude to demonstrating the Problem Analysis techniques. The Case of the Leaking Soybean Oil Filter may never make a best-selling mystery, but, as with most real-life mysteries, to the people who had to live with it, explain it, and correct it, it was of far more interest than any best-seller. Although Problem Analysis was used *after* the explanation had been arrived at (quite accidentally), it demonstrated—to the people who had worked on the problem inefficiently and unsuccessfully for several days—that a systematic investigation process would have produced the correct explanation within a matter of hours.

> Our client is a major food processor. One of the company's plants produces oil from corn and soybeans. The five units that filter the oil are located in one building. On the day the problem was first observed, a foreman rushed into his supervisor's office: "Number One Filter is leaking. There's oil all over the floor of the filter house."

The foreman guessed that the leak was caused by valves loosening up from vibration. This had happened once before. "Number One sits right next to the main feedwater pump and gets shaken up more than the other four filters." A mechanic tried to find the leak but couldn't tell much because the oil had already been cleaned up. The lid fastener looked all right. After examining the pipes, valves, and walls of the filter chamber, the mechanic concluded that the oil had spilled from another source.

The next day there was more oil. Another mechanic traced the leak to the cleanout hatch, but that didn't help much. Why should the cleanout hatch leak? It looked perfectly all right. Just to be on the safe side, he replaced the gasket even though it looked new. The hatch continued to leak. "Maintenance people just aren't closing it tight enough after they clean it out," someone volunteered. "There are a couple of new guys on maintenance here since the shifts were changed around last month. I wonder if they're using a torque wrench like they're supposed to. This happened to us once before because somebody didn't use a torque wrench." No one could say for sure.

The next day an operator slipped on the oil slick floor and hurt his back. The cleanup task was becoming more than irksome, according to some outspoken comments overheard by the foreman. A few people began grumbling about promises made at the last safety meeting to improve conditions in the filter house. Two days later the plant manager got wind of the situation, called in the supervisor and the foreman, and made it clear that he expected a solution to the oil-mess problem within the day.

That afternoon someone asked, "How come the gasket on the Number One Filter has square corners? They always used to have rounded corners." A quick check of the filters revealed that the other four filters still had round-cornered gaskets. This led to the discovery that the square-cornered gasket on the Number One Filter had been installed the evening before the leak was first noticed. It had come from a new lot purchased from a new supplier who charged 10 cents less per unit. This led to the question "How can they sell them for 10 cents less?" and to the subsequent observation "Because they don't work."

The new gasket was inspected and compared with the old gaskets. It was easy to see that the new one was thinner and uneven. It was equally clear that this gasket had never been designed to be used on this kind of filter unit. It would always leak. It should never have been installed. Additional gaskets were purchased from the original supplier and installed. The leaking stopped.

Looking back at the problem, a few people said they had had ideas about its cause but couldn't explain how the cause they had thought of could have produced the effect. Actions taken before the problem was solved had been based on experience, on similar problems in the past, on standard operating procedures, and on hunches. The faulty gasket had even been replaced with an identical (and therefore equally useless) one "just to be on the safe side."

Sometimes we stumble onto the cause of a problem. Sometimes we take an action that just happens to correct the effect, although the cause is never explained fully. In the latter case—cause is unknown and the action that solved the problem is one of many taken at the same time—a recurrence of the effect will mean that all those same actions may have to be repeated to ensure correction!

At other times the cause is neither discovered nor stumbled upon, and *no* action corrects the effect. An interim, or holding, action must be devised so that the operation can live with the problem until its true cause is found—or until problem-solving roulette produces a winning number. That happy accident occurs less often than managers would like. Interim action gradually becomes standard operating procedure.

The Case of the Leaking Soybean Oil Filter was reconstructed as a Problem Analysis for plant employees who were learning to use the techniques. It made the point very well that the roulette approach, however familiar, produces frustration and misunderstanding more often than results. Motivation to use a systematic approach grew as soon as the employees recognized that they had worked for several days on a mess that could have been corrected permanently in a matter of hours.

The remainder of this chapter is a step-by-step demonstration of Problem Analysis, exactly as it could have been used when the leaking oil filter problem was first observed.

STATE THE PROBLEM

Before we can describe, analyze, and explain a problem, we must define it. We do this with the *problem statement,* or the name of the problem. It is important to name the problem precisely because all the work to follow—all the description, analysis, and explanation we will undertake—will be directed at correcting the problem *as it has been named.* The name of this problem is "Number One Filter Leaking Oil."

This seems obvious enough. But suppose we had worded the problem statement "Oil on the Filter House Floor." Any way you look at it, oil on the floor is certainly a deviation from SHOULD. Yet it is of known cause, and all that a logical analysis can produce as an explanation is "Number One Filter Leaking Oil." This is where we want to begin our search, not end it.

However simple or complex a problem may seem at the outset, it is always worth a minute or two to ask, "Can the effect of this problem *as we have described it* in the problem statement be explained now?" If it can, as in "Oil on the Floor," we must back up to the point at which we can no longer explain the problem statement.

Vague or generalized problem statements that begin with such phrases as "Low productivity on . . ." or "Sub-standard performance by . . ." must be reworded into specific problem statements that name one object, or kind of object, and one malfunction, or kind of malfunction, for which we wish to discover and explain cause. We must describe exactly what we see, feel, hear, smell, or taste that tells us there is a deviation.

It is tempting to combine two or more deviations in a single problem-solving effort or to try to bunch a bevy of seemingly related problems into one overall problem. Nearly everyone has attended meetings during which two or more distinct problems were tied ankle to ankle in a kind of problem-solving sack race. This procedure is almost always inefficient and unproductive.

SPECIFY THE PROBLEM

Once we have a precise problem statement, the next step in Problem Analysis is to describe the problem in detail or to specify it in its four dimensions:

WHAT– the identity of the deviation we are trying to explain

WHERE– the location of the deviation

WHEN– the timing of the deviation

EXTENT– the magnitude of the deviation

FIGURE 3

SPECIFY THE *IS*

	SPECIFYING QUESTIONS	IS—PERFORMANCE DEVIATION
WHAT	WHAT specific object has the deviation?	Number 1 Filter
	WHAT is the specific deviation?	Leaking oil
WHERE	WHERE is the object when the deviation is observed (geographically)?	At the northeast corner of the filter house
	WHERE is the deviation on the object?	At the cleanout hatch
WHEN	WHEN was the deviation observed first (in clock and calendar time)?	3 days ago, at the start of the shift
	WHEN since that time has the deviation been observed? Any pattern?	Continuously, on all shifts
	WHEN, in the object's history or life cycle, was the deviation first observed?	As soon as oil goes into the filter, at the start of the shift
EXTENT	HOW MANY objects have the deviation?	Number 1 Filter only
	WHAT is the size of a single deviation?	5-10 gallons of oil leaked per shift
	HOW MANY deviations are on each object?	N/A
	WHAT is the trend? (…in the object?) (…in the number of occurrences of the deviation?) (…in the size of the deviation?)	Stable—leaks daily, about the same amount

THE NEW RATIONAL MANAGER

Information on the effects of any deviation will fall within one of these four dimensions. Within each we ask *specifying questions* that will flesh out our description of how the deviation presents itself to our senses. The answers to the questions will give us exactly the kinds of information that will be most useful for the analysis. See Figure 3.

In the dimension of EXTENT, the response to "How many deviations are on each object?" is N/A—not applicable. This illustrates the fact that every problem is unique, and its context reflects that uniqueness. As a result, one or more of the specifying questions may not produce useful information. Nevertheless, we ask. We always attempt to answer every question. Skipping questions that probably don't matter destroys the objectivity we are working so diligently to maintain.

Given only a few variations in wording, any problem can be described by answering the specifying questions—whether the problem concerns a unit, a system, part or all of a function, or human performance. Our choice of wording should indicate that our five senses have detected a problem. When we are dealing with a human performance problem, however, we must alter the questions to reflect the fact that we are observing people and behavior, not units and malfunctions. There are other variations on the basic techniques. When we are working with human performance, we usually need to use a combination of Rational Process ideas—not only those found within the Problem Analysis process. For these reasons, human performance is dealt with separately in Chapter Eight, after all the Rational Processes have been explained.

Once we have described our problem in the four dimensions of WHAT, WHERE, WHEN, and EXTENT, we have the first half of the total specification we want. It is the second half that will render it a useful tool for analysis.

IS AND IS NOT: A BASIS OF COMPARISON

We know that our problem IS "Number One Filter Leaking Oil." What would we gain by identifying a unit that COULD BE leaking but IS NOT? Or the locations at which oil COULD BE observed to leak but IS NOT? Such data would give us what we need to conduct an analysis: *a basis of comparison*. Once we have identified COULD BE but IS

NOT data, we will also be able to identify the peculiar factors that isolate our problem: exactly what it is, where it is observed, when it is observed, and its extent or magnitude. These peculiar factors will lead us closer to the problem's cause.

Suppose for a moment that you have two identical potted plants growing in your office. One thrives but the other does not. If you take the wilting plant out of the office and ask someone about the probable cause for its sorry appearance, you will get any number of educated guesses. But if the same person observes that the two plants have not been receiving identical treatment (the thriving plant is on a sunny window sill; the wilting one, in a dim corner), speculation as to the cause will be immediate and more accurate than it could have been without a basis of comparison. *Regardless of the content of a problem, nothing is more conducive to sound analysis than some relevant basis of comparison.*

In Problem Analysis, we conduct the search for bases of comparison in all four dimensions of the specification. We will now repeat our problem statement and the specifying questions and answers, and add a third column called Closest Logical Comparison. In this column, we will establish the problem as it COULD BE but IS NOT in terms of WHAT, WHERE, WHEN, and EXTENT. The closer the comparison, the more tightly the dimensions of the problem will be defined. Let us see how this works out in Figure 4.

Note that the second specifying question in the WHAT dimension does not suggest a close, logical comparison. In this case, leaking oil cannot be compared usefully with any other specific malfunction with the hatch. The decision as to what is close and what is logical must rest with the judgment of the problem solver or the team. In many cases, it is extremely important to identify the malfunction that COULD BE but IS NOT in order to narrow the scope of the search for cause. Each Problem Analysis is unique to the content of each problem.

Once we have identified bases of comparison in all four dimensions, we are able to isolate key distinguishing features of the problem. This approach is similar to describing the outlines of a shadow. With the completion of the IS NOT data in our specification, the outlines begin to suggest the components capable of having cast the shadow.

THE NEW RATIONAL MANAGER

FIGURE 4

SPECIFY THE PROBLEM

PROBLEM STATEMENT: Number One Filter Leaking Oil

SPECIFYING QUESTIONS	IS—PERFORMANCE DEVIATION	IS NOT—CLOSEST LOGICAL COMPARISON
WHAT WHAT specific object has the deviation?	IS Number 1 Filter	COULD BE but IS NOT Numbers 2-5
WHAT is the specific deviation?	IS leaking oil	(No logical comparison)
WHERE WHERE is the object when the deviation is observed (geographically)?	IS observed at the northeast corner of the filter house	COULD BE but IS NOT observed at other filter locations
WHERE is the deviation on the object?	IS observed at the cleanout hatch	COULD BE but IS NOT observed at other filter locations, at cleanout hatches of Numbers 2-5
WHEN WHEN was the deviation observed first (in clock and and calendar time)?	IS first observed 3 days ago, at the start of the shift	COULD BE but IS NOT observed before 3 days ago
WHEN since that time has the deviation been observed? Any pattern?	IS observed continuously, on all shifts	COULD BE but IS NOT observed when the unit is not in use
WHEN, in the object's history or life cycle, was the deviation first observed?	IS first observed as soon as oil goes into the filter, at the start of the shift	COULD BE but IS NOT observed at a time later on in the shift
EXTENT HOW MANY objects have the deviation?	IS Number 1 Filter only	COULD BE but IS NOT Numbers 2-5
WHAT is the size of a single deviation?	IS 5-10 gallons of oil leaked per shift	COULD BE but IS NOT less than 5 or more than 10 gallons per shift
HOW MANY deviations are on each object?	N/A	N/A
WHAT is the trend? (...in the object?) (...in the number of occurrences of the deviation?) (...in the size of the deviation?)	Stable—leaks daily, about the same amount	COULD BE but IS NOT increasing or decreasing in frequency or in size

DEVELOP POSSIBLE CAUSES FROM KNOWLEDGE AND EXPERIENCE OR DISTINCTIONS AND CHANGES

KNOWLEDGE AND EXPERIENCE

We usually have ideas about the possible causes of a problem, but, given the benefit of the IS/IS NOT comparison, some new ideas may come to mind while others may seem less plausible. Experts and those close to the problem may have ideas about possible causes but will still find the information in the specification useful. Brainstorming is an effective technique to use to quickly list many ideas without evaluating or discussing them. The purpose is to cast a large net in search for the true cause.

In all cases, a short statement that describes how the cause works is needed. Simply pointing to the gasket as the cause will not help us confirm or eliminate it as a cause. What about the gasket creates the leak? Is it too large, too small, too hard, or too soft? Saying that uneven surfaces of gaskets allow leakage suggests a different cause and, perhaps, a different fix than saying that the square corners cause the gasket to seal incorrectly.

If this search yields only implausible causes, or produces far more causes than can reasonably be evaluated in the time available, then consider distinctions and changes.

DISTINCTIONS

Number One Filter leaks; Numbers Two through Five might, but they do not. What is *distinctive* about the Number One Filter *compared with the others?* What stands out?

As the question "What is distinctive about...?" is applied to all four dimensions of a problem, our analysis begins to reveal important clues to the cause of the problem—*clues*, not answers or explanations. Let us return for a moment to the wilted potted plant in a dim corner of the office. With a basis of comparison (the identical plant that thrives on a sunny window sill), we quickly see a factor that is highly suggestive of cause. We said earlier that anyone observing this difference in treatment is likely to offer a quick opinion about the plant's wilted appearance. This natural cause-and-effect thinking pattern that we all employ ensures that we all use this kind of reasoning when confronted with a problem *provided that we observe a distinction that taps something in our experience.*

At this point in Problem Analysis, we identify the distinctions that characterize the problem in terms of WHAT, WHERE, WHEN, and EXTENT when compared with the WHAT, WHERE, WHEN, and EXTENT that *might* characterize it but do not. We will now repeat all the columns we have already developed and add a column headed What Is Distinctive About…. This is shown in Figure 5. The question we ask to elicit distinctions is this: "What is distinctive about (the IS data) when compared with (the IS NOT data)?"

The four dimensions of a specification yield distinctions of differing quantity and quality. One or more dimensions frequently yield no distinctions at all. Obviously, the goal is quality: new information that is not already in the specification and that is *truly a distinction* for only the IS.

In Figure 1, the arrowhead indicates change at a point between past acceptable performance—at which time the SHOULD was being achieved—and current unacceptable ACTUAL performance.

Managers who may never have heard of Problem Analysis know that a decline in a formerly acceptable performance suggests that something has changed; common sense tells them to look for that change. But such a search can be extremely frustrating when the manager is faced with an array of changes—changes that are known and planned, changes that are unforeseen or unknown, which continually creep into every operation.

Instead of searching through this mass of changes to find that one, elusive, problem-creating change, we examine the one, small, clearly defined area in which we can be sure of finding it: distinctions in the IS data when compared with the COULD BE but IS NOT data. This is the next step in Problem Analysis.

FIGURE 5

USE DISTINCTIONS

PROBLEM STATEMENT: Number One Filter Leaking Oil

	SPECIFYING QUESTIONS	*IS—PERFORMANCE DEVIATION*
WHAT	WHAT specific object has the deviation?	IS Number 1 Filter
	WHAT is the specific deviation?	IS leaking oil
WHERE	WHERE is the object when the deviation is observed (geographically)?	IS observed at the northeast corner of the filter house
	WHERE is the deviation on the object?	IS observed at the cleanout hatch
WHEN	WHEN was the deviation observed first (in clock and calendar time)?	IS first observed 3 days ago, at the start of the shift
	WHEN since that time has the deviation been observed? Any pattern?	IS observed continuously, on all shifts
	WHEN, in the object's history or life cycle, was the deviation first observed?	IS first observed as soon as oil goes into the filter, at the start of the shift
EXTENT	HOW MANY objects have the deviation?	IS Number 1 Filter only
	WHAT is the size of a single deviation?	IS 5-10 gallons of oil leaked per shift
	HOW MANY deviations are on each object?	N/A
	WHAT is the trend? (…in the object?) (…in the number of occurrences of the deviation?) (…in the size of the deviation?)	Stable—leaks daily, about the same amount

IS NOT—CLOSEST LOGICAL COMPARISON	WHAT IS DISTINCTIVE ABOUT...
COULD BE but IS NOT Numbers 2-5	The Number 1 Filter, when compared with Numbers 2-5? *The Number 1 Filter has a square-cornered gasket; the other 4 have rounded gaskets.*
(No logical comparison)	
COULD BE but IS NOT observed at other filter locations	The northeast corner of the filter house when compared with other filter locations? *This location is nearest to the feedwater pump, exposing the Number 1 Filter to higher vibration levels than the other 4 filters.*
COULD BE but IS NOT observed at the cleanout hatches of Numbers 2-5	The cleanout hatch when compared with other cleanout hatches? *(No information not already noted above.)*
COULD BE but IS NOT observed before 3 days ago	3 days ago, at the start of the shift, when compared with the period of time before that? *There was a monthly maintenance check just prior to the start of the shift 3 days ago.*
COULD BE but IS NOT observed when the unit is not in use	Continuous leaking, on all shifts, when compared with not leaking when the unit is not in use? *Oil flows through the unit under pressure only when the filter is in use.*
COULD BE but IS NOT observed at a time later on in the shift	The start of any shift when compared with any time later on during the shift? *It's the first time oil comes into the filter under pressure. The cleanout hatch is opened and refastened daily at every shift.*
COULD BE but IS NOT Numbers 2-5	(No information not already noted above.)
COULD BE but IS NOT less than 5 or more than 10 gallons per shift	5-10 gallons of oil leaked per shift when compared with less than 5 or more than 10?
N/A	N/A
COULD BE but IS NOT increasing or decreasing in frequency or in size	N/A

What changes are most likely to suggest the cause of our problem? Those that are most relevant to its peculiar features of WHAT, WHERE, WHEN, and EXTENT. Suppose there had been eight operational and/ or maintenance changes in the filter house over the past six months. Even if we knew the exact number and kind of changes that had occurred, which ones would we want to examine first? Six changes that affected all five filters? Or two that affected only the Number One Filter? Or seven that affected operations during the past six months? Or one that was instituted only a day or a week before the problem was first observed?

When we ask the following question of each distinction, "What changed in, on, around, or about this distinction?", we are going straight for the changes capable of suggesting cause. We are bypassing any changes that *may have occurred but are not relevant* to the key features of this problem. The relationship of distinctions and changes and the relationship of both to the generation of possible causes are very important.

Suppose that, when the problem was first recognized, a problem analyst had been presented with the distinction of the square-cornered gasket on the leaking filter. He or she might not have grasped its significance. Why not? Because unimportant distinctions abound between one thing and another and between one period of time and another. Compare any two pieces of equipment that have been in place for a few years and you will usually find a number of distinctive features about each. Parts have broken and been repaired. New, perhaps slightly different, parts have replaced worn-out ones. Operating procedures may vary slightly from one to the other for any of a dozen reasons.

The leaking filter might have had a different type of gasket for five years yet never have leaked until recently. *But when this distinction is appreciated as representing a change*—and a change that occurred the evening before the leaking was observed—*its significance as a clue is greatly heightened.*

To the distinctions of the IS data as compared with the IS NOT data, we now add the change question and the answers to it. This is shown in Figure 6.

THE NEW RATIONAL MANAGER

FIGURE 6

USE CHANGES

PROBLEM STATEMENT: Number One Filter Leaking Oil

	WHAT IS DISTINCTIVE ABOUT...	*WHAT CHANGED IN, ON, AROUND, OR ABOUT THIS DISTINCTION?*
WHAT	The Number 1 Filter, when compared with Numbers 2-5? *The Number 1 Filter has a square-cornered gasket; the other 4 have rounded gaskets.*	The square-cornered gasket is a new type, installed for the first time 3 days ago at the monthly maintenance check.
WHERE	The northeast corner of the filter house when compared with other filter locations? *This location is nearest to the feedwater pump, exposing the Number 1 Filter to higher vibration levels than the other 4 filters.*	Nothing. Location and vibration levels have been the same for years.
	The cleanout hatch when compared with other cleanout hatches? *(No information not already noted above.)*	
WHEN	3 days ago, at the start of the shift, when compared with the period of time before that? *There was a monthly maintenance check just prior to the start of the shift 3 days ago.*	A new type of square-cornered gasket was installed for the first time 3 days ago, as noted above.
	Continuous leaking, on all shifts, when compared with not leaking when the unit is not in use? *Oil flows through the unit under pressure only when the filter is in use.*	Nothing.
	The start of any shift when compared with any time later on during the shift? *It's the first time oil comes into the filter under pressure. The cleanout hatch is opened and refastened daily at every shift.*	Nothing. Nothing. The filter has been cleaned, hatch refastened on every shift for years.
EXTENT	(No information not already noted above.)	N/A
	5-10 gallons of oil leaked per shift when compared with less than 5 or more than 10?	Nothing.
	N/A	N/A
	N/A	N/A

Somewhere in the distinctions and changes that emerge during Problem Analysis lies the explanation of cause—provided that all relevant information about the problem has been obtained and included. Several possible causes will sometimes emerge. In some cases, pieces of information must be knitted together to provide a satisfactory explanation of the problem's cause. Two changes operating in combination may produce a performance deviation that one of those changes alone cannot.

We identify possible causes by asking the following question of each item in the categories of distinctions and changes: "How could this distinction (or this change) have produced the deviation described in the problem statement?" Again, as with using knowledge and experience, it is necessary to develop statements that explain how the cause creates the deviation. Beginning at the top of Figure 6—distinctions and changes relative to WHAT—we immediately notice the combination of a distinction and a change:

Possible Cause: The square-cornered gasket (a distinction between the Number One Filter and the other four) from the new supplier (a change represented in that distinction) is too thin and unevenly constructed. This caused the Number One Filter to leak oil.

Other possible causes can be generated from the distinctions and changes in our analysis. Knowing the true cause, they will not appear to be strong contenders, but they are possible. We will describe them in order to help explain the testing step of Problem Analysis in the following section.

One possible cause can be derived from the WHERE dimension. It was noted that the northeast corner of the filter house, where the Number One Filter stands, contains the feedwater pump. This distinction has some significance: The leaking filter is exposed to considerably greater vibration than the other four filters. This represents no change. It has always been that way. We know from the specification, moreover, that the current leakage is occurring at the cleanout hatch, not at the valves. When vibration caused leakage in the past, it occurred at the valves. Nevertheless, at this point in Problem Analysis, we should generate all reasonable possible causes, without focusing only on the problem's true cause. Vibration is given the benefit of the doubt.

Possible Cause: Vibration from the feedwater pump in the northeast corner of the filter house (distinction in the dimension of WHERE) causes the Number One Filter to leak oil.

TEST POSSIBLE CAUSES AGAINST THE SPECIFICATION

The last statement is listed as a possible cause simply because it is possible. That's important. By including *all* possible causes, we lose nothing, maintain our objectivity, and reduce the incidence of conflict and disagreement in the explanation of a problem. In the testing step of Problem Analysis, we let the facts in the specification perform the function of judging the relative likelihood of possible causes.

We ask of each possible cause, "*If* this is the true cause of the problem, then how does it explain each dimension in the specification?" The true cause must explain each and every aspect of the deviation, since the true cause created the *exact* effect we have specified. Effects are specific, not general. Testing for cause is a process of matching the details of a postulated cause with the details of an observed effect to see whether that cause could have produced that effect. For example:

If vibration from the feedwater pump is the true cause of the Number One Filter leaking oil, **then** how does it explain **why**:

WHERE: Leaking IS observed at the cleanout hatch; IS NOT observed at the cleanout hatches of Numbers Two through Five.

WHEN: Leaking IS observed three days ago; IS NOT observed before three days ago.

Vibration previously affected the valves and *not* the cleanout hatch. It doesn't make sense to say that vibration causes a cleanout hatch to leak. Why would vibration cause leaking to begin three days ago and not before? Unless we are willing to make some rather broad assumptions, we cannot make this possible cause fit the observed effects. Our judgment tells us that this is an improbable explanation at best.

Another possible cause is suggested by the distinctions and changes found in our analysis:

Possible Cause: New maintenance people (a distinction that also represents a change in the WHEN dimension) are not using a torque wrench to close the cleanout hatch. This is causing the Number One Filter to leak.

Testing this possible cause with our "If. . .then. . ." question, we quickly find ourselves at a loss to explain why the leaking occurs only on the Number One filter and not on the other four. After all, the same people are responsible for maintaining all five filters. If they failed to use a torque wrench on the Number One Filter, why would they do so on all the others? We would have to make broad assumptions to make the cause fit the observed effects: "Well, they probably use the torque wrench on the other four. But back in the northeast corner of the filter house, where it's so dark and there's all that vibration from the feedwater pump, they choose to forget it and don't tighten the cleanout hatch the way they should." This explanation is more improbable than the other one.

The actual cause fits all the details of the effect as specified: a new, thinner, square-cornered gasket that was put on the Number One Filter three days ago during the monthly maintenance check. It explains the WHAT, WERE, WHEN, and EXTENT information. It requires no assumptions at all to make it work. It fits as hand does to glove, as cause and effect *must* fit. There is less likelihood of the other possible causes being true.

DETERMINE THE MOST PROBABLE CAUSE

By now in our analysis, we will have identified *the most likely possible cause* that explains the deviation better than any of the other possible causes. But this most likely possible cause seldom proves to be, beyond the shadow of a doubt, the true cause. Of course this is not always the case. Often, several possible causes, including the true cause, carry assumptions that must be true if the cause is to be true. We compare assumptions by asking "Which cause has the fewest assumptions? Which cause has the most reasonable assumptions? Which cause has the simplest assumptions?" Our selection of the most probable cause may depend as much on the quality of the assumptions as on the quantity. Sometimes judgment is needed to select the most probable cause. To improve our chances of success, however, we need to spend time and effort in confirming the cause.

VERIFY ASSUMPTIONS, OBSERVE, EXPERIMENT, OR TRY A FIX AND MONITOR

Confirmation is an independent step taken to prove a cause-and-effect relationship. It depends on bringing in *additional information* and taking *additional actions*.

To *confirm* a likely cause is to *prove* that it did produce the observed effect. In our example all we need to do is simply look at the gasket in operation and see whether it leaks (observe). Or, we can trade the gasket from the Number One Filter for the non-leaking gasket from one of the other filters (experiment). Or, we can obtain a gasket with rounded corners from the old supplier, install it, and see whether the leaking stops (try a fix and monitor). Any of these would prove that the leaking resulted from the installation of a new, thinner, square-cornered gasket bought at a bargain price.

Sometimes no *direct confirmation* is possible and we must rely on our assumptions. A rocket booster explodes in flight. Most of the tangible evidence is destroyed. We would certainly not want a second such accident. All that can be done is to verify assumptions generated during the testing against the specification. "If *this* happened, then *that* would make sense…." Devise ways to verify the assumptions. The assumptions must be true in order for the cause to be true.

Confirmation is possible in most problem situations. What it consists of will depend on the circumstances. We want to use the safest, surest, cheapest, easiest, quickest method. A mechanical problem may be duplicated by consciously introducing a distinction or a change that seems highly indicative of cause. Many problems are confirmed by "putting on the old gasket"—that is, reversing a change to see whether the problem stops (try a fix and monitor). In that case, confirmation provides corrective action. Resolution coincides with the last step in the process of Problem Analysis.

FAILURE

Of course, we may fail. While the most common cause of failure is too little data in the specification, there are three other major reasons for failing to solve a problem despite using Problem Analysis:

▷ Using inaccurate or vague information to describe the problem.

▷ Insufficiently identifying key distinctions and changes related to the IS data in the specification.

▷ Allowing assumptions to distort judgment during the testing step. The greater the number of assumptions we tack onto a possible cause in order to label it "most probable," the less chance there is that it will survive confirmation. There is nothing wrong with making assumptions as long as we regard them as such and do not prematurely grant them the status of fact.

A PROCESS, NOT A PANACEA

Thousands of people have used these techniques to solve problems that seemed otherwise unsolvable or solvable only by far greater expenditure of time and money. On the other hand, many of these same people have failed to solve other problems they were sure they could crack—"if only they had stayed with the process." Problem Analysis enables us to do a good job of gathering and evaluating information about problems. However, there are limitations to the power of the process to produce the right answers. If we cannot track down the key facts needed to crack a problem, that problem will continue to defy solution. No approach or process, however systematically or meticulously applied, will unlock its secret.

CHAPTER SUMMARY

The shadows cast by our problems may be perplexing. Yet the *structure* of *all* problems is always the same. It is knowledge of this structure that enables us to move systematically from definition to description to evaluation to hypothesis to confirmation of cause.

▷ The **Problem Statement** is a concise description of both the object of our concern and the deviation or malfunction for which we want to find the cause. In our example, that statement was "Number One Filter Leaking Oil."

▷ The **Specification** of the problem is a comprehensive description of the problem's WHAT, WHERE, WHEN, and EXTENT—as it IS and as it COULD BE but IS NOT. The Number One Filter IS leaking; each of the other four COULD BE but IS NOT. The location of the leak IS the cleanout hatch; the leak COULD BE but IS NOT observed at the cleanout hatches of Numbers Two through Five. From the identification of this IS... COULD BE but IS NOT data, we assemble bases of comparison that will lead us to an understanding and resolution of the problem.

▷ Our own **Knowledge** and **Experience**, or that of experts, may suggest possible causes. Using the specification as a guide, we look to generate as many possible causes as we reasonably can. We then test these against the specification.

▷ If we have too many or too few causes to consider, or if all of the causes we generate fail to test against the specification, we look for **Distinctions**—features in all four dimensions that characterize only the IS data. We ask, "What is distinctive about the Number One Filter when compared with Filters Two through Five?" We carry this kind of questioning through the other three dimensions. The result is a collection of key features that characterize the WHAT, WHERE, WHEN, and EXTENT of our problem.

▷ We then study each distinction to determine whether it also represents a **Change**. It is at this point in our analysis that we recognize the square-cornered gasket on the leaking filter—not only as a distinctive feature of that filter but also as a change. Until the day before the problem appeared, the Number One Filter had been equipped with the same type of round-cornered gasket used on the other units.

▷ When all the distinctions and changes have been identified, we begin to **Identify Possible Causes**. Each distinction and change is examined for clues to cause. Each resultant hypothesis of cause is stated to illustrate not only what caused the problem but how it did so: "The square-cornered gasket from the new supplier is too thin and unevenly constructed. This caused the Number One Filter to leak."

▷ Each possible cause we generate is then **Tested** against the specification. It must explain both the IS and IS NOT data in each dimension. To graduate to the status of **Most Probable Cause**, it must explain or withstand all the facts in the specification. Unless we make some farfetched assumptions, "greater vibration in the northeast corner of the filter house," for example, cannot explain either the leak at the location on the filter or the time period that characterized this problem. Vibration, as a possible cause, is less likely to have produced the problem than the installation of the new gasket.

▷ The final step in Problem Analysis is **Confirmation** of the true cause. We are hoping to demonstrate, as closely as possible, the cause-and-effect relationship. The confirmation is carried out in the work environment if possible. In our example, this can be done either by duplicating the effect suggested by the cause or by reversing the change suspected of having caused the problem to see if the problem stops.

If no possible cause that has been generated passes the testing step, or if no cause that does pass it survives the confirmation step, the only recourse is to tighten up the prior work. We may need more detailed information in the specification, in the ensuing identification of distinctions of the IS data, and in the identification of changes in and around the distinctions. This may lead to new insights, to the generation of new possible causes, and, finally, to a successful resolution.

If we fail to find the true cause of a problem through these techniques, it is because we failed to gather and use information appropriately. We cannot use information that we do not have. If we get the information but use it carelessly, the result may be no better.

The logic of Problem Analysis defends conclusions that support facts; it sets aside those that cannot. It is a process that makes use of every bit of experience and judgment we possess; it helps us to use both in the most systematic and objective way possible.

Problem Analysis enables people to work together as a team, pooling their information in a common format, to determine the cause of a problem. Most deviations are so complex that one person alone does not have the information necessary to find, test, and confirm the cause. When all those who hold important data have a mechanism for integrating it, they can begin to find the unknown cause. Otherwise, that discovery may be stalled by misunderstandings and other barriers to communication.

THREE

THE USES OF PROBLEM ANALYSIS

IN THIS CHAPTER

Acquiring the Habit of Problem Solving
Problem Analysis Questioning at the Managerial Level
The Abbreviated Use of Problem Analysis
Situations in Which Actual Performance Has Never Met Expectations
Use of Problem Analysis Techniques by the Management Team

ACQUIRING THE HABIT OF PROBLEM SOLVING

This chapter presents ways in which organizations have solved problems through improved use of cause-and-effect thinking.

Some years ago, we asked a commanding general of a large United States Air Force base what results he had expected of the Kepner-Tregoe program, which had been installed throughout his command two years earlier.

"The day I assumed this command," he said, "people were lined up outside my door. 'We thought we ought to see you before we do anything on this' was a typical opening line. In short, they were asking me to take responsibility for their actions—not, I believe, because they really wanted me to but because they thought they had to operate that way. I had to convince them that they did not have to and that I didn't want them to. But you cannot just tell people, 'Look, you've got to solve your own problems!' You must provide them with both the skills and the confidence to do that.

"That was why we installed the Kepner-Tregoe program as a core feature of our overall organization development effort. With that we were able to say, 'Now, you've been given problem-solving techniques that have been very successful for a great many people. We expect you to use them. The time to go to your superior is when you think you have the solution to a problem, when you're ready to present your case.'"

Throughout what the general referred to as his "homemade organization development program," there was great emphasis on giving and taking responsibility. He believed this attitude would lead to a healthier and more productive organization. His tenure as commanding officer proved him right.

> He related an incident that had occurred about a month before our meeting. One Saturday (a non-working day for top-level technical people), he had stopped in at the base to find some sixty of his staff carrying out a multifaceted Problem Analysis. They were trying to determine the cause of cracks in the walls of fighter aircraft engines.

> "Nobody had told me a thing about it. I had no idea the group had decided to spend their Saturday working on the problem. It was their decision as a team." Several days later the group presented the general with their analysis of the problem. After asking a number of questions, he approved their recommendations and forwarded the analysis to the Pentagon. He strongly suggested that the analysis be accepted and the proposed course of action be adopted as soon as possible. One week later, as a direct result of that suggestion, the Pentagon ordered nearly $9 billion worth of aircraft grounded for detailed inspection and repairs.

Most applications of Problem Analysis result, to be sure, in less dramatic conclusions. But the conditions that produced these particular conclusions were typical of conditions that have always produced the best results: The people who carried out the analysis had been given systematic problem-solving techniques. They knew how to apply them to actual problems on their jobs. They were rewarded for making the effort. They were not afraid of failure. To one degree or another, these conditions for habitual and successful problem solving are evident in all the examples that follow.

Chapter Two laid the groundwork for fully understanding the following examples of Problem Analysis in action. The examples touch on four general subjects:

▷ Problem Analysis questioning at the managerial level.

▷ Abbreviated use of the process.

▷ Resolution of situations in which a performance ACTUAL has never achieved the designated SHOULD.

▷ Use of the techniques in a team situation.

PROBLEM ANALYSIS QUESTIONING AT THE MANAGERIAL LEVEL

Full step-by-step application of the process, documented on chartpad or notepad, is most often required for concrete problems whose identity can be directly observed or easily visualized. These are largely mechanical, tangible situations.

At the management level, however, application of the process often consists of using the *ideas* of the process. Using the ideas includes discussing the facts of a situation in all its dimensions rather than formulating hypotheses based on experience. It means being attentive to the distinctions in WHAT, WHERE, WHEN, and EXTENT rather than relying on informed speculation alone. Further, it is testing possible causes against the facts rather than immediately acting on the cause suggested by informed speculation.

Data may be recorded and notes taken, but use of the process by managers is usually observable in the character of the questioning and in the nature of the investigation. We observe people using the common language of Problem Analysis to organize their information, communicate it, and put it into perspective. They are sharing information through the channels of a systematic process. They are using words that will clarify each individual's contributions.

Busy managers are not avoiding their responsibility when they tell employees, "I want you to solve your own problems." They have neither the time nor the information to personally guide their employees' problem-solving efforts. The truth of the matter is that managers who become directly involved in problem solving are subject to criticism for failing to set priorities on their own time or to delegate appropriately—

in short, for failing to *manage* their operations. Managers need not have all the right answers. What is required of them are the ability and willingness to ask the right questions. The kind of questioning we use in specifying, in identifying distinctions and changes, and in testing possible causes lends itself well to the process of assessing the logic and the contributions of others to resolving a problem.

CASE HISTORY: SHRINKING BANK ACCOUNTS

One kind of problem that taxes our ability to ask the right questions is the problem that drifts in like fog, very gradually, until visibility has dropped to near zero. Some gradual change in conditions has occurred, and by the time the situation has become serious enough to gain everyone's attention, its critical elements may be lost to view.

A major bank in California had a number of branches in the Los Angeles area. The operating results of all branches are reviewed monthly by the Executive Committee. At a July review, the Hawthorne branch showed a volume of transactions slightly below plan. All the other branches were right on target or above.

In August, the Hawthorne branch slipped a little further; in September, even more. In October, the news was worse yet. Members of the Executive Committee began an investigation. One vice president suggested exploring the subject of **change**, saying he had already given it some thought. He pointed out that when the decline in transactions was observed, the new branch manager had been in his position for about two months. "Look, he represents a change all right. He came in just before the branch started to slip. I thought we were making a mistake then, and I'm sure of it now."

The committee went on to consider who might take over that position if the bank let the new manager go. After a long discussion, the chairman suggested that they might be jumping to cause on the basis of a single fact. He wanted the committee to consider the decline in terms of an informal specification—to discuss the WHAT, WHERE, WHEN, and EXTENT of the decline. He wasn't taking anything away from the vice president's assessment. He just wanted to make sure the situation was investigated thoroughly and objectively before taking action that would seriously affect the branch manager's career.

Despite some disagreement, they began an objective analysis. In the dimension of WHERE, the committee named the Hawthorne branch as the IS. It was in Hawthorne alone that the decline was observed. All other branches represented the IS NOT. The question "What is distinctive about the Hawthorne branch when compared with all other branches?" led to a discussion of its proximity to the airport and the factories of two large defense contractors.

"Wait a minute," someone said. "Both contractors have been stretching out work on their current defense contracts and reducing the workforce for some time. And one is transferring a lot of its work from Hawthorne to Long Beach...."

After discussing the gradual local economic decline that had resulted from these actions, the committee concluded that the new manager deserved the benefit of the doubt. Because the economic situation in Hawthorne was not characterized by a sudden, sharp, and immediately identifiable change, the committee had found it easier to seize on the new manager's performance as the likely cause of decreasing transactions. His appointment, after all, had been a more visible and recent change. Attention subsequently was focused on the new line of reasoning, supported by the efforts of at least one committee member to consider this as the cause of the problem.

SUMMARY

By insisting on asking and answering questions in all dimensions of the problem situation—including but not confined to the new manager's performance—the chairman played a vital role in the process. He made it possible for the discipline of Problem Analysis to absorb responsibility for producing a reasonable possible cause for the decline, one that could respond to *all* the facts surrounding it. There was no loss of face nor was anyone blamed or fired for a situation that in no way could be termed mismanagement.

It was simple to check the theory of local economic decline as the true cause of the problem:

▷ When did the volume first begin to fall off at Hawthorne? In early July.

▷ When did layoffs begin at the defense contractors? In late May and early June.

▷ How long after a round of layoffs would the impact be felt in the bank? No more than two or three weeks.

▷ How would the impact show up initially? By a reduction in deposits, then an increase in withdrawals.

Confirmation consisted of a few hours of telephone research to check out the experience of other banks nearby. The same story was told by all.

PROPER USES OF THE TECHNIQUES

To make the techniques of Problem Analysis pay off on a day-to-day basis, there must be a commitment to use them properly. There must be a willingness to ask *all* the questions needed to define a problem situation fully and to allow the facts surrounding that situation to speak for themselves. Speculation is useful only to the extent that it is made within the structure of the process. On the other hand, speculation that overrides the structure or that is couched in the language but not the spirit of the process can be devastating. Note that the vice president suggested "exploring the subject of *change....* " His suggestion that the new branch manager was at fault was presented to the group on the basis of what has aptly been labeled a "process trinket."

Listen to the manager who coined this term: "People occasionally come to me with some idea they want to push through, and they've covered the whole thing with these 'process trinkets.' If it *looks* like Problem Analysis, if it *sounds* like it, then the idea will have a better chance of acceptance."

It is quite possible to give the *appearance* of systematic analysis to a recommendation that represents a solitary, biased viewpoint. Yet whoever controls the questioning and the assessment of that recommendation controls its *management*. As one of the aides to the above-mentioned general once told us, "The general expects you to come to a recommendation based on your own analysis. But you would not like to be in the position of defending it to him if it were not strictly on the up-and-up."

CASE HISTORY: REJECTED CIRCUITS

The simple question "Why?" is a poor substitute for the four-dimensional questioning we use in Problem Analysis. Yet whenever something goes wrong, it is second nature to ask "Why?" and then review the flood of answers in the hope that one of them will instantly suggest the problem's actual cause. The usual rationalization for the "Why?" approach is that people have been hired for their expertise and experience. If they can't come up with answers to problems that occur in the operation, then those people don't belong in their jobs. Concrete results arising from the combination of systematic techniques and technical expertise are the only things that will convince a manager that *questions are as important as answers*.

An electronics manufacturing company is involved in the demanding task of producing miniaturized printed circuitry. One day, the production quality fell off sharply and the number of rejected circuits skyrocketed. "Why?" demanded the manager. "Why?" echoed the employees. "Temperature in the leaching bath is too high," said one technician. So temperatures were lowered.

A week later, when rejects climbed still higher, temperatures were raised, then lowered again, then systematically varied up and down for days. Rejects remained astronomical. "Cleanliness is not what it should be. That's what's causing the trouble," someone offered. So everything was scrubbed, polished, filtered, and wiped. The rejects dropped, then rose again. Acid concentration was the next idea. Same results. Water purity was checked out on Wednesday, Thursday, and Friday. The possibility of oil transferred from the operator's fingertips received full scrutiny on the following Monday and Tuesday. Rejects were still high.

They might have remained high had one supervisor not begun to ask systematic questions. "What is wrong with the rejected pieces?" This produced the information that the acid leaching step of the printed circuit pattern was occurring unevenly—as if some waterborne contaminant in the leaching solution was inhibiting the action.

THE USES OF PROBLEM ANALYSIS   **55**

"When *does* it occur?" A check of the records showed that rejects were at their highest on Monday mornings, lower on Monday afternoons, and gone by Tuesday noon.

This cast a different light on everything. Now nobody was asking "Why?" about the cause of a general, ill-defined deviation. Instead, they focused on **what was distinctive about Monday mornings** compared with the rest of the week. They focused on what might have been changed that bore a relationship to this timing. An immediate distinction was recognized: "Monday morning is the first work period following the non-work period of the weekend." And what changed on Monday morning? On each Monday, as soon as the tap was turned, water that had stood in the lines over the weekend came into the printed circuit leaching laboratories.

The water used in the process had to go through intensive purification, since purity standards of a few parts per billion are required. A quick search turned up the fact that some valves had been changed several months before. These valves used a silicone packing material. As water stood in the lines over the weekend, enough of this silicone packing material had begun to diffuse into the water to degrade the leaching process. The result? Many rejections on Monday morning, fewer in the afternoon, and none after Tuesday noon. By then the contaminated water had been purged from the system.

SUMMARY

The company could have asked "Why?" indefinitely without ever finding the cause of this problem. Once the question "When?" had been asked and answered, the people involved could focus their technical expertise where it would do the most good.

Regardless of the content of a problem, the search for specific and accurate answers demands specific and precise questions.

THE ABBREVIATED USE OF PROBLEM ANALYSIS

The best use of Problem Analysis is the use that works best. There is no particular virtue attached to slavish adherence to every step in the entire process if a brief, informal use of the ideas can reveal the cause of the problem. In fact, the longer people use Problem Analysis, the more adept they become at singling out fragments of the process that apply to the kinds of problems they face every day. When people begin asking questions like "Has anything changed in the timing of this operation lately?" or "What stage was this process at just before you noticed the trouble?" they have made the transition between an academic appreciation of Problem Analysis techniques and internalization of their practical role in daily problem solving.

CASE HISTORY: TROUBLE ABOARD *APOLLO XIII*

The vast majority of Problem Analyses never see pen and paper. This is especially true of the abbreviated application of the process. The seriousness of a problem does not necessarily determine the length or complexity of the analysis required to resolve it. Some extremely serious problems have been solved through abbreviated uses of the process. They were so data-poor that full use could not be undertaken. Fragments of the process had to be relied on and combined with educated speculation to arrive at a most likely cause.

Apollo XIII was on its way to the moon. Fifty-four hours and fifty-two minutes into the mission—205,000 miles from Earth—and all was well. Then John L. Swigert, Jr., duty commander at the time, reported: "Houston, we've got a problem here.... We've had a Main Buss B undervolt." This was an insider's way of saying that electrical voltage on the second of two power generating systems had fallen off and a warning light had appeared. A moment later the power came up again. Swigert reported: "The voltage is looking good. And we had a pretty large bang associated with the caution and warning there." Three minutes later, as the dimensions of the problem became clearer, he reported: "Yeah, we got a Main Buss A undervolt too.... It's reading about 25 1/2. Main B is reading zip right now." Apollo XIII, carrying three people toward the moon at incredible speed, was rapidly losing power and could shortly become a dead body. A disaster had occurred in space and no one was sure what had happened.

On the ground at Houston, NASA engineers put Problem Analysis questioning to work immediately. They began to build a specification of the deviation from the information that came in answer to their questions and from data displayed on their monitoring equipment. At the same time they started a number of contingency actions to reduce use of electrical power on board Apollo XIII. Thirteen minutes after the first report, Swigert reported: "Our O^2 Cryo Number Two Tank is reading zero... and it looks to me, looking out the hatch, that we are venting something... out into space... it's gas of some sort."

What had begun as an electrical problem—loss of voltage—became a sudden loss of oxygen in the second of two tanks, with a more gradual loss of oxygen from the first. Since oxygen was used in the generation of electricity as well as directly in life-support systems, the situation could hardly be more serious.

Although no one at the time could conceive of what **might** have caused the tank to burst, "Rupture of the Number Two Cryogenic Oxygen Tank" **would** explain the sudden loss of voltage and the subsequent loss of pressure. Further actions were taken to conserve both oxygen and electricity. A number of "IS ... COULD BE but IS NOT" questions were asked to get further data, and a series of system checks was undertaken to verify cause. In the end it was determined that the Number Two Tank had burst and vented all its oxygen, plus a large portion of the gas from the Number One Tank, through a damaged valve and out into space. The three men returned successfully to Earth but only by the narrowest of margins. Had the cause remained unknown for very much longer, they would not have had enough oxygen left to survive.

It was weeks before the root cause of this problem was established through on-the-ground testing and experimentation. Two weeks before the launch, a ground crew had piped liquid oxygen into the tanks in a countdown demonstration. After the test they had had difficulty getting the oxygen out of the Number Two Tank. They had activated a heater inside the tank to vaporize some of the liquid oxygen, thus providing pressure to force it out. They had kept the heater on for eight hours, longer than it had ever been used before. Although a protective switch was provided to turn off the heater before it became too hot, the switch was fused in the ON position because the ground crew had connected it to a 65-volt power supply instead of the 28-volt supply used in *Apollo XIII*. Later, in flight, the crew turned the heater on briefly to get an accurate quantity reading. The fused switch created an arc that overheated the oxygen in the tank, raised

THE NEW RATIONAL MANAGER

the internal pressure tremendously, and blew the dome and much of the connecting piping off into space.

SUMMARY

There was no time for NASA Houston to go through a complete listing of all the distinctions and changes they might observe. Instead, they asked "What *traumatic change* could cause the sudden, total failure in electrical generation?" Cutting off the flow of oxygen to the fuel cells would have that effect. They knew which fuel cells were inoperative when Swigert reported that the Number Two Tank was reading zero. They tested the cause—that the Number Two Tank had ruptured—and found that this would explain the suddenness and totality described in the specification. It would also account for the bang reported at the time of the first undervolt indication, a shuddering of *Apollo XIII* felt by flight crew members, and the venting of "something... out into space." It accounted for both the IS data they had amassed and for the IS NOT information that had come from their monitoring activities. More importantly, it explained a sudden, total failure within the system.

For the NASA Houston engineers, this cause was difficult to accept. They had unbounded faith in Apollo equipment, knowing that it was the best that could be devised. The idea of an oxygen tank bursting open in the depths of space was not credible. All this was justified from their experience. Without the bungling that had occurred on the ground two weeks before the launch, the tank would have gone to the moon and back just as it was designed and built to do. However, the Houston engineers stuck to the Problem Analysis process despite their incredulity, believing that the test for cause they had carried out had provided the correct answer. In fact, they proved this cause in record time. What saved the day was their knowledge of *Apollo XIII*'s systems and of what *could* produce the exact kind of sudden failure that had occurred.

In a case such as this, Problem Analysis is rendered difficult by two factors: secondary effects and panic. Sudden failure in a complex system usually causes other deviations that may obscure the original deviation. The shock of a sudden failure often precipitates panic, making a careful review and use of the facts even more difficult. A disciplined and systematic investigation is difficult in any case, but discipline becomes essential when a top-speed search for cause is undertaken and there is no possibility of amassing all the data that would be optimal in the investigation. In the NASA incident, the presence of a systematic approach enabled a team of people to work together as a single unit, even though they were separated from the deviation by nearly a quarter of a million miles.

CASE HISTORY: PLUGGED SPRAY NOZZLES

The NASA example illustrates the chief motivation for using an abbreviated version of Problem Analysis: lack of data and/or time needed to do a full-scale analysis. Another common motivator for short-cut Problem Analysis is expediency. It may simply be unnecessary to go into the full process in order to explain the deviation. The facts of WHAT, WHERE, WHEN, and EXTENT may suggest a reasonable, possible cause for the problem. If this possible cause can quickly be confirmed as the true cause, all the better.

A large city in California bought new spray equipment for painting white-and-yellow lines on roads. From the beginning the equipment gave the operators trouble, even though no new procedures had been introduced. No critical change existed. The equipment was brand new. It was cleaned with solvent before being taken out on the job. After a short period of operation, the spray nozzles plugged up. The operators then stopped work, cleaned everything, and reassembled the equipment. Within minutes the nozzles plugged up again. It didn't take long for this problem to make a shambles of the work schedule of the Street and Transportation Department.

A Problem Analysis was begun. The problem was specified. The only IS NOT available in terms of WHAT was the previously used paint sprayer. At that point, about two minutes into the analysis, someone said, "What if the solvent we are using is good for the old unit but not for the new one?" The manufacturer's instruction book turned up the fact that only ST-64 solvent must be used on the new sprayer. "What solvent are we using?" "Same one we always used, Ajax Super-Kleen. It's the best one we can get." Best for what? Not the new paint sprayer. ST-64 was introduced and the new sprayer worked perfectly.

THE NEW RATIONAL MANAGER

SUMMARY

"Best for what?" applies equally well to the use of Problem Analysis. If a possible cause leaps to mind two minutes into the specification and can be confirmed easily and quickly as the true cause, then that is the best use of the process for that situation. If a "Eureka" idea comes to mind in a minute and requires only minutes to confirm, how much time is lost even if it fails?

CASE HISTORY: SPOILED CATTLE FEED

Another useful abbreviation of Problem Analysis is focusing on one dimension in the specification. For example, distinctions and changes related to the timing of the problem may be studied intensively to the exclusion of everything else.

One of our clients produces cattle feed with soybean meal as an essential ingredient. Soybeans contain urease, an enzyme that reacts with urea to form ammonia. Urea is added to the meal to help the cattle convert it to protein. This means that the urease content must be controlled. If ammonia were produced, it could cause serious, even fatal, bloating in the cattle. So the meal is put through steam-heated toasters to control and reduce the urease. A laboratory analysis is run on urease levels every day.

For nine years there had been no trouble with urease levels in our client's plant. Carloads of cattle feed were produced every day. The laboratory analysis was run every day. Everything was as it should be. One day the routine laboratory test showed that the urease level was substantially above the standard. The results were reported immediately to the plant manager. All meal produced within the past forty-eight hours was embargoed, and the manager began to specify the problem. He quickly focused on the WHEN dimension: "The urease level had been high all day today but appeared to have been normal right up through last night. Almost certainly something had changed today, this morning, and had lasted all day." For the present he would look only in this direction.

He went to the feed line and questioned the operators. What had they changed? What were they doing differently today? Nothing, as far as they knew. Everything was just the same as it had always been. Then he went to engineering to find out about the equipment. "Anything changed today?" Nothing. He went to the laboratory to ask about the tests. Nothing. Then to maintenance with the same question. "Oh, yeah. We had a new guy replacing a packing gland on the steam line." It turned out that the repairman had run into trouble and so had turned off the steam to one of the toasters all day. He didn't realize that the reduced temperature meant that the urease would be uncontrolled and the feed spoiled for cattle consumption.

A closer check by the laboratory showed eleven carloads affected. Other markets were found for the feed where the higher urease level would not be a problem. No customers suffered.

SUMMARY

The plant manager understood that a change in some condition is what creates a deviation. He recognized that the change in this case probably had taken place during a very specific, recent period of time. If, after nine trouble-free years, serious trouble had developed this morning and continued all day, then a change within the past twenty-four hours was the thing to track in all functions that could possibly account for an increase in urease levels.

Once the purpose of each of the steps in Problem Analysis is understood and a manager has internalized the rationale behind the progression of these steps, they can be pulled apart and applied to suit the particular needs of a situation. The structure of each problem is the same: a deviation between actual and expected performance for which the cause is unknown. All the facts surrounding any problem fall into four dimensions: WHAT, WHERE, WHEN, and EXTENT. Comparative data in these four dimensions—the IS NOTs—provide the distinctions and changes that narrow the search for the cause of a problem. These and other basic tenets of Problem Analysis become second nature to people who use the process in part and in full on a daily basis. How much of it do you need to solve a problem? Just enough.

CONCLUSIONS

The Executive Committee chairman of the California bank knew that more was needed than a focus on one personnel change. The manager in the electronics company knew that "Why?" must be supplanted by "WHAT?" "WHERE?" "WHEN?" "EXTENT?" before he could recognize the direction in which the analysis should go. Mission Control on *Apollo XIII* knew that the only choice it had was to do less than the full Problem Analysis it would have liked to do. Time and data were distressingly inadequate. The operators trying to figure out why a paint sprayer plugged up knew they had used enough of the process just two minutes after they began their analysis, when the explanation jumped out at them. The plant manager in the cattle feed manufacturing facility, given the nature of his problem, knew that an investigation of a change in the dimension of timing was almost guaranteed to produce the right answers.

Examples of the successful use of abbreviated Problem Analysis all share one characteristic: They show that experience and judgment produce the best possible results when channeled through some or all of the elements of a systematic process.

SITUATIONS IN WHICH ACTUAL PERFORMANCE HAS NEVER MET EXPECTATIONS

When we begin a Problem Analysis that concerns the "has never worked" kind of problem, it is sensible to examine the performance SHOULD itself and perhaps do a bit of research.

Is the SHOULD realistic? Has it ever been attained, anywhere, by anyone? *Who* says it is the SHOULD? Based on what criteria and with what assumptions? Sometimes performance standards are set carelessly or are set purposely at a level higher than anyone really expects to achieve. And sometimes a performance SHOULD is communicated in one way but meant in quite another.

CASE HISTORY: THE "ON-TIME" MISUNDERSTANDING

A vice president for sales and marketing, complaining about the lack of drive in a recently hired salesman, was perplexed. The man had an excellent sales record with his previous employer.

We asked for an example of this lack of drive.

"OK, here's an example. I told him that when he's in town I expect him to be in the office by 8:30. At 8:30 on the dot, this guy walks through the door."

What is wrong with that?

"It irritates me that he walks in as the clock strikes. If nothing else, you'd think he'd show up before then to get his day organized. That's what I've always done. I guess I feel it's unprofessional behavior—like a kid slipping into his seat in class just as the bell rings."

Had any of this been communicated to the new employee?

"Of course not! It isn't the sort of thing you say."

Then how did the manager think the situation would ever resolve itself?

"I don't know...."

About a month later we received a letter from the manager that included these remarks:

"I bit the bullet and talked to the man about coming in here at 8:30 sharp. He laughed. He said his wife was taking a class at a local college that started classes at 8:15 a.m. He dropped her off there and then came into the office, which is just about fifteen minutes from the college. If I preferred, he told me, she could drop **him** off at 8:00! The outcome of this somewhat embarrassing misunderstanding is that I have thought a lot about how I communicate with my staff. I looked at their jobs in terms of what you call SHOULD and I decided that I make too many assumptions. I don't tell people what I actually expect. Naturally, they reciprocate by not doing it."

SUMMARY

Human performance SHOULDs must be communicated clearly and fully. Equally important is a commitment on the part of the manager to make these SHOULDs reasonable. If they are not communicated clearly, or if they are unreasonable, then performance will be perceived as unacceptable even though the person is doing the best he or she can. This classic cause of misunderstanding between manager and employee has been experienced by nearly everyone from one side of such a misunderstanding or the other. It does not have to occur.

Case History: The $27 Solution

A Day One Deviation from SHOULD is often only a small gap in performance. Something performs fairly well, perhaps almost well enough—but never quite as well as it was supposed to. Instead of achieving the standard 100 percent, we observe a 92 or 95 percent efficiency day after day. This is a typical problem in a production plant, where a 5 percent loss of efficiency on an important unit of equipment can result in substantial loss over time.

A chemical plant manufacturing a single product had one process unit that consistently produced at acceptable quality and quantity levels. When demand for the product increased, management decided to purchase and install a second unit. This was done and the new, virtually identical unit went on line. From the beginning it underproduced. It was always 5 to 7 percent less efficient than the original unit. Teams of technical people from the plant, the parent company, and the manufacturer worked the new unit over from top to bottom without discovering the cause.

The critical control on production yield depended on holding solids to a level of 15 percent at one point in the process. Samples were drawn from each of the units every hour and analyzed in the laboratory for solids content. Feeds, temperatures, and pressures were adjusted accordingly to maintain the 15 percent target. On the original unit the adjustment produced correct final yield. On the new unit—an exact duplicate of the original, according to the manufacturer—it did not. Final yields fluctuated regardless of adjustments.

After more than a year of investigation by experts, the plant manager authorized a team of five maintenance and repair personnel to have a go at the problem. All five had just been trained in Problem Analysis techniques. He felt they needed a miracle to come up with the cause of the fluctuating yield on the Number Two Process Unit.

The team made the initial assumption that the new unit could not be the identical twin of the original unit! Something within it or surrounding it must be different. Point by point, feature by feature, they made a comparative specification of the new unit (problem IS...) and the original one (problem COULD BE but IS NOT...). They set out to identify all distinctions relative to the WHAT, WHERE, WHEN, and EXTENT of the problem through examining the bases of comparison in their specification. After a great deal of work, only one substantial distinction could be found: Samples of product drawn from the new unit for laboratory solids analysis emerged at a point on the fractionating column just a bit higher than the draw-off point on the original unit. From this solitary distinction they postulated the following possible cause: "Samples drawn from the Number Two Unit give a misleading solids level due to the location of the draw-off point." They could not explain **why** this should be so, but it was the best they could do.

"So what?" shrugged the technical people. "We knew that when the unit was installed. According to the manufacturer's design, there are a number of optional locations for that draw-off point. We used the one that was most convenient."

The team insisted that this difference in the draw-off location might lead to inaccurate readings and affect control over the process. Moreover, it would cost a grand total of $27 to move the sampling location on the new unit to match the location on the original unit. Experts were against it, but the plant manager gave the go-ahead anyway. From the day the $27 was allocated, the 15 percent solids level on the new unit was achieved and maintained. The plant manager computed the value of lost production in the preceding year as something close to $700,000.

SUMMARY

Why there was a discrepancy in readings between one optional draw-off point and another could never be explained. There was a *critical distinction* between the units. There had to be. But even when found, this critical distinction was rejected by most people. It is noteworthy that a team of maintenance and repair personnel, without much technical expertise, was able to evaluate and solve this problem using simple, systematic techniques.

CONCLUSIONS

In many of our client companies, a Problem Analysis team always includes at least one member who has no technical expertise that bears directly on understanding the problem's *content*. This individual leads the process questioning. Time and again we have been told that inclusion of a non-expert has kept the team from getting bogged down in the details of the problem and giving undue weight to assumptions based on content expertise and technical background.

In a case in which performance has been acceptable up to a certain point in time, we know that we are looking for some kind of change in our search for cause. In a case in which performance has never been acceptable, we know that some *condition* necessary to achieve the SHOULD does not exist now and never ever has. So we must focus on the *conditions of performance that separate the problem as it IS from all that it COULD BE but IS NOT.* In other words, in the Day One Deviation, the search for cause must take place entirely in the area of distinctions.

USE OF PROBLEM ANALYSIS TECHNIQUES BY THE MANAGEMENT TEAM

To one degree or another, all the examples that have appeared so far in this chapter reflect the shared use of Problem Analysis techniques. In this final section, teamwork itself is our major focus: *how managers use the common language of the process to communicate and share information, thereby resolving problems they might not have been able to resolve individually.*

CASE HISTORY: POOR SALES OF THE MODEL A

A very large merchandising house sells a private brand of sewing machines. The machines are manufactured for the house in six different models. For over a year the sewing machine line had not been selling as well as expected even though it was well received when it was first introduced. The sales promotion manager, the merchandising manager, and the sewing machine buyer finally met to analyze the problem. They began to specify the deviation, each contributing his or her special knowledge.

Their problem statement was simple enough: "Sewing Machines Selling Poorly." They could not be more specific at the outset of the analysis, since the exact nature of the deviation—percentages of expected revenue achieved—was being explored in detail for the first time.

"What sewing machines?" was the first question, in the dimension of the problem's WHAT. They were prepared to say "All six models." But when they began to review their data, they were astonished to see that only Model A was selling poorly. Models B and C were selling somewhat better than A, and Models D, E, and F were selling quite well. None of the three managers had realized there were such marked differences in the rates of sales among the six models. Until then they had only been dealing with **average** figures. Almost immediately after beginning the specification, they went back to the problem statement and revised it to read "Model A Sewing Machine Selling Poorly."

They probed into the dimension of WHERE and found that low sales of Model A were nationwide. There were no distinctions to be gleaned in terms of geographical factors such as "better in the Midwest, worst in the Northeast." From coast to coast, Model A sales were poor wherever Model A was available.

They hit paydirt when they turned their attention to the dimension of WHEN. The records showed that the Model A machine had sold as well as expected in the first couple of months but then had fallen off sharply. Also, Models B and C had sold well initially and then sales had fallen off—but not as sharply as Model A. Models D, E, and F had sold well when first introduced and had continued to do so right up to the present time.

The discrepancies between the IS and IS NOT information were inescapable. They couldn't be ignored and they wouldn't go away. There was something distinctive about the Model A machine—and about the B and C models to a lesser degree—when compared with the models that were selling well.

The merchandising manager suggested an explanation: "Model A has fewer attachments and selling benefits. Perhaps it's simply a less desirable unit!" It was a neat explanation but unfortunately not so. "The fact is," said the sewing machine buyer, "there isn't much difference among the attachments of the six units." She thought it made more sense to look at differences in sales features.

"That won't wash," said the sales promotion manager. "Sales features for the six machines have been constant from the start. Anyway, how could that possibly account for a falloff on Model A beginning a couple of months **after** its introduction?"

The merchandising manager then brought up the subject of motivation. "Could there be some lack of motivation to **sell** Model A?" The sales promotion manager replied, "The salesperson makes the lowest commission on Model A, the next lowest on Models B and C, and the best commission on the other three. That's normal enough—and, besides, it doesn't represent any kind of change. It's always been that way."

After a few moments of silence, while everyone digested this information, the sewing machine buyer asked, "Wouldn't there be some lapse of time **after** a new item is introduced before the salespeople begin to receive their commissions and figure which sales bring in the greatest return? I mean, maybe the realization that the commission rate on Model A is substantially lower than on Models D, E, and F would take a little time to sink in. After a couple of months their motivation to sell Model A might have changed."

The team decided that this explanation was the most likely cause of Model A's poor sales. To confirm it, the sales promotion manager raised the commission rate on Model A, leaving price and all other variables the same. Within two months the Model A machine began to sell better.

SUMMARY

In this meeting, the three managers were able to contribute from their own areas of expertise. Equally important, each manager was able to question the team, within the structure of the process, to provoke ideas and expand their capability to truly *analyze* the problem, not just talk about it. "*Could* this be a distinction?" one asked another. "*Does* that represent any change?" Each manager had unique inputs to make, but all had the same understanding of the structure and progression of Problem Analysis. All were intent on the same goal: explaining the problem's cause. How different an approach it is from that in which each of three managers focuses on building a case to support a pet theory of cause.

CASE HISTORY: FAILING PUMPS

Sometimes a decision must be made about the way to correct a situation. Everyone agrees that *some* kind of corrective action is needed, but the decision makers do not understand the situation's cause sufficiently to say *what* kind of corrective action makes the most sense. This was the case in the following example, where Problem Analysis was required before the managers could move on to the decision-making process.

A United States Government manager had a tough decision to make: what to do about an irrigation project the U.S. was financing in a Middle Eastern nation. Pumps that had been installed in wells some eighteen months earlier were now failing. The local employees didn't know how to maintain them, and it was the manager's job to institute a training program. The government had $20 million in the project and was prepared to spend half a million more on training.

At first this manager didn't see the situation as one characterized by "cause unknown." To him the cause was obvious: The local employees didn't know how to maintain the pumps. Then, when one of his assistants began to ask some probing questions, he realized that he didn't know **for certain** what was causing poor maintenance.

He called a meeting of his entire staff to specify the problem. He was shocked to find that the IS specification described the deterioration of **everything** having to do with the project: wells, weirs, pumps, ditches, shacks, tools—the whole works. The IS NOT was nothing more than "Not pumps alone...." This knocked out the assumed cause, "Local Employees Don't Know How to Maintain Pumps." After all, how much technical expertise is required to maintain ditches, shacks, and weirs?

He went on to ask, "Where is the deviation?" "IS in Country X; IS NOT in Countries Y and Z." (Y and Z were countries in which a similar program was in effect. The level of technical expertise of local employees there was about the same as in Country X.) "When was the deviation first observed?" The IS specification, in Country X, was "from the inception of the program." The IS NOT, in Countries Y and Z, was there "had **never** been any difficulty with pump maintenance," even though the program in Country Y had been in effect nearly twice as long as in Country X.

"Extent?" In Country X "about 60 percent of the installations had deteriorated." The IS NOT was that "40 percent had not" and that "none had deteriorated in Countries Y and Z." The deviation had reached crisis proportions in Country X, threatening crop failure and famine.

THE NEW RATIONAL MANAGER

Staff members now began to ask what was **distinctive about Country X** compared with Countries Y and Z? And what was **distinctive about 60 percent of the Installations** in Country X, where there was deterioration, compared with the 40 percent where there was none?

"Well, one thing, obviously," said an agronomist on the staff. "Land ownership patterns. There are many more tenant farmers in Country X than in Y and Z—small farmers working land they don't own."

"They are little more than serfs of the landlord owners," added an economist. "I would say that about 60 percent of the installations in Country X are maintained by tenant farmers."

The team manager asked the economist how many installations in Countries Y and Z would probably be maintained by tenant farmers. "Why, practically none. It's a totally different pattern of ownership in those countries."

Now the situation took on an entirely different light. The installations that were going to pieces were maintained by tenant-serfs with no stake in the success of the project. Installations that continued to function were maintained by farmer-owners. This had been the case from the inception of the project, so there was no change to cause the deviation. A condition of life had produced a predictable outcome. People with an incentive to maintain wells, weirs, pumps, and other equipment had somehow managed to stretch their mechanical skills to do the job. By contrast, laborers who received no benefit from the project, but only an additional burden, had let things go.

SUMMARY

It is dangerous to assume the cause of a deviation when it has never been properly analyzed or confirmed. In this example, the experts all thought they knew the cause: "The local employees can't maintain something as complicated as a pump." This statement appeared plausible until it was tested against other facts. Its inadequacy as an explanation became apparent when the deviation was specified and distinctions were developed using the inputs of staff members.

A decision based on inaccurate understanding of the situation's cause is of little or no help; it may actually make matters worse. If the manager involved in the irrigation project had recommended a series of costly maintenance training schools, scattered about the country (as he had been about to do), a great deal of time and at least half a million dollars would have been wasted. The deviation would have continued to exist, and other equally useless actions would probably have been taken, further compounding the confusion. Only when the actual cause of the situation was known could an efficient incentive program be instituted—for it was motivation, not ability, that was the core of the problem.

CASE HISTORY: THE IMMINENT STRIKE

Before people have had actual experience with Problem Analysis in a team situation, they may sometimes imagine that the process is too rigid, that it deprives the team of spontaneity and creativity. They may visualize managers trudging a mental assembly line from problem statements to confirmed causes. If that perception were true, Problem Analysis would indeed cramp anyone's style. Fortunately, it is not so, as the following example makes clear.

The management of an automobile company are meeting to discuss an urgent labor problem. An issue about work rules has suddenly arisen in three stamping plants, and there is serious danger of a wildcat strike that will shut them all down. Shutting down the stamping plants will idle all the assembly lines within a few days, just when the peak sales period is rapidly approaching. The timing couldn't be worse. Union leaders from the three plants have made serious demands. Top management has given orders to avoid a strike if at all possible.

"Why an issue like **this**, and why **now**?" asks the group's chairman, thinking about the dimensions of WHAT and WHEN. "It doesn't make sense to me." The situation is discussed at length. "All three plants are making these demands, but the ones in Plant A are most strident," says another person, thinking of IS and IS NOT. "Why should Plant A be more interested in this than the others?" asks someone else, looking for a distinction. "Aha! It's the only plant of the three with a possible jurisdictional conflict. They have two unions fighting for power in this particular trade." This statement by the chairman, who spotted the distinction, is followed by a discussion of the union squabbles.

"You know," says one man, drawing on his experience to suggest a possible cause, "it **could** be that there's a jurisdictional dispute going on underground at Plant A."

"That," someone else puts in, "is pure speculation."

"Look," says the first man, "**if** it were so, then someone may have worked up a possible wildcat strike to get added leverage for his own position. And if so, then I'll bet it doesn't have a thing to do with the issue itself. The other two plants would be going along just to give support to that faction. I know all this is speculative, but it fits the facts."

"And I know what you're thinking," says the man who had interrupted him. "If there's something like that going on, then Charlie Olson is mixed up in it."

"It isn't hard to guess what he would want," the chairman interjects, doing a little mental testing of the possible cause. "He's president of one union. If he wants to freeze out another union, this could do it. Nobody has more to gain in a jurisdictional fight than Olson." To confirm the cause through the additional data, they make a phone call to Plant A. Sure enough, word comes back that Olson is deeply involved.

Based on extended speculation within the basic thinking pattern of Problem Analysis and confirmed by the involvement of a key person, the managers conclude that this is a jurisdictional matter. The dispute has nothing to do with work rules. They then develop a new approach: The company makes a quiet intervention at Plant A; the jurisdictional question is set to one side; and talk of a strike disappears overnight. A verbal Problem Analysis has come to its successful completion.

SUMMARY

What these managers did was *speculate on the facts of WHAT and WHERE* that, if true, *would* explain the situation. Then they checked them out. If their speculations had proven incorrect, nothing would have been lost. As it turned out, their speculations were totally correct. Their willingness to base their speculations on experience and to accept whatever facts developed from further investigation saved time. Had they not speculated, they might not have found the cause of the threatened strike in time. Had they not checked out whether Olson was involved, their problems might have increased tenfold. They would have kept looking for a red herring only to discover, at the last moment, that the real cause lay elsewhere.

CASE HISTORY: THE NASA CONTRACT DISPUTE

In our final example of how Problem Analysis is used by a management team, a serious and costly problem is analyzed not by one team but by several teams in two organizations.

An electronics company obtained a NASA contract to produce a complicated item originally designed by a prestigious research laboratory. The equipment was completed, delivered, and installed but failed to work.

NASA sued the company to recover $880,000 in payments already made. The plant manager argued that his company had manufactured the equipment exactly to the specifications given by NASA. NASA's position was that the equipment didn't work, so NASA should not and would not pay for it. At the electronics company, the plant manager's head office was under pressure for botching the job.

Looked at in one way, it was NASA's problem. But the responsibility for discovering the cause of the deviation in performance—total failure of operation—lay with the top technical group in the company that had produced the equipment, not with NASA. To make the equipment's basic design totally visible, several teams began breaking down its specifications into individual requirements. They then compared the test and performance data they had generated against the specifications to see whether their translation of the design into hardware had been at fault. They concluded that they had followed the design to the letter and that there was nothing wrong in what they had done. Now that the specifications had been broken down and laid bare, however, it became painfully evident that **the design itself was faulty**. One element of the design ignored a basic law of physics! In short, they had meticulously produced something that could not work. The plant manager took this analysis to NASA and convinced agency officials that his people had done their work correctly—and that no one could produce equipment that would work from such a design.

The suit was withdrawn and NASA turned its attention to the research laboratory that had produced the faulty design. Thus, the laboratory was presented not with a *problem*, in our terminology—for cause was now known—but with a *decision*, a requirement for some kind of action. More importantly, the laboratory faced the need to develop procedures to prevent similar disasters in the future.

CHAPTER SUMMARY

Problem Analysis was not developed with improved communication in mind. It was developed as a system that would make the best use of a manager's natural cause-and-effect thinking pattern. Yet, over the years, the process has gained an impressive reputation as a communications device because of its common language for problem solving and because it can be used by a team of people with various technical backgrounds, experiences, and outlooks. Managers continue to use the basic ideas of Problem Analysis in team situations because the ideas pay off time and again.

To receive the maximum contribution of relevant information from a number of people working on one problem, some kind of structure is essential. It is also essential that people understand each other's words. You have probably seen this little sign on an office wall or desk: "I know that you believe you understand what you think I said, but I am not sure you realize that what you heard is not what I meant!" It may be the truth, sometimes, but it isn't the SHOULD....

Problem Analysis techniques help people work together in organizing information so that cause-and-effect relationships can clearly be seen. The techniques provide both a way of testing cause and a framework of information to use in further confirming cause. The techniques provide a procedure for cutting into any deviation, regardless of its content, to arrive at a mutual understanding of its components. Finally, by providing effective conditions for investigation, the techniques give assurance and confidence to those doing the analysis. It also gives them a common orientation that reduces confusion, minimizes arguments, and encourages teamwork.

FOUR

DECISION ANALYSIS

IN THIS CHAPTER

The Conditions and Elements of Making Choices
The Major Elements of Decision Analysis
The Techniques of Decision Analysis

THE CONDITIONS AND ELEMENTS OF MAKING CHOICES

Decisions must be made and actions must be taken in all organizations. It is up to the appropriate people in the organization to select the actions, determine how to carry them out, and take responsibility for their successful implementation. Often, however, there is uncertainty over how to proceed. People find it hard to think together about the choices they must make. They cannot agree on where or how to start making the decision. As a result, they may overlook important information, fail to consult the proper people, and make mistakes. Organizational decision making is often not as good as it should be.

Although people enjoy being involved in decision making, many shun the task because of the controversy involved. Lacking commonly accepted, unbiased procedures, decision making becomes a shoving contest among those with differing points of view. The individuals with the most power prevail. Others accept decisions in order to save face and avoid direct confrontation.

When people are provided with a common approach to decision making, they find they can indeed work as a team. There is more sharing of relevant information. Differing positions are more successfully reconciled because the process of decision making is less biased. Inevitably, the quality of decision making improves.

THE THINKING PATTERN FOR MAKING CHOICES

Decision Analysis is a systematic procedure based on the thinking pattern we use when making choices. Its techniques represent expansion and refinement of the elements in this thinking pattern:

▷ We appreciate the fact that a choice must be made.

▷ We consider the specific factors that must be satisfied if the choice is to succeed.

▷ We decide what kind of action will best satisfy these factors.

▷ We consider what risks may be attached to our final choice of action that could jeopardize its safety and success.

We may employ this thinking pattern very swiftly, even unconsciously. Although we may skip one or more of the elements in a cursory analysis, each element plays some role in determining every choice we make. When we are confronted with simple, repetitive choices, memory and experience enable us to consider in a fraction of a second the specific factors that must be satisfied. This is seen typically in the choices we make when we drive an automobile. We would be incapable of driving without the ability to make decisions and choices quickly and automatically, unconsciously using all the elements of the choice-making thinking pattern.

Nobody needs to be told that excellence in making choices is critical to individual and organizational success. Everyone knows that choices made today influence our lives tomorrow. What is not so obvious is *how* to use the information available to make the decision today that will be lauded as excellent tomorrow and bring credit to everyone associated with it. Nor so obvious is *how* we ought to use that information, how we can avoid getting bogged down in details, how we can avoid missing the details that must be recognized, and how we can escape being confused and intimidated by the uncertainties of the future.

Behind most decisions lie a myriad details. Some are highly important, some insignificant. The quality of available information may not match our needs. There may not be enough information. There may be so much that it overwhelms us. Perhaps the degree of relevance of available information is unclear. Over every decision hovers some measure of uncertainty—for all decisions will play out their day on a stage somewhere in the uncertain future. Good decision making, like good problem solving, depends heavily on experience and judgment. In both areas of managerial responsibility, however, it is within the framework of a *systematic procedure* that experience and judgment produce successful results and a reputation for managerial excellence.

CASE HISTORY: HIRING A NEW R&D DIRECTOR

Making good choices depends on three elements: the quality of our *definition* of specific factors that must be satisfied, the quality of our *evaluation* of the available alternatives, and the quality of our *assessment* of the risks associated with those alternatives. It all sounds so straightforward that we wonder how bad decisions come to be made. Here is one simple and highly typical example.

"We need to increase the research and development capabilities of this organization." That was the statement made by a member of the Executive Committee of a fast-growing social research organization.

Over a period of two months, the committee discussed this need and considered alternative actions. With what result? The committee hired a new director of R&D, an individual who had worked for a competitor and was considered "the best."

"Best for **what**?" is the question that should have been asked when the statement of need was first made.

After the new director had been in the job for six months, the Executive Committee came to three conclusions: (1) The new director was not "best" for their organization; (2) The alternative of "new director" did not really address any of the firm's pressing R&D concerns; (3) The question of a suitable direction for R&D at that point in the company's life had never been adequately discussed.

The committee had made a poor decision. Why? Because the committee had no clear purpose to begin with, it had not discussed the organization's specific needs in matters of research and development. Consequently, the committee had not understood the kinds of alternatives most likely to benefit the organization. Yet, at the time the decision was made, everyone was positive and enthusiastic about the choice.

"What we said later," one member of the committee told us, "was that, given the information we had at the time, it seemed like the right way to go. But I don't buy it. Given the information we **could** have had and the actions we **might** have taken had we really thought through our situation, I don't believe that the decision to hire 'the best' away from a competitor would have seemed like the right way to go. Everyone was hung up on the assumption that there was somebody out there who could come in and work miracles. It was never put in just those words, but it was on that assumption that the whole decision was really based."

Many, many decisions are characterized by this kind of thinking. A good decision can only be made in the context of *what needs to be accomplished*. No alternative is any better than the opportunity it holds for us to do the job that has to be done.

The purpose of Decision Analysis is to identify what needs to be done, develop the specific criteria for its accomplishment, evaluate the available alternatives relative to those criteria, and identify the risks involved.

For the remainder of this chapter, we will explain the major elements in the process of Decision Analysis and show how the process is used. Our example involves a relatively simple, straightforward choice among four possible courses of action.

THE MAJOR ELEMENTS OF DECISION ANALYSIS

THE DECISION STATEMENT

In Problem Analysis, we begin with a *problem statement*, which names the situation to be resolved. In Decision Analysis, we will begin with the *decision statement*, or with naming the "choice" dilemma that is to be resolved.

Resolution in Problem Analysis consisted of a confirmable answer to the question "Why?" Resolution in Decision Analysis will consist of an answer to the questions "To what purpose?" "Which?" and "How?"

A decision statement provides the focus for everything that follows and sets the limits of the choice. The criteria to be developed will follow from it, describing in detail the requirements of the decision. The alternatives will be judged on their ability to meet these requirements. Because the decision statement sets all these activities in motion, it has another quality in common with the problem statement: *The way it is worded deserves careful attention.*

A decision statement always indicates a choice, some kind of action and its intended result: "Select a new director of quality" or "Choose a site for our new West Coast office." It also indicates the *level, or implied prior decisions,* at which the decision is to be made. "Select a new director of quality" indicates we have already decided that a new director is needed.

In the case we presented earlier—"We need to increase the research and development capabilities of this organization"—the decision failed chiefly because no thought was given to the level of the decision. In fact, it was not clear that there was even a choice to be made. The statement of purpose gave the decision-making team no guidance and set no limits, up or down, on the range of alternatives that would be considered. The only stage it set was one on which an alternative-driven solution could assume the starring role.

THE OBJECTIVES FOR THE DECISION

Objectives, in our terminology, are the criteria for the decision— the specific results and benefits the decision is to achieve. We establish these objectives once we agree upon the correct statement of our decision. We do this before discussing alternatives, sometimes even before identifying alternatives. Decision Analysis is the antithesis of identifying a course of action and then building a case to support it. Instead, we are moving from what needs to be accomplished toward the alternative that can best accomplish it. For example, if we want to hire a new executive, we are more likely to make a good choice if we *first* identify the qualities of an ideal candidate and *then* begin the interviewing process. No experienced manager needs to have this reasoning spelled out. Objectives are clear measures of the ends we want to achieve, for only with clear measures can we make reasoned choices.

MUSTs and WANTs

We divide the objectives into two categories: MUSTs and WANTs. The MUST objectives are *mandatory*; they *must* be achieved to guarantee a successful decision. They may not be our most important objectives. Rather, they are minimum requirements that any alternative must provide to be meaningful. When the time comes to assess alternatives against our objectives, any alternative that cannot fulfill a MUST objective will immediately drop out of the analysis.

These objectives must be *measurable* because they function as a screen to eliminate unacceptable alternatives. We must be able to say, "This alternative *absolutely* cannot fulfill this objective; it cannot meet a requirement that is mandatory for success." For example, a MUST objective in a hiring decision might be "Two years' experience as a supervisor in this industry." If that length of experience is mandatory, then there is no point in considering any candidate who hasn't put in the two years.

Of course, it is important to understand why an objective is mandatory. We might ask what benefit will we gain from a candidate with two years' experience. If there are other acceptable ways to gain that benefit, then two years' experience is not truly mandatory.

"Two years' experience" also needs to be a *reasonable* objective. Can we reasonably expect to find alternatives that satisfy this MUST objective? Given the remuneration for the position and our location, can we expect to find candidates with two years' experience? If we cannot and two years' experience is truly mandatory, then we may need to re-think the decision statement or some of the other objectives.

All other objectives are categorized as WANTs. The alternatives we generate will be judged on their *relative* performance against WANT objectives, not on whether or not they fulfill them. The function of these objectives is to give us a comparative picture of alternatives—*a sense of how the alternatives perform relative to each other.*

An objective will be stated frequently as a MUST and then be rephrased as a WANT so that it can perform both functions. For example, "Two years' experience in this industry" (MUST) may be rephrased as "Maximum experience in this industry" (WANT). Now, when we come

THE NEW RATIONAL MANAGER

to evaluate the alternatives, we can make two kinds of judgments. First, candidates with less than two years' experience will be eliminated. Second, the remaining candidates will be judged relative to each other based on how many years of experience each has had.

Here is an example of a high-priority objective that could not be used as a MUST: "Interacts well with managers at all levels." No matter how important this objective may be, it concerns an ability that can be measured only in a subjective way. All four job candidates may meet this objective, but *some will meet it better than others*. This is exactly what we want to know: Who meets it best? Who is equally good? How well do others compare to the best performer?

Unlike a MUST objective, we are less concerned with finding alternatives that satisfy the objective minimally and more concerned with how the alternatives perform relative to each other. A WANT objective is not necessarily less important than a MUST; it simply serves a different purpose.

Someone once succinctly described the functions of these two kinds of objectives by saying, "The MUSTs decide who gets to play, but the WANTs decide who wins."

ALTERNATIVES

An ideal alternative perfectly fulfills every condition set for it without adding new difficulties. Unfortunately, ideal alternatives are rare. We must, therefore, evaluate each available alternative by measuring it against all of our objectives. It is the relative quality of that fit that concerns us.

If we must choose among several alternatives, we will have to decide which one will best fulfill our objectives with the smallest acceptable risk. In other words, we try to make a *balanced choice*. An alternative that best accomplishes the objectives but carries severe risks may not, after all, be the best choice. Another alternative, perhaps less exciting but safer, may be the best balanced choice.

If there is only one alternative, we must decide whether it is good enough to accept. In this case, our evaluation will focus on its relative worth compared with a perfect, but unobtainable, alternative.

If we must choose between a current and a proposed course of action, then we consider both to be alternatives. We evaluate their performance against our objectives just as we would if both had been proposed. Whatever is currently being done is, after all, an alternative; the choice is whether to continue that way or find another, better way.

If, in the absence of *any* alternative, we must create something new, we can usually build an alternative from available components. We then choose the best and most feasible combinations, treat each as a separate alternative, and evaluate all of them against an ideal model of an alternative.

In the next chapter, we will examine true examples of these situations and explore the sources of alternatives.

THE CONSEQUENCES OF THE CHOICE

The final step in Decision Analysis is the search for possible adverse consequences of all feasible alternatives.

The negative consequences of any action are as tangible as its benefits, sometimes more so. Once a decision has been made and implemented, any of its negative effects will eventually become real problems. The effects of decisions—good or bad—always outlive the decision-making process that produced them. And which effects—good or bad—are longest remembered? "The evil that men do," wrote Shakespeare, "lives after them, the good is oft interred with their bones...." Some things haven't changed at all in almost four hundred years.

We must thoroughly explore and evaluate the possible adverse consequences of any alternative *before* we make a final decision. This is the only opportunity we will ever have to deal with such effects at no cost beyond a little intellectual effort. We must recognize possible adverse consequences before they occur and take them into consideration as part of our decision. Having recognized and assessed them, we may be able to avoid them altogether or take steps in the present that will reduce their effect in the future. A risk attached to an alternative is not necessarily a totally damning factor—*provided that someone sees it while there is time to do something about it.* Any evaluation and choice that omits a disciplined, systematic search for potential negative consequences is an invitation to disaster.

Decision Analysis seldom deals with certainties. The further into the future a proposed action extends, the less certain it can be. It is because of these uncertainties that the process of Decision Analysis depends on our judgments, evaluations, experience, and intuitive feelings. All of these supply the valid data we need to support the correct decision we must make.

To set aside feelings, instincts, and the inner voice that says, "I don't feel right about this," is to throw away a valuable resource. It leads to such errors as hiring a person you don't like and can't work with just because "the résumé looked so good, and I was trying to be objective." That is not good decision making. A good decision is one that will work. Overlooking factors that make a choice unworkable is a fundamental mistake. A reasonable selection and a good decision always depend on thorough study and careful evaluation of *all* relevant information.

Decision Analysis is a methodical, systematic process. But it is also as creative and innovative a process as its users choose to make it.

THE TECHNIQUES OF DECISION ANALYSIS

The techniques of Decision Analysis are divided into these activities:

▷ State the decision.

▷ Develop objectives.

▷ Classify objectives into MUSTs and WANTs.

▷ Weigh the WANTs.

▷ Generate alternatives.

▷ Screen alternatives through the MUSTs.

▷ Compare alternatives against the WANTs.

▷ Identify adverse consequences.

▷ Make the best balanced choice.

STATE THE DECISION

CASE HISTORY: PURCHASING THE BEST PERSONNEL INFORMATION SYSTEM

The following situation illustrates the use of Decision Analysis techniques. It concerns the selection of software from among four potential suppliers.

Our client's decision statement was: "Select the Best Personnel Information System for [Our] Corporation." The people involved in making this decision were the vice president of operations, the vice president of human resources, the director of management information systems, and one of the firm's attorneys. They worked as a team to decide three things: the level of the decision, who was to delegate necessary research tasks to others in the firm, and who was to use the resulting information to reach the final conclusion. The team was not involved in the research required to make the evaluation.

Operating this way, the team arrived at its conclusion after three one-hour sessions held over a period of two weeks. Compared with previous, similar decision situations, this was considered a tremendous saving of time and effort.

The decision statement indicated not only the purpose of the decision but also the level at which it would be made. It set the stage for the *kinds* of alternatives that would be considered. Had the statement been worded: "Select a method to improve our method of personnel information recording and reporting," the character of the decision would have been different. The selection of a new system would have appeared as one of several alternatives.

A decision statement is, in a way, the product of previous decisions. The team had already decided that it needed a new system to replace all the present methods and procedures. Thus, the wording of the decision statement immediately vetoed a dozen other possible decisions that might have been made.

DEVELOP OBJECTIVES AND CLASSIFY
INTO MUSTS AND WANTS

What must the new system do? What would the team *like* it to do in addition? What constraints affect the choice of a new system? Such are the questions that every team of decision makers has to ask in order to begin setting objectives. The answers to these questions will result in a list of objectives. The objectives will then be classified as MUSTs or WANTs.

Among our client's MUST objectives for the new personnel information reporting system were these:

MUST be capable of:

• Meeting Equal Employment reporting standards.

• Providing reporting to management, using Report Writer.

• Capturing compensation information.

Each of these objectives was considered mandatory, and each was measurable: a system could offer these features or it could not. These objectives were also considered reasonable. Several alternatives were known to meet these minimum requirements.

The list of WANT objectives represented additional desirable, but not mandatory, criteria. Following are five of the seventeen WANT objectives that appeared in the analysis:

• Captures individual job histories and special capabilities.

• Can be implemented within six months.

• Meets Health and Safety reporting requirements.

• Reduces current paperwork.

• Protects employee confidentiality.

WEIGH THE WANTS

Once the WANT objectives had been identified, each one was weighed according to its relative importance. The *most* important objective was identified and given a weight of 10. All other objectives were then weighted in comparison with the first, from 10 (equally important) down to a possible 1 (only one-tenth as important).

No attempt was made to rank the objectives. The purpose of the 10 to 1 weighting scale was simply to make visible the relationships among these objectives. What mattered most? What could be done without, if necessary?

When the time comes to evaluate the alternatives, we do so by assessing them *relative to each other* against all the WANT objectives—one at a time. This is why it is critical at the outset to identify the most important objectives. It is pointless to know that a particular alternative satisfies nine out of ten WANT objectives if, in fact, it is the tenth that is most crucial to the success of the decision. We must also examine the *balance* of WANT objectives and look for certain danger signals:

▷ Too many high numbers may indicate either unrealistic expectations or a faulty perception of which objectives can guarantee success.

▷ Too many low numbers suggest that unimportant details may be smothering the analysis.

▷ Too many objectives reflecting the vested interest of a single stakeholder may lead to an unworkable decision. This is especially true if other stakeholders are equally affected by the final decision.

▷ Loaded objectives—those that guarantee a smooth passage for a certain alternative and penalize all others—can make a mockery of an analysis.

These are the weights our client team assigned to the five WANT objectives:

- Captures individual job histories and special capabilities 9
- Can be implemented within six months 10
- Meets Health and Safety reporting requirements 8
- Reduces current paperwork 5
- Protects employee confidentiality 3

GENERATE ALTERNATIVES AND SCREEN
THROUGH THE MUSTS

In this case, alternatives were fairly clear-cut. The team identified four leading suppliers of the system they wanted and then launched the evaluation.

In this evaluation, an alternative either meets all the MUST objectives (GO) or does not (NO GO). A NO GO is immediately dropped from further consideration.

The MUSTs, you may remember, were:

- Meeting Equal Employment reporting standards.

- Providing reporting to management, using Report Writer.

- Capturing compensation information.

To the surprise of most people on the team, one highly regarded system failed at this point. It could not provide the Report Writer feature. The alternatives are shown in Figure 7.

Note that the information columns in Figure 7 tell us *why* an alternative has passed or failed. By listing this information, the process has become visible. Facts, opinions, and judgments are on record. A written summary exists for future reference, leaving nothing to be memorized or forgotten. And necessary information is available for anyone who must approve the final decision.

Having eliminated Company D, the team now carried the three remaining alternatives into the next phase: comparative evaluation on the basis of the WANT objectives.

COMPARE ALTERNATIVES AGAINST THE WANTS

Beginning with the first WANT objective—"Can be implemented within six months" (weight of 10)—the team evaluated the information it had gathered about Companies A, B, and C.

Company A had given an estimate of six months with a guarantee; Company B, six months but would not commit to a set date; Company C, four months and seemed reliable. The vice president of operations was less certain about Company B. He had heard that two of B's customers had reported slightly delayed implementation; otherwise, they were satisfied with the service they had received.

Based on this information, the team decided that Company C, with a reliable estimate of four months, *best* met the implementation objective. They gave Company C a score of 10 on that objective, and gave relative scores of 9 to Company A and 5 to Company B. What purpose do these numbers serve? *They help to reflect our judgments.*

At this point in the analysis, all objectives have been sorted out and made visible, and the WANTS have been weighed. Now the alternatives will be sorted out, permitting us to judge the relative advantages of each one. For example, how good an implementation job can Company C do *compared with Companies A and B?* As each company is scored against each of the WANT objectives, its relative overall performance and ability to produce desirable results will gradually become clear.

Figure 8 shows the judgments the team made of the relative performances of the three alternatives, scored against all of the WANT objectives.

People sometimes are bothered when none of the alternatives seems to deserve a 10. They are even more disturbed when none of

FIGURE 7   **ALTERNATIVES SCREENED THROUGH MUST OBJECTIVES**

MUST OBJECTIVES	COMPANY A	GO/NO GO	COMPANY B	GO/NO GO
Meets Equal Employment reporting standards	Meets government requirements. More detail available	GO	Meets government requirements. More detail available	GO
Provides management reporting using Report Writer	All reports use Report Writer	GO	Standard reports can be exported to Report Writer	GO
Captures compensation information	In standard package and can be added to	GO	In standard package	GO

      THE NEW RATIONAL MANAGER

the alternatives performs well on a particular objective. We give a 10 to the alternative that comes *closest* to meeting the objective, and score the other alternatives *relative to it*. We are not seeking an ideal through this comparative evaluation. What we are seeking, instead, is an answer to the question: "Of these (real and attainable) alternatives, which best fulfills the objective?"

There is one caution: If, during the scoring step, a statement such as "none of the alternatives is much good" comes up repeatedly from one objective to the next, then something is obviously wrong. Either more alternatives are needed or the objectives are unrealistic, and no *real and attainable* alternative can fulfill them. But this is a rare circumstance. People in a decision-making position are usually there because they have a good grasp of what is feasible; they do not devise unattainable objectives.

At the other extreme, all alternatives may perform well on nearly all objectives. This is caused by a set of objectives so loose that any of a number of similar alternatives will be equally good at satisfying the requirements of the decision. The simple remedy is to go back to the list of WANT objectives and make them tighter, more demanding, and more numerous. The alternative that really does offer more will then stand out.

COMPANY C	GO/NO GO	COMPANY D	GO/NO GO
Meets government requirements. More detail available	GO	Meets government requirements using standard reports. Cannot be modified	GO
Standard reports can be exported to Report Writer	GO	Cannot use Report Writer	NO GO
In standard package and can be added to	GO	—	

Now we need answers to two questions: How does each alternative perform across the board? How does it compare to the other alternatives on total performance against WANT objectives? We can answer the questions by computing the weighted scores of each alternative.

A *weighted score* is the score of an alternative multiplied by the weight of the objective to which the score refers. For example:

Company A scored 9 on the WANT objective "Can be implemented within six months." That objective has a weight of 10. Therefore the **weighted score** of Company A on that objective is 90 (9 x 10).

We continue by computing Company A's weighted scores for *all* the WANT objectives. Then we add up all of the weighted scores to produce the *total weighted score* for the Company A alternative. We complete this step by repeating the procedure for the other alternatives, producing the results that appear in Figure 9.

The total weighted scores function as *visible comparative measurements* of the alternatives. Their numbers indicate that one alternative is more viable than the others, that one course of action is apparently more valuable than the others. There is nothing magical about

FIGURE 8   **ALTERNATIVES COMPARED AGAINST WANT OBJECTIVES**

WANT OBJECTIVES	WEIGHT	COMPANY A	SCORE
Captures individual job histories and special capabilities	9	Can be written into program	6
Can be implemented within 6 months	10	6 months with guarantee from vendor	9
Meets Health and Safety reporting requirements	8	Exceeds requirements; very flexible	10
Reduces current paperwork	5	Minimum forms required; can use current documentation	10
Protects employee confidentiality	3	Can customize security	10

THE NEW RATIONAL MANAGER

the numbers. A base of 10 to 1, for both the weighting of WANT objectives and the scoring of alternatives, is a simple, logical, and productive means for producing good results.

As Figure 9 indicates, the total weighted scores were 304 for Company A, 218 for Company B, and 302 for Company C. As we have said, this is a sampling of the full-blown analysis that included seventeen WANT objectives. For the record, the complete scores were: 1009 for Company A, 752 for Company B, and 878 for Company C. Company A, then, satisfied the objectives of the decision to a greater degree than either of its competitors.

Under certain conditions we can vary the way we assign numerical weights. If a manager must work with fifty or a hundred objectives, for example, these can be broken down into categories, with a weight (or percentage of influence) given to each category. In this instance, a single WANT objective may bear a weight of 10, but belong to a category with a comparatively low weight. While the logic of the Decision Analysis process remains unchanged, this modification of technique reflects the particular requirements of the decision.

COMPANY B	SCORE	COMPANY C	SCORE
In standard package	8	In standard package and can be added to	10
Vendor says maybe 6 months	5	4 months	10
In standard package	7	In standard package	7
Uses minimum forms; cannot customize	5	Uses minimum forms and can make custom forms	7
No security on data file but can be added	5	Password security on Report Writer	7

The total weighted score gives us a tool for selecting a *tentative choice*. Although the tentative choice often graduates to the status of *best balanced choice*, it should never do so before we explore the potential risks involved. Four decades of experience have shown us clearly that elimination of this final step of Decision Analysis—because "one alternative is so obviously the leader"—can negate the value of all work done up to this point.

IDENTIFY ADVERSE CONSEQUENCES

If exploring potential risks is so important, why do people often fail to do this step? There are several understandable reasons. If an analysis of three alternatives produces total weighted scores of 700, 350, and 210, it may seem a waste of time to brainstorm for potential risks. In another case, someone may be reluctant to inject a dose of pessimism when the rest of the team enthusiastically exclaims, "We've done all this work! And we've produced this great alternative!" That

FIGURE 9   **ALTERNATIVES AND THEIR TOTAL WEIGHTED SCORES**

WANT OBJECTIVES	WEIGHT	COMPANY A	SCORE	WEIGHTED SCORE
Captures individual job histories and special capabilities	9	Can be written into program	6	54
Can be implemented within 6 months	10	6 months with guarantee from vendor	9	90
Meets Health and Safety reporting requirements	8	Exceeds requirements; very flexible	10	80
Reduces current paperwork	5	Minimum forms required; can use current documentation	10	50
Protects employee confidentiality	3	Can customize security	10	30
Total Weighted Scores				**304**

one doubtful member of an optimistic decision-making team may very well hide those negative opinions. One last and very common reason for dropping the step of risk exploration is this: We are often unable or unwilling to apply the lessons of the past to the decisions of today.

One manager told us that, early in his career, he had meekly suggested to his boss that the potential problems of an alternative under consideration had not been adequately considered. Even more meekly he reminded his boss that a decision made in another department had seriously backfired several months before. "That," his boss replied scornfully, "was *them* and *then*. And this is *us* and *now*." The subject was dropped. The decision proved to be a good one, but that did not prove the young manager wrong. A year or two after a decision is implemented, nobody regrets the time spent probing its risks. It is a mere fraction of the time spent in regret over a risk that should have been explored but was not.

In the earlier steps of Decision Analysis, we try to make our objectives as comprehensive and our evaluation of alternatives as rigorous as possible. But these activities go just so far. They must be followed

COMPANY B	SCORE	WEIGHTED SCORE	COMPANY C	SCORE	WEIGHTED SCORE
In standard package	8	72	In standard package and can be added to	10	90
Vendor says maybe 6 months	5	50	4 months	10	100
In standard package	7	56	In standard package	7	56
Uses minimum forms; cannot customize	5	25	Uses minimum forms and cans make custom forms	7	35
No security on data file but can be added	5	15	Password security in Report Writer	7	21
		218			302

by the most creative and difficult step in the process: *considering the consequences of alternatives*. This entails answering at least the following questions.

If we choose *this* alternative:

▷ What are the implications of being too close to a MUST limit?

▷ Where might information about this alternative be invalid? What are the implications?

▷ What could go wrong, in the short- and long-term, if this alternative were chosen?

▷ What could keep this decision from being successfully implemented?

In this step of the process, we try to destroy our best alternatives one at a time. We become destructive, negative, and pessimistic. The degree to which managers accept this process is determined largely by how experienced they are. Experience teaches us that there are no awards for past optimism over current failures. This fact is borne out by the difficulty of finding out who, in any organization, was really responsible for the very worst decisions that were ever made.

We begin this step with the *tentative* choice—the alternative with the highest total weighted score. We examine it by itself. We examine its probabilities of failure or potential trouble. Remember that this is *never* an exercise in comparisons. We do *not* say, "Alternative A is more likely to produce this problem than Alternative B." Comparison is not a useful approach. Each alternative must be examined separately.

We then rate the adverse consequences of an alternative on the basis of *probability and seriousness*: What is the probability that this (adverse consequence) will occur? If it (the adverse consequence) does occur, how serious will it be? We can use ratings of High, Medium, and Low (H,M,L) or a scale of 10 (highly probable/very serious) to 1 (unlikely/not at all serious). The 10 to 1 system is fine—provided that we avoid the temptation to start multiplying: "Probability of 9 x Seriousness of 3 = 27." (We did this in our first book, *The Rational Manager*, and went on to add these numbers for each alternative. This produced "adverse consequence totals" for all the alternatives. We have found over the years that this is not useful information.) If we permit the numbers to obscure the information that produced them, we can lose sight of the serious adverse consequences.

We will not lose any sleep over an adverse consequence of low probability and minimal seriousness. But we will be very attentive if an adverse consequence is considered both highly probable and very serious.

Following are some of the adverse consequences for the alternatives that scored the highest. These were identified during the final step of the Personnel Information System decision.

Company A:	If the company is to be sold soon, then support could be affected.
Probability?	Medium
Seriousness if it occurs?	High
Company C:	If this is a new company with inexperienced employees, then they may not meet future needs.
Probability?	Low
Seriousness if it occurs?	Medium

Three factors determine the number and importance of potential adverse consequences we identify for the alternatives: the extent of their existence, our ability to find them, and our willingness to address those we find.

MAKE THE BEST BALANCED CHOICE

Having clearly identified the value each alternative can deliver and the risks each alternative poses, we are prepared to weigh the potential gains against the potential pitfalls. We ask ourselves whether or not we are willing to accept the risks of a choice to gain the benefits. If the answer is yes, then we should commit to the choice. If not, we should consider less risky, more beneficial choices.

How useful is the Decision Analysis process if potential adverse consequences can knock out the very alternative that scored the highest on the objectives we worked so hard to develop? It is *because* of the previous steps in the process, the visibility of information, and the tracking of our thinking from the decision statement to this point that we can best assess the potential adverse consequences. It is only now, with all the data before us, that we can stretch our imaginations beyond the body of facts we have amassed, survey it all, and ask: "What did we miss? Can we afford the risks involved with this choice?"

The outcome of this particular case was that our client chose to go with Company C, the runner-up in the numerical scoring. Some-one had picked up a rumor that Company A might sell out within the next three years. The rumor was never substantiated but was there just the same. Moreover, Company C's youth and relatively small size seemed to offer at least as many potential advantages as disadvantages. Its management team was aggressive, ambitious, and preoccupied with service as a means of getting and retaining new business. Our client's service needs were unlikely to outstrip Company C's ability to meet them. The team made the best decision possible based on the avail-able information and on the experience and judgment of the team members.

So how did it all turn out?

Company A did not sell out within three years. But by that time its reputation for service had been eclipsed—by Company C, the team's choice. Company C did an excellent job. It had the system in full op-eration within four months as promised, and it continued to treat our client as a key customer. The decision-making team remained satisfied that it had made the right choice and never regretted having consid-ered the rumor about Company A in its deliberations.

In three one-hour sessions conducted over a period of two weeks, the team had reached a prudent decision that produced exactly the results they had hoped for: a balanced, reasoned choice of action that all could subscribe to and support—a *choice that worked* for the organization.

CHAPTER SUMMARY

Through the process of Decision Analysis, we expand from a concise statement of purpose to a number of criteria for completely defining the achievement of that purpose. These criteria give us something specific against which to evaluate available alternatives. Then, by narrowing those judgments through a systematic method of evaluation and risk assessment, we reach a final conclusion.

The power of the process lies in the ability it gives managers to make *productive* use of all available information and judgments. The process does not guarantee that perfect decisions will be made every time. Given human fallibility and the usual inadequacy of available information, there can always be errors. At the very least, however, the Decision Analysis process enables the manager to reduce the incidence of errors by providing a systematic framework for evaluating alternatives. Going beyond this simplest level of efficiency, the examples in the next chapter illustrate how much more effective Decision Analysis can be when creative and innovative managers apply the basic logic of the process to their most important choices.

The Uses of Decision Analysis

Types of Decisions

Every decision we make requires us to think in terms of *objectives, alternatives*, and *potential risks*. That choice may involve a thousand criteria plus the inputs and deliberations of a hundred or more people. Or, it may involve only five criteria and ten minutes of deliberation by one person. The dimensions are immaterial because the basic process is always the same. And the final judgment is always: "This is what ought to be done."

In this chapter, we will describe how managers have applied the systematic process of Decision Analysis. The true cases we cite illustrate individual approaches to the development and evaluation of objectives, alternatives, and potential risks in a number of common decision-making situations. In each case, a manager or management team has adapted the procedure to match specific requirements.

These decision situations fall into five categories:

▷ The complex decision that requires examination of a large amount of information and involves the judgment of many people.

▷ The "Yes/No" decision that involves only two alternatives: to take or reject a course of action; to do something in a different way or to continue as before.

▷ The decision as to whether a single proposed course of action is sound enough to be implemented.

▷ The decision in which an original alternative must be developed by the decision-maker or team.

▷ The routine decision: hiring, purchasing of equipment or services, developing of personnel policies, and other everyday decisions.

A final section is devoted to *adverse consequence thinking*—the protection of decisions.

THE COMPLEX DECISION

CASE HISTORY: REMOVING OREBODY PILLARS

This example, illustrating full and detailed use of Decision Analysis, clearly demonstrates each step in the thinking process.

Our client operates one of the world's largest underground mines. In the company's primary mining (its first cut-through), it takes out about 40 percent of the ore. The remainder is left behind as pillars to prevent collapse of the tunnels. In the secondary stage, the tunnels are filled in to support the ceilings, and the pillars are mined out. This is critical, dangerous work: A mistake can result in trapped miners as well as loss of a great deal of ore. The best way of backfilling and mining out the pillars depends on the specific characteristics of the mine, the ore, and the surrounding strata. How this is done is never treated as a cut-and-dried decision; it always entails close evaluation of many possibilities.

The company had to make a decision concerning the removal of pillars on the 2,500- and 2,800-foot levels. About $200 million in ore remained underground. Two methods had been suggested: "sub-level cave" and "high-rise with sub-level cave." Both were sound, accepted practices; neither method had an apparent advantage over the other. Since opinions of the top technical people were about evenly divided between the two alternatives, the organization named a task force of thirteen to study the situation and arrive at a decision. Among them were senior production people, geologists, safety engineers, ventilation and scheduling personnel, and cost control personnel. Each group of experts on the team had a somewhat different point of view and knowledge of the business.

They first discussed the conditions required for successful pillar removal. They recognized that there were four groups of considerations. These were listed as: "Metal Recovery," "Mining Conditions," "Cost," and "Operation." From these four groupings, they developed twenty specific objectives for the decision. These included: "Maximum metal recovery," "Minimum siltstone in ore," "Safety," "Least cost per metal unit," and "Minimum cement in ore stream." With these as the ideal model of a perfect removal procedure, they began to evaluate the two available methods. Each method was evaluated against each criterion to determine which came closest to the ideal. They considered all aspects of the two methods point by point, using a numerical system to record and keep track of the judgments they made as they went along.

When they had finished evaluating the relative advantages of the two methods, they found that the sub-level cave procedure appeared to be 25 percent better than the high-rise procedure. Even the proponents of the sub-level cave method were surprised at the degree to which it outperformed the high-rise method.

The team then looked at the adverse consequences of adopting each method. They found that the "high-rise" alternative carried somewhat more penalty and risk than the other. The choice was clear: The "sub-level cave" method more nearly approximated the ideal and carried fewer potential penalties. That method was put into operation, and the $200 million in ore was recovered without incident. Their analysis, excluding information on adverse consequences, is outlined in Figure 10.

FIGURE 10

DECISION ANALYSIS TO SELECT A REMOVAL METHOD FOR
THE OREBODY PILLARS AT 2,500-2,800 FEET

OBJECTIVES

MUST OBJECTIVES
Meet schedule

Retain stability 18c Sub
Be profitable

WANT OBJECTIVES	WEIGHT
Maximize metal recovery	10
Minimize cost/metal per ton	10
Provide safe mining conditions with regard to ringfirers, brow firers	10
Minimize reliance on fill and stability of structures	10
Maintain good ventilation conditions	8
Maximize flexibility of production	8
Maximize recovery of metal in rib pillars	8
Defer advance south of primary stopes	7

ALTERNATIVES

SUB-LEVEL CAVE

INFORMATION	GO/NO GO
On present schedule	GO
Ref. JPD/OPS MIN 4.2	GO
Memo reference JL/2.1/MIN 8.10.2 November 1	GO

HIGH-RISE WITH SUB-LEVEL CAVE

INFORMATION	GO/NO GO
Alternative schedule but would need some tons from 2G/2B block	GO
Ref. SBL/RCM MIN 4.2	GO
Memo reference FoS/2.1/MIN 8.10.3 dated October 29	GO

INFORMATION	SCORE	WEIGHTED SCORE
186,000 tons	10	100
$228/ton	7	70
Least exposure for workers	10	100
Least reliance on fill and stability of structures	10	100
No problems	10	80
Multiple draw points required	10	80
More problems due to ribs being surrounded by cement fill on two sides and unconsolidated fill on two sides	7	56
No problems	10	70

INFORMATION	SCORE	WEIGHTED SCORE
177,000 tons	9	90
$190/ton	10	100
Moderate exposure	7	70
Some reliance on fill and stability	5	50
Need to get fresh air to the hanging wall through pillars and cement drives	7	56
Few draw points available	7	56
Less unconsolidated fill surrounding rib pillars	10	80
Would require primary stopes earlier than using sub-level cave	2	14

FIGURE 10 continued

OBJECTIVES

WANT OBJECTIVES	WEIGHT
Ensure simplicity of operation	5
Minimize development in fill	5
Minimize siltstone in ore stream	5
Minimize number of workers required	4
Minimize development footage	4
Minimize equipment requirements	4
Minimize new equipment purchases	3
Minimize casual water	2
Provide good roadways	2
Minimize cement in ore stream	1

Total Weighted Scores

ALTERNATIVES

SUB-LEVEL CAVE			HIGH-RISE WITH SUB-LEVEL CAVE		
INFORMATION	*SCORE*	*WEIGHTED SCORE*	*INFORMATION*	*SCORE*	*WEIGHTED SCORE*
Repeated straightforward operation	10	50	Some complications	7	35
No development needed	10	50	4,000 feet of development in fill	1	5
Would tend to get more through dilution in the cave	8	40	Minimum	10	50
Some extra requirements	8	32	Would expect more tons/shift	10	40
Refer memo JL/2.1/MIN 8.10.2	8	32	Refer memo FoS/2.1/MIN 8.10.3	10	40
More drilling equipment required	9	36	Minimum	10	40
Minimum special demands	10	30	Will need small load haul dump units for development through fill and also may need special support equipment	8	24
Water will drain and not necessarily be on production subs	10	20	More washing out water as in open stopes	7	14
Good roadways	10	20	Fill provides poor roadways when affected by water	8	16
Minimum cement	10	10	More mining through cement	8	8
		976			**788**

SUMMARY

This is an interesting example because, at the outset, even the experts could not see any marked advantage of one method over the other. They had preferences, but no one ever suggested that either method was dangerous, unsound, or even inadequate. After the experts had considered and clarified the exact conditions for successful pillar removal, however, they were able to evaluate the two methods *in detail, relative to each other, against an ideal.* As a result, they found a decided difference between the two.

This is nearly always the outcome in such a situation. When there is too much detail to juggle mentally, some systematic way must be found to evaluate the many judgments that have to be made. We have to remember that the human computer in all of us, no matter how overloaded, will stagger along, doing the best it can. But "doing the best it can" may not be good enough. In our example, the managers helped themselves by breaking down their task into steps and taking each step in turn.

The mining decision involved hundreds of separate technical considerations, and thousands of independent judgments were made in the course of the deliberations. Yet none of this information was lost. It was gathered into categories and groups of judgments and made visible. Then these summary evaluations were pulled together into an overall evaluation of the two methods. The adverse consequences were studied next. Finally, all judgments were integrated into a single judgment to answer the question: "*On balance*, comparing the two alternatives, how well does each perform against the defined set of necessary conditions?"

A decision arrived at through Decision Analysis may sound no different from one arrived at through experience and without a systematic process. But the validity of the former is a thousand times greater, for all elements that go into the decision remain accessible and visible. The decision can be reconstructed logically in all its detail. Every step in thinking and in dealing with information can be shown and duplicated. This allows for error-checking and for augmentation as new information becomes available. And it simplifies communication and explanation of the decision. As has been made visible in the example, anyone outside the team, asking why the sub-level cave method was judged 25 percent better than the high-rise method, can be shown point by point exactly why this was so. If objectives are correct and facts accurate, then the conclusion is inarguable—particularly in the eyes of an expert.

SHOULD WE TAKE OR REJECT A COURSE OF ACTION? YES OR NO?

When managers are first introduced to Decision Analysis, they learn to use its techniques through the kinds of examples we have presented. Objectives are set, alternatives are identified and evaluated, risks are examined. After managers become familiar with the basic procedure, one of the first concerns they raise goes something like this: "That's all well and good if you have three or four alternatives to choose from. But most of the time, my real-life judgments are going to consist of Yes or No. What good is Decision Analysis when the choice is that limited?"

The Yes/No decision is very prevalent in government bureaucracies. And rarely is the necessity of communicating the background of a decision so important.

CASE HISTORY: ASSESSING THE WATER QUALITY PROPOSAL

The following letter was written by an executive of the Department of Natural Resources for a state in the southern United States. It was addressed to the director of the Bureau of Pollution Control in a city located in that state. The city had proposed a plan for managing the water quality of the river on which it is located. The Department of Natural Resources is responsible for accepting or rejecting such proposals. Yes/No decisions are indeed the reality of the job for the department in all these cases. The department uses Decision Analysis to approach all such decisions, as well as to reach and communicate its conclusions.

Dear Mr. _____:

This letter is in response to your request [date] for a detailed written explanation of why [the division] rejected your proposal for storing effluence as a part of the overall plan to meet X River water-quality standards.

Since this is a very complex issue, we attempted to be as systematic and comprehensive as possible in considering all aspects of your proposed action and in anticipating its impact. We started with the following decision statement: **Decide whether the concept of flow variable wastewater discharge to the X River from Y City's facilities is acceptable.**

We then **identified objectives that should apply for any water-quality control strategy** for the X River. These objectives were separated into MUST objectives and WANT objectives. To be a MUST, the objective has to be both measurable and mandatory. If an objective is not both measurable and mandatory, it is a WANT. We assigned a weight to each WANT objective using a scale of 1 to 10, with 10 signifying the maximum importance or desirability. The objectives we identified are listed below.

MUST Objectives

1. Meet existing water-quality standards in the X River.

2. Be equitable for all types of discharges to the X River.

3. Maintain a minimum reserve capacity of 15 percent for ultimate oxygen demand at all flows in the X River.

WANT Objectives	Weight
1. Provide protection for potential water supplies downstream	10
2. Maximize water quality in the X River	8
3. Maximize reliability of wastewater treatment control systems	8
4. Minimize present worth of treatment/control systems	8
5. Minimize organic loading to the river and reservoir	7
6. Minimize nutrient (nitrogen and phosphorus) loading to the reservoir	7
7. Maximize enforceability of effluent standards for treatment/control systems	4

WANT Objectives	Weight
8. Increase reserve capacity for ultimate oxygen demand	4
9. Expedite the construction grants process	4
10. Optimize the use of X River waste assimilative capacity	3

All these objectives are not necessarily compatible with each other, but they are rational objectives that should be considered. **The weights for each objective were the consensus of our highest levels of management and most experienced staff members.**

The next step in our decision process was to identify alternatives and to determine how well each alternative would satisfy the objectives. (Note: The MUSTs are not weighted because any alternative not satisfying every MUST is unacceptable; we seek an alternative that will satisfy all MUSTs and that will satisfy WANTs better than the other alternatives.) **In this case, we have only two alternatives to consider: Yes, the concept of flow variable wastewater discharge is acceptable; and No, the concept is unacceptable.**

The No alternative satisfies all MUSTs; it is equivalent to saying that the waste load allocations determined for all X River discharges and transmitted to the city in our letter of [date] will be followed. These allocations will allow water-quality standards to be met, they are equitable for all discharges, and they provide a 15 percent reserve assimilative capacity.

The Yes alternative would have a number of technical questions to be resolved (such as the specifics of an equitable policy, since other governments would have to be allowed the option of flow variable discharge; and the specific allowable discharges from all waste source points in the range of X River flows). We assumed that the technical questions could be resolved; thus, it was considered that the Yes alternative could be made to satisfy the MUST objectives.

In comparing how well the alternatives would satisfy the WANTs, we could assign a score, on a scale of 1 to 10, to each alternative against each WANT. Then multiply the score by the weight of each WANT to get a total weighted score for each alternative. Or, we could simply signify the relative merits of an alternative by positive and negative signs. (This was done, for example by [Company] in its ABC Water Quality Management Plan.)

By either method, the end product in this case is the same. The No alternative satisfies all WANTs better than the Yes alternative, except for WANTs 4, 5, and 10. The No alternative is superior to the Yes alternative on WANTs 1, 2, 6, and 8 basically because there will be fewer loadings of most pollutants discharged. The No alternative is superior on WANTs 3, 7, and 9 because it will result in a system that is less complex to design, operate, monitor, and control. The extensive technical work that would be needed before engineering could commence for the Yes alternative would mean significant delays in the completion of Y City's facilities plans. The Yes and No alternatives rank about equally for WANT 5: the amounts of phosphorus discharged would be the same. However, the No alternative might be somewhat more favorable, since a lesser loading of total nitrogen might be possible and since upgrading existing systems now might make it easier to effect phosphorus removal, if found necessary, in the future. The Yes alternative is superior on WANTs 4 and 10, since it would almost surely have a lower present worth and since it would obviously make more use of the natural assimilative capacity of the river.

The final step in our decision process was to identify and compare the adverse consequences of implementing either alternative. We identified eight such consequences and tried to quantify the probability [P] and seriousness [S] of each. This also was done on a scale of 1 to 10, with 1 representing very low probability and seriousness and 10 representing very high probability and seriousness. The results follow.

Adverse Consequences	Yes		No	
	P	S	P	S
1. Delays in the grants process for all [State] facilities	10	9	8	3
2. Loss of momentum	7	8	3	8
3. Difficulty in enforcing effluent standards	9	3	4	3
4. Adverse effects on Z Reservoir	5	7	3	3
5. Non-acceptance by City of G	1	7	6	7
6. Non-acceptance by other local governments	8	8	1	8
7. Non-acceptance by [United States Environmental Protection Agency]	9	10	1	10
8. Non-acceptance by environmentalist groups	9	9	1	9

The values assigned for probability and seriousness, like the weights for WANT objectives or the scores for alternatives satisfying each WANT, can be debated. However, these values are the consensus of our management and experienced staff. It is obvious that the Yes alternative, if chosen, would have higher probabilities of serious adverse consequences. In fact, we feel that non-acceptance by EPA and environmentalists would be almost certain if [this division] were to agree with the concept of flow variable discharge. We also feel that strong opposition of one or both of those groups would ultimately prevent implementation of that alternative.

Based on all of the above rationale (which, incidentally, is similar to that used by the City's consultants in their evaluation of the return flow concept versus keeping existing discharges in the X and T Rivers), it is the decision of [this division] that the concept of flow variable wastewater discharge to the X River from Y City is not acceptable or approvable.

We believe that we understand the city's reasons for wanting to pursue this matter, and it is our sincere hope that the city can understand and agree with [the division's] position. We are ready to discuss the matter further with you if you so desire, and we will provide all possible assistance in bringing this project to a timely conclusion.

Yours sincerely,

How radical a departure this letter is from other rejection letters that focus only on the negative aspects of a proposed action. The rejection was presented as the logical conclusion of an evaluation of many factors that were clearly understood by everyone concerned with the decision. Although the rejection was not entirely palatable to the city, its objective and thoughtful manner aided in its acceptance.

SUMMARY

All Yes/No decisions are open to rephrasing and to objective analysis. The fundamental criticism of the typical Yes/No decision is that it bypasses a careful thinking-through of objectives. Instead of first considering the purpose of the decision and the characteristics of a good choice, the decision maker plunges immediately into an evaluation of *one* of the available alternatives. This often amounts to building a case against that alternative, producing a shortsighted view of the issues. People do this when they have no other method of evaluating such a choice. At the same time, they may fear that a bad alternative will slip through unless they make a strong case against it. When the Decision Analysis procedure is used carefully in this kind of decision, it is impossible for a truly inadequate or seriously risky alternative to look better than it is.

SHOULD WE CHANGE OR CONTINUE AS BEFORE? YES OR NO?

Sometimes we must decide either to change a certain operation or to continue as before. The decision "Yes, we should change" is always accompanied by many unknown factors. On the other hand, the decision "No, we should not change" has obvious flaws—otherwise, the proposal to change would never have been made. However, familiarity with the status quo is a compelling attribute of the "No" choice.

CASE HISTORY: TO CENTRALIZE OR STAY DECENTRALIZED

One of the world's largest insurance companies carried all its accounts and business records in computers located in twelve business regions throughout the United States. Every month these accounts were closed, forwarded to the Central Office, and entered into the central computer to be combined into a single record.

A proposal had been made to eliminate the twelve regional computer records, handle **all** business through a master computer at the Central Office, and downgrade the twelve regional offices to administrative entities. The Executive Committee faced a Yes/No decision: Should the company conduct business in this new way or continue on in the decentralized manner? After debating this issue, the Executive Committee rejected the new method as too risky and complicated.

An assistant to one of the Executive Committee members felt that rejecting the proposal on a Yes/No basis had been inadequate. Although the new method was suspect because it entailed change, there had been no close comparison of the **relative advantages and disadvantages** of the two systems. He asked his manager, a vice president, if he could conduct a full-fledged Decision Analysis on the proposal as an exercise in the technique. With the vice president's grudging permission, the young man began by listing what he thought might be the criteria of an **ideal** insurance accounting system. The next day he took his set of criteria to the vice president, explained them, and asked his advice. After they discussed the requirements of such a system, the vice president added one item and reworded another. Then the assistant asked, "I wonder how the other vice presidents would see these? Would they agree with our list?" The vice president took this as a challenge and had the list of objectives circulated among the other Executive Committee members for comment.

Where suggestions were received and incorporated, the young man said to the vice president, "Some of these are more important than others, but I don't know enough about the insurance business to assign the correct weights." The vice president reviewed the list and added weights to the criteria. Again, the assistant raised the question as to how the other members of the committee would see them. The list was circulated for further comment and approval. As before, suggestions were received and incorporated into the list of criteria.

The assistant took the completed, weighted criteria to experts in both present and proposed systems, gathered relevant data, then submitted this to disinterested managers for an evaluation of the two systems. Their conclusion was that the centralized system would perform **more than twice as well** as the present one against the criteria. On the grounds of "some interesting data I've developed," the assistant requested and received approval for a fifteen-minute presentation to the Executive Committee.

To prepare for the meeting, the assistant assembled a large chart to display the criteria, some of the supporting information available, and the evaluation of the two systems against the objectives. One could see at a glance that the proposed system was better on almost all counts. On the day of the presentation, the assistant brought in experts to answer substantive questions, put up his chart, and explained his findings.

There is much to learn from this example. The Executive Committee had never really framed a decision statement. A sales presentation extolling the virtues of the new centralized system had been made to the committee by a computer consultant. Most of the discussion that followed was about hardware. No comparison was made with the performance characteristics of the present system. Then the committee had been asked to make a decision. "Yes, we buy the new system" would imply change and probable headaches; "No" would presume an understanding of the relative performance of the two systems. However, this understanding was impossible without a set of criteria against which "Yes" and "No" could be transformed into distinct alternatives, each with its advantages and disadvantages.

When the young assistant developed these criteria, it made all the difference in the world. A system first seen as too complicated, risky, and troublesome could now be recognized for its real advantages over the old decentralized system.

Two meetings, each about three hours long, were held to discuss and explore all aspects of the two systems. The Executive Committee then voted unanimously to overturn its previous rejection of the proposed computer system. The new system was purchased and installed. In the first year of operation, it saved more than $400,000 over the former system. In each year that followed, savings exceeded $500,000. These savings would not have been realized if the two systems had not been compared independently against adequate operational objectives.

IS IT GOOD ENOUGH?

In another kind of decision, the question that must be answered is: "Is this proposed alternative good enough to adopt?" Clearly, the current way of doing things is recognized as inadequate. No one is pressing to maintain the status quo. An attractive alternative has been developed or presented, and the people who must make the final decision are almost, but not quite, ready to give it a "Yes."

CASE HISTORY: THE IDEAL DISTRIBUTION SYSTEM

Executives of a paper and wood products company had to deal with a unique and very difficult situation. Their mill and production facilities were located more than seven hundred miles from their primary market area. Their competitors' mills were much closer, some within the market area itself. This meant that the company was at a disadvantage in cost of distribution and customer service. This disadvantage had been balanced out by lower production costs in their mill area, but that was no longer the case. For the present and the foreseeable future, the higher distribution cost would constitute a major handicap to doing business competitively.

The company had worked with a consulting firm for the past two years, searching for ways to reduce this handicap. An efficient, highly automated distribution system had been designed, based on a set of warehouses within the market area to which unit trainloads of product would be shipped. Now the plan had been completed, with an implementation budget of $11 million. The chairman of the board, the president, and all the senior vice presidents had the task of reviewing the proposed system to decide whether or not to accept the consultants' recommendations. Their decision statement was: "Is this proposed distribution system good enough to adopt?"

The group's first step was to set out the criteria of an **ideal** field distribution system—that is, a model that did not appear to be attainable in reality but would incorporate all desirable characteristics. Using this model, the group would be able to judge the quality and performance of the proposed system. Their final set of objectives consisted of six MUSTs and twelve WANTs. All of the WANTs plus only one of the six MUSTs (for brevity's sake) are listed in Figure 11. Again, for brevity's sake, we have chosen not to include the information on which the scores were based. The group assigned weights to the WANTs to reflect degrees of importance; the top weight was 25 rather than the usual 10. The first WANT, "Increase per share earnings of common stock," was given a weight of 25. Although this objective was not mandatory (therefore not a MUST), its extreme importance warranted a position as a highly weighted WANT. The other WANTs, listed in declining order of importance, received weights relative to this highest one.

Since their model was an ideal distribution system with optimum performance, each of its objectives was assigned a score of 10. Multiplying each score by the weight produced a total weighted score of 1,120 for the model. The group now had something against which to compare the proposed system. They went through the consultants' plan point by point, evaluating its projected performance against the ideal.

On the first WANT, the plan performed well on four out of five possible ways to "Increase per share earnings of common stock"; that gave it a score of 8. On the second WANT, "Better, faster service," the group gave the plan a score of 10. But on the third WANT they hit a snag: They could not justify "Maintain premium sales prices" on the basis of service alone. They would also have to maintain market leadership by having the best quality, most progressive product available in the market area. Since the plan did not provide for a heavy, continuing R&D effort, it scored only 5 against this WANT.

The same thing happened on the next WANT. The company could only "Reduce production costs from present, maintain at lower level" if it spent several million dollars in modernizing the present production equipment. And the plan did not provide for that. The next difficulty was in the ability to "Guarantee continuous supply of product from mill to field warehouses." This, too, would hinge on modernizing the present production equipment.

The complete list, with all the scores computed, appears in Figure 11.

The plan scored only 883 points against an ideal of 1,120, or 79 percent. That was not considered to be good enough. Cost estimates were developed for an R&D effort that would ensure continued product leadership and for modernizing production equipment. The total went far beyond the MUST of "Total system implementation cost no more than $11 million." Since an improved plan was too expensive, it was ruled out as a NO GO.

But there is a sequel to this story. Having made the weaknesses in the proposal visible, the company and the consulting firm quickly modified the plan. The plan would provide money for accelerated R&D and equipment modernization, yet still obtain most of the desired distribution advantages. The modifications raised the total weighted score for the new system to 1,007. This was 90 percent of the theoretical ideal. The modified plan was accepted and put into effect. It succeeded.

FIGURE 11 **DECISION ANALYSIS TO DETERMINE IF A PROPOSED
DISTRIBUTION SYSTEM IS GOOD ENOUGH**

OBJECTIVES AND CHARACTERISTICS OF AN IDEAL DISTRIBUTION SYSTEM		MODEL		PLAN	
MUST OBJECTIVES					
Total system implementation cost no more than $11 million		GO		NO GO	
WANT OBJECTIVES	*WEIGHT*	*SCORE*	*WEIGHTED SCORE*	*SCORE*	*WEIGHTED SCORE*
Increase earnings of common stock	25	10	250	8	200
Provide better, faster service than any competitor in the market area	15	10	150	10	150
Justify, maintain premium sales prices	12	10	120	5	60
Reduce production costs from present, maintain at lower level	10	10	100	3	30
Reduce transportation cost, mill to market area	9	10	90	10	90
Guarantee maximum 3-day delivery, any customer in market area	9	10	90	10	90
Maintain complete inventory, full line of products, at minimum cost	8	10	80	9	72
Guarantee continuous supply of products from mill to field warehouses	7	10	70	5	35
Provide truck delivery to all customers	6	10	60	10	60
Maintain minimum costs of handling at warehouses	5	10	50	8	40
Provide modular sealed plastic packaging and handling throughout	4	10	40	10	40
Minimize handling damage to product	2	10	20	8	16
Total Weighted Scores		**1,120**		**883**	
Percentages		**100 percent**		**79 percent**	

Until the executives of this company had a standard against which to evaluate their plan, they had no way of knowing whether the plan was good enough to accept. Once they developed a model of the ideal distribution system, however, they were able to assess the consultants' proposal and see how close it came to the ideal. This made visible two mammoth weaknesses that neither the consultants nor the company personnel had previously recognized. Success of the plan depended on having the best products available in the market area and on maintaining optimum production costs—two factors that had been ignored. If the executives had considered this matter merely as a Yes/No decision, they undoubtedly would have approved a plan that would have failed entirely or required extensive overruns to keep it alive. It was their clear view of the deficiencies of the proposed system—*as measured against the model*—that triggered the necessary modifications for a successful plan.

SUMMARY

How good is good? A model can be constructed that is so idealistic and visionary that it is useless as a standard against which to judge real-life alternatives. The other extreme is to have too low an aspiration, to create a model no further advanced than the common practice of the day. As in so many aspects of Decision Analysis, informed judgment has a big role to play in selecting a realistic vision of the future. A reasonable model must be constructed, perhaps unattainable in its totality, yet within reach in some of its more important aspects.

There is a caution to attach to the evaluation of "How good is it?" If decision makers settle for an inferior alternative, they block the possibility of their finding a better one. A somewhat parallel situation is the medical practice of giving a placebo to a patient. Although the placebo sometimes has a beneficial psychological effect, that patient is unlikely to seek an active medicine that will actually alleviate or cure the sickness. In the same way, a quick and slipshod analysis—ending in the conclusion, "Great idea! Let's buy it!"—is deceptive and dangerous. It has the effect of deluding people into thinking that an inferior decision is better than it really is. Careful analysis, on the other hand, tends to expose weaknesses and show how far from the ideal

THE NEW RATIONAL MANAGER

an alternative is. At the very least, careful analysis provides a realistic platform from which to build improvements and make rational choices.

SUBDIVIDED EVALUATIONS

In its use of Decision Analysis, Florida Power and Light Company has adapted the "How-good-is-it?" format for use in purchase of equipment, services, and supplies. The company evaluates vendor and product separately, having found that quality in both are requisites for satisfactory performance. The evaluation is divided into sub-parts. For the vendor these include "Commercial considerations," "Technical assistance (capabilities)," "Quality," and "Delivery and storage." Under each heading are a number of performance criteria, totaling twenty-six separate items. Under "Commercial considerations," for instance, the company looks at such criteria as the vendor's financial stability, past performance on claims and adjustments, the completeness of the vendor's bids, and adherence to previous commitments. Each of these sub-parts is given a weight reflecting its importance relative to the other criteria. "Commercial considerations" has a weight of 15 percent in the overall judgment of the vendor. "Technical assistance" is also worth 15 percent. "Quality" of service is judged to be three times as important, warranting a weight of 45 percent. "Delivery and storage" is worth 25 percent. Based upon Florida Power and Light's past experience with the vendor, each item is scored and the weighted scores are accumulated.

Using a similar process, the company makes a separate evaluation of the vendor's product. Here, the number of sub-parts varies with the item being evaluated. One product, for example, has categories of "Mechanism," "Linkage," "External tank" (a major component), and "Internal tank," with a total of twenty-four specific components or features listed under these headings. As before, weights are assigned and the weighted scores accumulated.

At this point, Florida Power and Light moves into a third step: reconciling these evaluations with the price bids made by different vendors. Vendor A, for example, may have a lower price than Vendor B but does not provide the same degree of service. The company introduces debits and credits to compensate for the price differences, bringing all values down to a common, equitable comparison. It warns that this procedure does not always result in the contract's going to the lowest bidder, but rather to the vendor offering the best bargain determined by the analysis. This procedure has resulted not only in savings of hundreds of thousands of dollars but also in confidence that the company is getting the most for its money. *How good is the contract being proposed?* Florida Power and Light has used this kind of Decision Analysis to find out. The procedure may not guarantee 100 percent success in the purchasing-bidding transaction, but it does minimize the possibility of overlooking or misunderstanding factors of potential importance.

DEVELOPMENT OF AN ALTERNATIVE

Another kind of decision is when no ready alternative exists, and the decision maker must decide *how best* to meet a specific need. When there is no acceptable known way to do that, this decision-making process starts from zero. The assignment, in short, is "Figure out a way to do X."

"Figure out a way" means that we must select from all available components a series of components that will be feasible and will get the job done effectively. To do this, we must clearly understand the nature of X—what it is we are trying to accomplish in the first place.

CASE HISTORY: IN SEARCH OF A STABLE CANE SUPPLY

A large sugar company in a tropical country faced a problem for which there was no known solution. Its mills buy cane from local growers and reduce it to crude sugar. The sugar is then exported through a government-controlled consortium at controlled prices. The company buys cane according to its sugar content and sells the crude sugar to the government at a fixed price. The only way the company can be profitable, therefore, is to produce economically. The crushing season lasts about five months. Early cane has low sugar content and brings less money to the planter. Late cane also brings a lower return. Cane harvested at the peak of the season brings the most money. But not all of the cane that is cut at the peak of the season can be crushed at that time, for the volume available far exceeds the optimum volume of the plant. This is shown in Figure 12. The decision faced by the company was this: Find ways to encourage the delivery of more early and late cane for processing, thereby permitting the plant to operate for a longer period at its optimum level. As indicated in Figure 12, the company's intention was to fill up the hatched areas, representing early and late cane processing. But how could this be done within the limited options of a controlled economy?

The top people in the organization came together to address the situation. Their decision statement was: "Find the best way of ensuring a stable, optimum cane supply to the Santa Elena Mill."

They then set out criteria that would characterize acceptable actions to encourage or guarantee a stable supply. A good action, for example, would be "Legally acceptable" at "Lowest cost" with "High probability of success." The team listed these actions as WANTs, and assigned a weight of relative desirability to each one. The complete set of WANTs is shown in Figure 13.

The team then generated ideas and actions that might ensure a stable cane supply. Some ideas had been talked about for years. Some actions had been used in the past, either by the company or its competitors. Some suggestions were fragments that had been used piecemeal; they were not a part of any coordinated plan for dealing with the cane supply.

FIGURE 12   **SUGAR CANE PROCESSING**

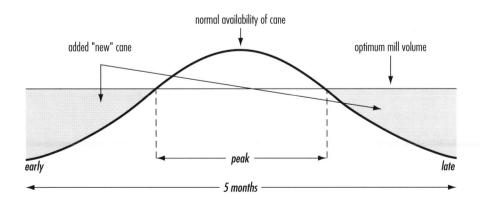

FIGURE 13

DECISION ANALYSIS TO FIND THE BEST WAY OF ENSURING
A STABLE, OPTIMUM CANE SUPPLY TO THE SANTA ELENA MILL

WANT OBJECTIVES	WEIGHT
Minimize cost	10
Legally acceptable	9
Maximize probability of success	10
Minimize complications of normal operations	7
Minimize risk of overload, plant breakdown	4
Feasible, easy to implement	5
Allows predictable schedules	5
Low risk of interruption by external factors	2
Low risk of retaliation by competitor mills	3
Low risk of offending planters, government officials	4
Low risk of being cheated	8
Avoids unfavorable precedent, next crushing season	10

Total Weighted Scores

ALTERNATIVE ACTIONS

Trucking allowance	Free railroad transportation	Graded, improved access roads	Reduced unloading time	Towing, repair service	Spot cash payment	Advanced payments on contract basis	Guaranteed price regardless of sugar content	Premium price for early, late cane	Profit sharing with planters	Discounts on trucks, parts, fuel, and oil	Discounts on tires	Discounts on fertilizer, farm equipment	Kickbacks to drivers	Pleasant waiting area for drivers	Polevault payments to planters
5	8	7	4	7	10	8	4	6	3	6	7	7	8	9	7
50	80	70	40	70	100	80	40	60	30	60	70	70	80	90	70
10	8	8	10	7	7	9	6	7	2	8	8	8	3	9	1
90	72	72	90	63	63	81	54	63	18	72	72	72	27	81	9
10	5	5	10	6	8	9	8	10	6	7	6	6	7	4	6
100	50	50	100	60	80	90	80	100	60	70	60	60	70	40	60
10	5	8	4	9	6	5	5	7	1	9	9	9	10	8	5
70	35	56	28	63	42	35	35	49	7	63	63	63	70	56	40
4	7	6	8	10	6	8	8	10	6	10	10	10	7	10	4
16	28	24	32	40	24	32	32	40	24	40	40	40	28	40	16
5	7	6	3	6	8	5	5	7	1	6	7	5	9	8	10
25	35	30	15	30	40	25	25	35	5	30	35	25	45	40	50
2	4	2	10	2	1	4	2	10	3	2	2	2	4	1	2
10	20	10	50	10	5	20	10	50	15	10	10	10	20	5	10
7	6	5	8	6	9	4	5	7	1	7	8	7	3	10	2
14	12	10	16	12	18	8	10	14	2	14	16	14	6	20	4
5	9	7	8	7	5	8	10	6	7	8	5	6	2	8	1
15	27	21	24	21	15	24	30	18	21	24	15	18	6	24	3
8	9	7	6	9	8	7	7	3	2	6	7	6	1	10	1
32	36	28	24	36	32	28	28	12	8	24	28	24	4	40	4
4	8	9	10	2	2	4	1	8	2	1	1	3	1	9	4
32	64	72	80	16	16	32	8	64	16	8	8	24	8	72	32
1	3	5	10	1	2	1	1	5	1	3	4	4	2	10	3
10	30	50	100	10	20	10	20	50	10	30	40	40	20	100	30
464	**489**	**493**	**599**	**431**	**455**	**465**	**362**	**555**	**216**	**445**	**457**	**460**	**384**	**608**	**328**

There were plenty of opinions but very few facts. No one knew for sure what had worked and what had not. About all anyone knew was that the present methods were inadequate and a better way must be found. Now, for the first time, management was going to assemble **systematically** all that was known in order to devise an overall program.

Cane is cut in the field when it reaches peak sugar content, when labor is available, when the weather is good, or when the planter's horoscope and intuition tell him that it's time to cut. Since most planters do not have their own trucks, they must hire trucks and drivers. The roads are very bad, the trucks are in terrible mechanical condition, and the loads are three or four times the maximum rated weight for the vehicle.

The planter is often a free agent who can sell his cane anywhere. He leaves it up to the truck driver: "Go wherever you can get the best price." At the mill there may be two hundred to three hundred trucks waiting to unload at any time. A truck and driver may stand in line for thirty-six hours before unloading.

The longer the waiting time between cutting and crushing, the lower the cane's sugar content. A delay means less money for the planter.

Some planters have mortgaged their crop to the bank and are obligated to sell their cane to a specific mill. The mill pays the bank, not the planter. To get desperately needed cash, the planter may "polevault"—that is, send a truckload or two to another mill, receive payment himself, and leave the bank wondering why his crop is so small this year.

Because the mill must run at between 95 percent and 100 percent of capacity to make a profit, it offers special inducements to planters and drivers. If it loses cane by being outbid by competitors, the mill will run at below the magical 95 percent mark. If the mill becomes greedy and overloads rickety, poorly-maintained equipment, the machinery may break down, putting the mill out of business. The sugar industry in this tropical country is a cutthroat, brutally competitive affair.

When the team evaluated each of the ideas and actions against the weighted criteria, as shown in Figure 13, the results were surprising. For brevity's sake, only the scoring is shown. The lowest-rated alternatives clearly were kickbacks to drivers and allowing "polevaulting" payments to planters—two favorite strategies used by their competitors. The highest-rated idea was to provide a pleasant waiting area for the drivers—

a shaded, open-air place for lounging, talking, playing cards, drinking beer, and socializing. It would cost little and be enormously successful.

The company owned a railroad that wound through the cane plantations and was used infrequently. Cane could be loaded from trucks to the railroad cars to achieve stockpiling. This would involve double handling rather than the triple handling of cane off-loaded onto the ground. Free railroad transport to the mill could be tied in as an added incentive. Improving the roads leading to the mill was another good idea: It would greatly influence drivers who owned their own rigs and had to pay for breakdowns. Paying a premium price for early and late cane would also help smooth out the production schedule.

Thus, a collection of actions jointly created a feasible and effective method for the mill to operate at a much higher level of profitability than ever before.

SUMMARY

The directive "Figure out a way" is often misinterpreted by managers. When they respond by meeting to "get all the ideas out on the table," the procedure is fairly predictable: Lists of alternatives are proposed *even before* all objectives are stated and clearly defined. As a result, the alternatives may satisfy one or more of the general objectives expressed at the meeting without serving as logical steps to a successful solution.

On the other hand, a group that begins with a well-defined set of objectives has an immediate structure within which it can create and evaluate options. In this context, the options themselves tend to be of higher quality. The admonition "Don't prejudge ideas or you will stifle creativity" holds true within this format as well. In the case of the sugar mill, the idea of a pleasant waiting area for the drivers was greeted at first with derision. No one had ever heard of such a thing. It was considered trivial. But since it was neither impractical nor irrelevant, this idea performed very well against the company's criteria.

Working from a set of objectives does not stifle creativity. On the contrary, this format focuses attention on the task at hand and prevents waste of time and energy on suggestions that are clearly irrelevant. It also enables earlier recognition of a good idea. An inadequate basis for evaluation invariably stifles creativity, for it works against the recognition of an excellent idea that may appear to be revolutionary or peculiar.

THE ROUTINE DECISION

When Decision Analysis is practiced continually and successfully within an organization, its use invariably becomes *required* for certain decisions and *habitual* in choice making at all levels. The Decision Analysis habit is very clear in the following example from a large chemical company.

CASE HISTORY: MARKETING SCRAP FIBRE

The company, which produces synthetic fibers, had a standard procedure for dealing with a substandard product. The rejected fiber went into a warehouse, where it stayed until a large quantity had been amassed. The plant manager then would phone the head office and request permission to dump a few tons of scrap. This gave the head office an idea of the amount of substandard material being produced. Permission was automatically granted, the plant manager cleared out the warehouse, and the rejected fiber went to the county dump.

But one day, in the middle of such a phone call, the manager at the head office suddenly asked, "What are my objectives? We're supposed to be making money, and dumping tons of fiber like this is crazy!" Permission was denied and the plant manager was told to find a non-conflicting market for the fiber that would return some of the revenue to the organization.

The plant manager was shocked. Marketing wasn't a plant manager's job. This seemed an impossible, unreasonable assignment. But the head office didn't yield. So some inquiries were made and five days later a new market for the synthetic scrap fiber was found: It was to be cut into short lengths as pile stuffing for sleeping bags. The entire lot was sold for $50,000.

This market for scrap fiber now contributes significantly to the overall revenue of the company. The scrap fiber is used as synthetic pile in ski jackets, coat liners, sleeping bags, and in a hundred other items. Imagine how much potential revenue had been trucked to the city dump in the years before one person asked "What are my objectives?" and decided that there must be a better way.

DECISION ANALYSIS AS A STANDARD PROCEDURE

The requirement to use Decision Analysis for certain kinds of choices is standard operating procedure in many of our client organizations. All that is necessary is that the top management of the organization set the example and set the rules. For example, a number of companies now require that all hiring, transfer, and promotion of employees be conducted using the Decision Analysis format. This accomplishes many goals. To begin with, everyone is using the same guidelines. All objectives for personnel decisions are clear, visible, and documented.

CASE HISTORY: OBJECTIVES FOR NEW HIRES

What follows is a Memo to File written by an executive in a United States Government agency. Accompanying all proposals for new hires, the agency requires a list of objectives for the position to be filled. If the proposal is approved, this list of objectives, or an amended version, will be used as the standard against which candidates will be evaluated.

Everyone involved in selecting the new hire receives a copy of these objectives or the revised version. And, in this agency, each candidate also receives a copy before being interviewed.

MEMO TO FILE

From: [Manager]

To: [Director of Human Resources]

Subject: Proposal to Hire Planner for the _____ Study

Decision Statement: Select a Planner for the _____ Study

Objectives	MUSTs	WANTs	Weight
Minimum 6 months planning experience	X		
Degree in engineering or planning	X		
Experience as study director		X	10
Registered engineer or planner		X	2
Data processing experience		X	5
Available for extensive work in [city]		X	8
Can and will work without guidance		X	6
Good communicator at meetings		X	8

CASE HISTORY: THE ROUTINE SELECTION

Most routine selections at the L.D. Schreiber Cheese Company, Green Bay, Wisconsin, begin in just the same way. The implementation of a new acid-handling system for the firm's head plant was the final result of a team decision based on the objectives that follow.

Once the use of Decision Analysis is required and has become habitual, once it becomes "the way we do things here," as it is at L.D. Schreiber, it is a self-perpetuating system.

To: [Managers Involved]

From: [Initiating Manager]

Subject: Objectives of Acid-Handling System

Decision Statement: Select an Acid-Handling System for Acetic and Lactic Acids

MUSTs

1. Machinery capable of handling strong acids

2. Meter directly into cooker

3. Personnel will not handle acids manually

4. Adaptable with small ($600) changeover cost to batch blending

5. Usable in existing system

WANTs	WEIGHT
1. Cost under $4,000 to implement	10
2. Adaptable as is to batch blending	10
3. Read out quantity on meter that goes into cooker	10
4. Accurate	10
5. Simple to operate	8
6. Simple to maintain	8
7. Similar to present water-addition system	8
8. Non-pressurized system	8
9. Push button to activate	7
10. Digital readout	6
11. Put on line by September 15	5
12. Usable in other plants	4

CASE HISTORY: THE "MILLION-DOLLAR ALTERNATIVE"

Many routine selection decisions at Florida Power and Light Company are put through a complete Decision Analysis, just to be sure that everything of importance has been considered. One such typical use of the process concerned the selection of a site for a new service yard in the Miami area.

Residential expansion in the northwest area of the city had quickly saturated the capability of the Transmission and Distribution Department, which is responsible for installing and maintaining customer service. Its employees work out of yards where they park the service vehicles and draw supplies and tools. A new yard was needed, but a seemingly "routine selection decision," once looked at from the perspective of Decision Analysis, showed that the decision would be more difficult than anyone had expected.

To begin with, a utility service site needs space to park many trucks and store bulky equipment and supplies. For a northwest site, an initial MUST objective would concern sufficient space for at least fifty service trucks. Some eighty service personnel might be headquartered at the location. Adding it all up, Florida Power and Light Company needed between seven and ten acres of industrial-zoned land in a neighborhood that had become a prime residential area. Utility service yards normally are set up in industrial districts or in outlying areas, where there are few neighbors to take a dim view of applications for zoning changes. This surely was not a characteristic of northwest Miami. Suitable and available sites would be few and expensive.

Although the alternatives had a broad range and permitted considerable flexibility, unprecedented expense continued to be a primary factor regardless of which alternative was examined. Transmission and distribution managers considered all sites that met the primary MUSTs of size and location. Some sites would require draining and clearing of swamp land. Others did not have the right zoning but were considered on the basis of possible rezoning approval.

Eight sites evolved. One site that seemed favorable before Decision Analysis turned out to have long-established industrial zoning—but a bare minimum of usable space. In the same way, the process made visible all the trade-offs among various alternatives. Ultimately, the transmission and distribution team recommended the purchase of a $1 million parcel of land. Previous service yards had been built on sites costing no more than $300,000.

How could this very costly alternative have emerged as the best one? With all the information visible and plugged into the analysis, one fact became apparent to the managers making the decision: Failing to establish a successful, suitable facility with growth potential to meet future probable needs would be the most expensive alternative of all. Florida Power and Light Company had already felt the effects of developing residential areas, overcrowded and inefficient conditions at existing yards, and wasted time and lengthy trips between service locations. Decision Analysis proved the soundness of the "million-dollar alternative." The choice was approved on the grounds that thrift today would prove no bargain tomorrow.

Thousands of Decision Analyses have been conducted at Florida Power and Light Company. One, "the computer modernization decision," called for spending millions of dollars over a five-year period for equipment, system development, reprogramming, and many other requirements. Technical advisors established the performance specifications for the new equipment and its support software and services. In effect, the specifications that evolved became the basis for the analysis. These specifications were included among the objectives for the decision and became "result objectives"—what the decision was ultimately expected to produce for the company.

MUST objectives totaled 30, WANTs 120. Florida Power and Light considered that a less comprehensive effort might fail to identify objectives that would turn out to be crucial after the fact. The lengthy analysis was reviewed by operating management and then passed on to the Budgetary Committee. The committee reached its decision in one week—unprecedented speed for a decision of this magnitude.

Because all the information that was critical to the decision was sorted, classified, sifted, and considered systematically—*and kept visible*—everyone who was affected by the decision and was essential to implementing it was able to quickly review and consider all aspects of the situation.

The technical expertise of the people who conducted this Decision Analysis was not enhanced or altered in any way because they had learned to use the process. *Enhanced skill in gathering and using information* had translated into the ability to fully utilize all technical inputs. It was this ability that expedited the decision and led to its ultimate success.

ADVERSE CONSEQUENCES

No decision is so small; no alternative so excellent in comparison to its rivals; no situation so patently fail-safe to ignore the possibility of adverse consequences before implementing a choice. If we were to look for the time bomb in decision making, *lack of attention to adverse consequences of a choice* is second only to failure to devise a sound decision statement. The examples that follow alert us to this peril.

CASE HISTORY: AN OBVIOUS QUESTION NOT ASKED

An East Coast commuter railroad wished to improve its service and attract more customers by adding modern, high-speed equipment. Two complete trains of radically new design were obtained from Italy. These low-slung aluminum cars, pulled by special diesel-electric locomotives, were put on the Boston-New York run with a great deal of attendant publicity. They made one trip and were retired, never to be used again.

Something vital had been overlooked. The new trains were low to the rails, but the station platforms along the line were high, built that way to accommodate American-style cars. There was no way for the passengers to get on or off the new supertrains. Some tried jumping, and several were hurt when they slipped and fell. In desperation the new trains were stopped a quarter of a mile outside the stations, and the passengers were invited to walk. Again some people slipped and fell on the rails. The trains, standing on the main line a quarter of a mile outside the stations, blocked the tracks so that other trains were held up.

The fiasco was so embarrassing to the officials of the line that they decided to junk several million dollars worth of rolling stock rather than admit they hadn't asked obvious questions about consequences before ordering the equipment. It was their hope that the error would soon be forgotten. It was. Bankruptcy followed a couple of years later.

In light of the incomplete nature of the information that is usually available for a decision, people will make mistakes. But no one has to make the mistake of ignoring information that can be obtained, or refusing to think about things that experience and imagination tell us may go wrong with a decision.

CASE HISTORY: THE EXPENSIVE QUESTION NOT ASKED

An executive in a food processing company heard about a couple of reclusive old men working in a makeshift laboratory who had developed a method of making superlative orange crystals. (Orange crystals, the ingredients that impart fresh flavor and aroma to an orange cake mix, are difficult to manufacture, but they provide the competitive edge between a fair product and an outstanding one.) The executive met with the developers, and the partners agreed to sell small amounts of the orange crystals to the company at a very high price. Sales of the company's orange cake mix went up, and the decision was made to buy the partners out. That was the decision statement, "Buy them out." After much negotiation and payment of an astronomical price, the deal was closed. The food processing company moved some of its people into the ramshackle laboratory, ready to make orange crystals. But it turned out that none of the employees who had remained in the laboratory knew exactly or altogether how to make the crystals. The process was a secret held only by the developers. By the time the food processing company found all this out, the secret of the orange crystals had been sold to its competitor for even more money than the company had paid for the laboratory. The sellers had retired to Mexico and could not be reached for comment.

This poor decision may be criticized in two ways. Had the decision statement been worded "Choose an orange crystal *process* to acquire," the food processing company would have begun by aiming at the product, not at its outer wrappings. But even with the decision statement "Choose an orange crystal *plant* to acquire" ("Buy them out"), disaster could still have been avoided by asking, "What could go wrong?" *This is what adverse consequence thinking is all about.* Then someone might well have posed the question, "What if we are unable to duplicate the product exactly?" Attention would then have gone back to the process—where it should have been focused in the first place.

We have said that the adverse consequences of a decision should be examined for probability of occurrence and seriousness should they occur. Depending on circumstances, the meaning of "serious" varies a great deal. Consider its meaning to John in the following example, a case of an adverse consequence with very low probability of occurrence.

John had been in his government's foreign service for fifteen years. He had done well, receiving promotions as rapidly as the system permitted. When he was stationed in the capital city of a Southeast Asian country, five top officials of the service were scheduled to arrive during the next months. Many meetings and social events were being scheduled for their visit, and John suggested that a luncheon for the visitors be provided at his home.

John's house was situated on a charming, quiet canal near the heart of this water-bound city. Although the canal was lined with palm trees and masses of bougainvillea, it was not far from the downtown dock of the city's largest, busiest, most heavily used canal. John suggested that the visitors could board a chartered boat at the main dock, see the city's business center from the water, and within ten minutes be transported to the pier in front of his house. After lunch, they could be driven to their afternoon meeting.

John's boss thought the idea was a great one and told him to make all the arrangements, which he did in meticulous detail. As a part of his arrangements, John chartered a motorboat adequate for ten passengers—the five visitors, John, three of his colleagues, and the driver. The boat was in good condition, and the driver was experienced.

What could go wrong? Every day the boat carried ten people, trip after trip up and down the canal. Unfortunately, they were rather smaller in build than the Western government officials who climbed into the boat to be transported to the luncheon. Fifty yards from the dock, it became exceedingly clear that the boat was about to sink. It did. Everyone aboard could swim, though none had done so in a business suit before or in any body of water as polluted as this one. All the swimmers made for the nearest dock and were pulled out by patrons of a waterside noodle shop who had been cheering their progress all the way. A larger crowd gathered to watch as the officials were hosed down by the patrons of the noodle shop, and everyone on the dock waved gaily while three taxicabs departed with the group for the trip to John's house. There they took proper showers and put on an assortment of items from John's wardrobe while they waited for fresh clothing to be brought to them. Nobody was very hungry.

John's career did not go downhill as a result of this incident. As he put it, "The week after was awful. I wanted to go back to that dock and tie a rock to my foot and jump off. But after about a month, everyone except my boss was laughing about it. I had thought of everything *but* 'What if the boat sinks?'" How probable was it that such a thing would happen? Very probable, once you realize that each Westerner in the boat weighed at least one-half times more than the average passenger who rode it every day of the year. So the boat sank.

QUICK AND CONTINUING USE

Quick and continuing use of Decision Analysis pays off handsomely. At every turn, managers should be questioning the recommendations and decisions brought to them: "What are your objectives?" "What are your MUSTs?" "What are your WANTs?" "What adverse consequences have you identified?" "What can you do about them?" By supervising and managing the decision process in this way, managers can have a significant impact on their organizations.

In our experience, most catastrophic decisions come about because no one asks such questions. Something obvious is overlooked, usually because no one thinks to look. The initial decision statement is not questioned, so the wrong decision is made. No one thinks to state the MUSTs explicitly, so a laboratory is bought and a much-needed formula is not. It is assumed that there are no adverse consequences worth mentioning, but when it is too late, it is discovered that a devastating one has been missed.

We can make it a habit to ask questions about the *process* followed in making decisions. Ask the questions twenty times and very little turns up. On the twenty-first try, an oversight is discovered that makes it all worthwhile. In person or over the telephone, in a meeting or in a conversation over lunch, managers should constantly be aware of their obligation to check on the process that produces the decision. It is one of the most important things that any manager can do. Like the concepts of Decision Analysis themselves, process questions *work*.

CHAPTER SUMMARY

Decision Analysis provides the decision maker with a basis for saying what is preferred on balance after all factors are considered. Parts of the process may be used in situations that do not require a complete analysis to gain comfort with a decision. Listing objectives in advance of the need to make a choice can save time and trouble later on. Asking "What could go wrong?" before an action is decided upon can prevent major and minor disasters.

The more complex and difficult the decision, the more important it is to take it one step at a time, paying full attention to each of the three elements of the decision-making process: objectives, alternatives, and potential risks. The more intangible and qualitative the data, the more we need to consider involving others in making the decision, using a systematic method for handling information and separating judgments to produce a successful conclusion.

Decision Analysis is intended to be flexible, to be used in full and in part, to be modified and adapted to meet the unique requirements of each situation. It may be used by an individual, a casual group, or a formally constituted task force. It may be used routinely as standard operating procedure for certain kinds of decisions.

Its single greatest advantage for the organization may be that it provides a common language and approach that removes decision making from the realm of personal preference or idiosyncratic behavior. Some people, to be sure, will always be able to contribute their ideas and communicate their reasoning better than others. Natural ability of this kind varies tremendously. When a common language is used in a systematic framework for decision making, however, everyone involved will understand *how* to contribute and communicate ideas. *Team decisions* based on productive individual contributions become a reality.

SIX

POTENTIAL PROBLEM (OPPORTUNITY) ANALYSIS

IN THIS CHAPTER

Future Events and Their Consequences
The Basic Activities
A Different Kind of Process
When to Use Potential Problem (Opportunity) Analysis

FUTURE EVENTS AND THEIR CONSEQUENCES

Organizations are forever concerned with the future. How an organization will fare in the years ahead will be determined largely by what is being done now. So prudent managers try to look into the future to read the portents they can identify. Yet organizations do not deal with the future as efficiently as they might. Whose responsibility is it to make predictions? And who is to decide what actions are to be taken against speculated but unprovable future demands? Looking into the future remains primarily an individual activity; its results are guided primarily by individual motivation and concern.

It is only when managers share a common method for looking into the future that they can begin to effectively prepare for possible threats and opportunities. This common method helps them identify and assess threats and opportunities. It helps them share relevant information and thus improves mutual understanding of how to avoid threats and benefit from opportunities. Only then does responsibility for how future concerns will be addressed become clear. Approached in this fashion, the future offers opportunity, not just uncertainty.

Potential Problem (Opportunity) Analysis is a process that enables us to walk into the future, see what it may hold, and then return to the present to take action now—when it can do the most good. Potential Problem (Opportunity) Analysis is the pattern of thinking that enables us to change and improve the future, rather than allow the future to arrive entirely on its own terms. This analysis is a protective and enhancing process through which we ensure that the future will be as good as we can make it.

In contrast, Problem Analysis and Decision Analysis are used whenever they are needed to resolve immediate, visible concerns. The use of Problem Analysis and Decision Analysis is demanded by the events of the moment; the use of Potential Problem (Opportunity) Analysis is a voluntary act of prudence.

It will come as no surprise that Potential Problem (Opportunity) Analysis is used less often and less thoroughly than the other Rational Processes we have described. It takes determination to make time for deliberating on imponderables and remote possibilities. In fact, many of the people who use the techniques of Potential Problem (Opportunity) Analysis to protect and enhance plans, projects, and operations within their organizations have had to learn its value the hard way.

CASE HISTORY: THE HIGH COST OF COMPLACENCY

A few years ago, one division of a United States paper manufacturing company enjoyed a near monopoly in its most profitable line: fine clay-coated papers for quality color and black-and-white printing. At that time, two thirds of all the prestige magazines in the United States were printed on this division's papers. Its 90-pound, clay-surfaced product was considered unexcelled, and the division was scarcely able to keep up with the demand. If the executives and technical people of the division were somewhat complacent about their success, who could blame them?

Then disaster struck. The United States Congress voted to allow a substantial increase in postal rates on magazines and published materials. Publishers immediately called the paper company and asked for an equivalent paper that would weigh less than half as much per sheet. The division responded by saying that a 40-pound surfaced paper of similar quality could indeed be developed—perhaps within a year's time. The publishers' general response was: "A year's time? Didn't you people ever consider the possibility that this would happen? Thanks, but no thanks."

Within two weeks the division had lost 70 percent of its business. Customers shifted en masse to a plastic-sized, 40-pound paper that was available immediately from a competitor. It wasn't quite as good as the heavier clay-coated paper, but it was cheaper and cost only one third as much to send through the mail. And that is what counted most with the customers.

Later, a vice president of the company talked to us about what had happened. "Every element of that disaster was perfectly predictable. We knew our paper was expensive. We knew it was heavy. We knew the Post Office Department had been trying for years to increase third-class rates. But that paper was the golden goose, and as long as it was laying all those golden eggs, there was a sense of security. It would go on forever."

After having lost the major portion of their business, division executives found it difficult to formulate an explanation that would mollify the Board of Directors. The members of the board held that executives were paid to know whether a situation was loaded or not. And it didn't help to add, "But conditions changed!" Conditions are always changing. Change is what life is all about. Success and survival depend on being able *to anticipate change, to avoid being swallowed up by its negative effects, and to seize the benefits it offers.* That is what this chapter is all about.

People do not ignore the future just because they are busy with the issues of the moment. It is hard to think about the future, to know *how* to think about it. Of course, the managers at the paper company might have foreseen a postal rate increase and known its effect on the marketability of their product. Potential Problem (Opportunity) Analysis must incorporate such common sense to be useful, but it goes beyond that. Potential Problem (Opportunity) Analysis is a systematic *process* for uncovering and dealing with potential problems and opportunities that are reasonably likely to occur and, therefore, worthy of attention.

The basic questions we ask in Potential Problem Analysis are:"What could go wrong?" and "What can we do about it *now*?"The basic questions of Potential Opportunity Analysis are "What could go better than expected?" and "What can we do now to make the most of it?" The specific sub-questions that lead to specific answers constitute the pragmatic and flexible process of Potential Problem (Opportunity) Analysis.

THE BASIC ACTIVITIES

The techniques of Potential Problem (Opportunity) Analysis are few and easy to understand. The process has been compared to the game of chess: A person may learn how to play in a few hours but then spend the next twenty years learning how to play well. For this reason it is not suitable to present a lengthy explanatory example of Potential Problem (Opportunity) Analysis in one chapter and examples of its use in the next, as we have done with Problem Analysis and Decision Analysis. Instead, we will look at the basic activities that provide the framework for Potential Problem (Opportunity) Analysis and then devote the rest of the chapter to illustrating how managers can operate within this framework to deal with a variety of future-oriented situations.

The techniques of Potential Problem (Opportunity) Analysis are divided into these activities:

▷ State the action—the basic goal or end result of the plan or action to be implemented.

▷ List potential problems (or opportunities)—future undesirable (or desirable) deviations to be addressed one at a time.

▷ Consider causes for the potential problem (or opportunity)—factors that could create or bring about the anticipated deviation.

▷ Take actions to address likely causes—ways to prevent the likely causes from creating the problem or ways to encourage the likely causes to create the opportunity.

▷ Prepare actions to reduce (or enhance) likely effects—ways to minimize the impact of the problem, should it occur, or ways to maximize the impact of the opportunity, should it present itself.

▷ Set triggers for contingent (or capitalizing) actions—systems that indicate that a potential problem or opportunity has occurred.

A Potential Problem Analysis is done separately from a Potential Opportunity Analysis, but in both the thinking is future-oriented. Separate Potential Problem and Opportunity Analyses can be done on the same action, but the difference will be the focus on either desirable or undesirable deviations and their causes and effects.

The actions that are taken may be large or small, complex or simple. Determination of the kind of action to take—preventive, contingent, promoting, capitalizing—will depend on the subject of the analysis, economics, feasibility of implementation, and common sense. Every action has a cost: It calls for an allocation of resources against some future return. The best bargain, naturally, is high return at minimum cost. A simple preventive action is a good investment when it significantly reduces the likelihood of having to face a serious problem in the future. A complicated, expensive program is a poor investment when it is aimed at preventing a lesser problem that is unlikely to occur.

Even though you may not be an expert in the economics of the paper industry, try to imagine two or three actions that might have been taken to prevent the heavy-paper disaster or to mitigate its seriousness once it occurred. Then think for a moment about the subject of cost versus benefit received. What actions might have been taken a year or two before the postal increase that would have saved the company from such staggering loss and would not have been unjustifiably expensive? Would a small developmental project on lightweight papers have made sense? Would research into alternative coatings have been in order? What other kinds of future-oriented actions would have been prudent?

This is as good a place as any to point out that it is always easier to conduct a second-hand Potential Problem Analysis on behalf of other people and their potential problems rather than on our own behalf—

particularly when other people's potential problems have already become actual ones.

Potential Problem Analysis may sound very similar to the adverse consequence thinking that is done at the end of Decision Analysis, but the two are quite different both in purpose and process. The potential adverse consequences of alternatives compared in a Decision Analysis are *identified* to help us reach the best balanced choice: an alternative that fulfills most of our important objectives at minimal risk. In Potential Problem Analysis, by contrast, we are constructing a plan of *action*; we are going to *do* something, perhaps many things, to eliminate or reduce potential problems. There is one juncture at which adverse consequence thinking and Potential Problem Analysis meet as natural starting points for action. Managers often conduct a Potential Problem Analysis to protect the implementation of a decision. When they do, any adverse consequences of the selected alternative are addressed in the course of the Potential Problem Analysis.

It is not uncommon for a management team to choose an excellent alternative that has a couple of substantial risks attached to it. This is because they believe those are risks that they can handle with Potential Problem Analysis. In other words, although the risks are real, they represent potential problems that can be prevented. If they do occur, the effects can be controlled through contingent actions. A few of our clients require their employees to not only do a Decision Analysis for all routine selections but also a Potential Problem Analysis on the final choice. This may seem like a lot of extra work, but in reality it usually amounts to one page appended to the Decision Analysis. This page spells out any potential problems attached to the final choice, and supplies the preventive and contingent actions that have been generated to handle them.

Whatever the details of the situation, the first step in Potential Problem (Opportunity) Analysis is to feel concerned about the future of some project, situation, or event. This is a matter of attitude and motivation. It is the kind of concern that presses us to begin thinking about potential trouble spots or opportunities, about our experiences with similar situations, about what we can do to prevent or mitigate problems that have occurred in the past and are likely to occur again, or about how to obtain the most benefit from changing circumstances. Potential Problem (Opportunity) Analysis must begin with a positive posture, a belief that one can and does have a degree of control over the future. One manager said to us: "I have that positive belief that I can change things. I always ask myself, 'Where could we get killed tomorrow?'"

Many people are afraid to look into the future. "Don't go borrowing problems" is an old adage. The message is clear enough. If you look into the dark recesses of the future, you are likely to find trouble lurking there. It is better not to look. Let trouble find you if it must.

By looking ahead with Potential Problem (Opportunity) Analysis, we are taking the initiative. The usefulness of the procedure depends entirely upon what it turns up. The value of the time we spend in Potential Problem (Opportunity) Analysis becomes known only after the fact. Perhaps nothing new was discovered. On the other hand, a future problem may have been recognized or a chance to seize some unforeseen benefit may have been spotted. Either way, the manager who looks ahead is the winner.

For the moment, we will focus on Potential Problem Analysis. Consider the following example of a manager who did look ahead and how his use of the basic activities of Potential Problem Analysis affected the event that he had planned.

STATE THE ACTION

CASE HISTORY: PLANNING AN INAUGURATION

A new, multimillion-dollar laboratory at a United States Government facility was to be inaugurated within a few weeks. A senior executive at the facility had been designated to manage the inauguration. It was to be a highly publicized open house with many Washington dignitaries and a few high-ranking officials from other nations as guests. The executive decided to use Potential Problem Analysis to plan, monitor, and protect the success of this one-time event. To be successful, the executive first needed to be clear that the action to be protected included only the inauguration and not the events before, or operations after, the open house.

Even administered systematically, the inauguration would entail a nightmare of details. It would bring a huge influx of visitors to a facility that had not been designed to accommodate large numbers of people. Because the facility was engaged in scientific work that had received a great deal of publicity, visitors' expectations were sure to be high. Conceivably, a great many things could go wrong.

Nobody can deal with every possible problem that might occur under such circumstances and trying to do so is usually counterproductive. Most of us have known managers who unwittingly allow huge problems to develop because the managers are detail-oriented without being priority-oriented. So where should we begin?

LIST POTENTIAL PROBLEMS (OR OPPORTUNITIES)

The next question this executive asked was: "Where in our plan are we *most vulnerable* with respect to the success of this inauguration?" What were the most likely potential problems that could disorganize, disrupt, or otherwise seriously jeopardize the smooth operation of such an event? He drew on his experience, judgment, and common sense to arrive at the most likely answers:

▷ *Weather:* Rain or high wind could disrupt the proceedings.

▷ *Program:* VIPs on the program might not attend.

▷ *Facilities:* These could be inadequate to handle the large number of people who might turn out.

▷ *Confusion:* People may not know where to go or what to do.

▷ *Appearance:* The site could be untidy.

The vulnerabilities in this kind of situation all have to do with the failure to fulfill plans. It had been planned, for example, that Senator Cramer, a long-time supporter of the facility and its work, would give the keynote address. If he were delayed or absent, the effect on the program would have been devastating. Vulnerabilities are often identified by looking at what has been planned, then thinking of what would hurt most if the plan were to fall apart.

Another common way to ferret out vulnerable areas in a plan is to approach an upcoming event chronologically. Set out the steps in the plan by asking, "From right now until the conclusion of the whole event, what must be done?" When the steps have been identified, the vulnerable areas will stand out. *Anything that has never been done before* suggests a vulnerable area. So does *overlapping responsibility or authority* for any activity—a situation notorious for converting potential problems into real ones. *Tight deadlines* represent vulnerable areas, as do a*ctivities* that must be *carried out at long distance* rather than under the direct control of the person responsible for their success.

Weather, the first vulnerable area identified, is something of an anomaly. One does not plan the weather; one can only assume what the weather will most likely be. The entire plan for the inauguration was based upon good weather. What if the weather were bad?

No plan ever comes off completely as envisioned. So it could be predicted with 100 percent confidence that this plan for the inauguration would have its gaps and omissions. Most of these would be annoyances that would be suffered and soon forgotten. But some could be of the never-to-be-forgotten, horror-story variety: "Remember that inauguration out at Botch City?" We all know stories that begin with similar words. Identifying the extreme vulnerabilities can prevent a further contribution to the lore. There are not many incidents so damaging that they jeopardize the overall success of an entire event, so there are few excuses for failing to search for those that might.

There is a vast difference between setting out the steps in a plan in order to identify vulnerable areas and simply listing things to do. In Potential Problem Analysis, the purposeful identification of specific potential problems leads to specific actions. And this is the vital distinction between intention and process.

Identifying specific potential problems involves describing those areas in which we might have problems and exactly what those problems might be. Simply identifying the area—for example, weather—is too broad and general. What specifically could have gone wrong concerning the weather? Considering the time of year, the inauguration could have been threatened by two specific potential problems: heavy rain and wind. A thunderstorm, with a torrential downpour, could have occurred late in the afternoon. Weather statistics gave this a 10 percent probability—too high to ignore. High winds, with blowing sand and dust, would have been less disconcerting. Statistics gave this a lower probability—less than 5 percent.

Having narrowed the vulnerability of weather down to "10 percent probability that heavy rain will disrupt proceedings," the executive had something tangible to work with. It was possible to assess the threat of thunderstorms to the plans, and possible mitigating actions could be thought of. The threat of high winds was deemed too insignificant to warrant further concern.

The executive's third identified area of vulnerability was "Facilities might be inadequate to handle the large number of people who turn out." There were two kinds of facilities: those for VIPs and those for the general public.

Because the general public represented a crowd that the facility was not designed to handle, inadequate facilities were seen as a likely and very serious potential problem.

Each of these specific potential problems could be described in detail. Each could be assessed independently: How serious a threat would it be to the successful outcome of the event? At the end of a few minutes, the executive had a list of the specific problems that would have to be dealt with in order to protect the success of the inauguration.

CONSIDER CAUSES FOR THE
POTENTIAL PROBLEM (OR OPPORTUNITY)

To take actions that can prevent or reduce the chances of a potential problem, it is first necessary to know what is likely to cause the problem. If the cause is not removed, then the problem is likely to happen.

Given the time of year, afternoon thunderstorms were the most likely cause of heavy rain.

Another potential problem involved Senator Cramer, the keynote speaker. He could have been delayed, or he might have cancelled at the last minute. Similarly, other critical speakers might have become unavailable. Competing priorities and forgotten schedules were seen as the most likely causes of these potential problems.

One cause for the facilities having been inadequate was that more people might have attended than were expected, but this was not a cause the manager wanted to remove. The purpose of the event was, after all, public relations. However, what aspects of the facility's design would have caused it to be overwhelmed by a large crowd? The manager identified several on-site inadequacies:

- Parking was insufficient for cars and tour buses.
- Sanitary facilities were largely inaccessible, in locked and secure areas of the building.
- Water fountains were not located near the inauguration area.
- Seating was inadequate.
- Trash cans were too few.

The executive reviewed the remaining potential problems and thought of as many causes as possible. Not every cause was ultimately addressed, but having an exhaustive list enabled him to spot most of the more probable causes.

TAKE ACTIONS TO ADDRESS LIKELY CAUSES

The executive searched first for ways to prevent each of the specific potential problems identified. What could be done to prevent a thunderstorm? Nothing. But a thunderstorm could be prevented from disrupting the proceedings. Since storms usually occur late in the afternoon, the inauguration speeches were rescheduled so that they would be completed shortly after 1 p.m. Tours of the facility could follow the dedication ceremonies. If it rained later in the day, no harm would be done.

To prevent the event from falling off the speakers' schedules, the executive arranged a call to the Senator two weeks, then one week, then two days before the date to make sure that nothing untoward had come up. He had the same person check on the other

VIPs scheduled to attend. The purpose was to jog memories and re-confirm invitations. Since control of the guests' priorities and travel plans lay outside the executive's domain, there was little more he could do to prevent these potential problems.

"Facilities might be inadequate" did lie within the executive's domain. Temporary areas were cleared and marked off for extra parking space. Mobile restrooms were rented from a local contractor. Temporary water fountains were installed, and trash containers were borrowed from other parts of the facility and placed around the inauguration area. Extra seating was arranged. Point by point, the identified causes of the facilities being inadequate were corrected.

Most of the entries on the long list of specific potential problems could be countered by simple and inexpensive preventive actions. A typical problem was "Confusion about where to go." In order to identify what would cause this confusion, the executive had a staff person drive onto the facility, pretending never to have been there before. This action enabled him to check traffic signs for clarity and placement. The signs were found to be too few, too small, and too close to turning points to permit a driver to react in time. Large cardboard signs were printed, and the executive arranged to have them placed in appropriate areas on the morning of the inauguration. Other signs, giving times of events on the program, were also prepared and put up. Because the specific causes of these potential problems were identified well in advance, a number of preventive actions could be found that virtually eliminated them—and the problems that would have resulted from them.

PREPARE ACTIONS TO REDUCE (OR ENHANCE) LIKELY EFFECTS

Some specific potential problems simply could not have been prevented. What if Senator Cramer, in spite of all the phone calls, failed to arrive to give his speech? The manager arranged for a backup speaker who could step in at the last minute. In fact, a backup activity for every event on the program was arranged. A canvas roof was placed over the speaker's stand for protection in case of early rain, or for shade if the day was sunny. A reception area was organized in a nearby building, should VIPs have to run for cover. No matter what might happen, the show would go on.

Room arrangements were made with a second hotel in the event that VIP reservations went awry at the first hotel or unexpected guests attended. Although additional government vehicles had been requested to prevent transportation problems for VIPs, a few staff members who owned station wagons were organized as an emergency on-call group.

In case the contractor failed to clean the site properly, a Boy Scout troop was enlisted as a last-minute cleanup crew, in return for a promised private tour of the facility later on. The Boy Scouts also agreed to remain on duty, collecting trash, during the ceremony itself. Extra bins and containers were provided to make the task easier.

These contingent actions, designed to minimize the effects of unpreventable problems, would have handled the most irritating and troublesome potential situations. This would have left the manager and the staff free to deal with other unforeseen problems. They could look forward to the great day with confidence that they had done everything within their power to ensure that the event would run smoothly and professionally. The inauguration would not be marred by disorganization and mistakes.

SET TRIGGERS FOR CONTINGENT (OR CAPITALIZING) ACTIONS

A contingent action is a wasted resource if it remains unused when needed. Some mechanism must be put into place to monitor the potential problem and activate the contingent action at the correct time. Someone had to monitor the VIP transportation and alert employees to use their station wagons. How would VIPs know that they were to go to the backup hotel if their reservations were lost? The best triggers usually begin the contingent action automatically. The canvas roof required no human interaction to prevent the rain from falling on the VIPs. However, there are times when judgment is required. For example, someone had to decide that the weather was bad enough to postpone the ceremony and that the VIPs needed to move to the reception area.

THE RESULTS

It did not rain early. It did not rain late. In fact, the weather was so good that the crowd was nearly double the expected size.

Because of a death in his family, Senator Cramer, the keynote speaker, canceled the engagement less than eight hours before the program was to begin. The backup speaker stepped in as promised. The proceedings went off without a hitch. The extra parking areas, filled almost to capacity, provided enough space for everyone. Traffic moved without incident. The facilities were adequate in spite of the large crowd. The orderly crowd showed little frustration or confusion. And the Boy Scouts ran in and out, picking up litter, so that the extra trash containers were all utilized.

Until the very last minute of the inauguration, the affair was an exercise in perfection, a model of organization. But it wouldn't be fair to end the story here. Despite the thorough planning that uncovered most of the problems, people who were there still do say, "Remember that inauguration at Botch City? WOW!"

The Air Force had been invited to provide a flyby as the ceremonies came to an end. And that is what was provided. A transonic flyby. This was in the early days of faster-than-sound flight, and there still were some things to learn. Three jets screamed by at low level, dragging a monstrous sonic boom behind them. More than three hundred windows in the new laboratory were shattered, and a number of concrete support pillars developed instant cracks. The laboratory was opened at 1:30 p.m. and closed at 1:45 p.m.—for nine weeks of repair. There were a few injuries, by some miracle all superficial.

Everyone who attended agreed it was the most memorable and exciting inauguration they had ever witnessed.

The moral of this story is that you probably can't win them all, no matter how hard you try. But if you provide a good backup speaker and adequate facilities, your public will enjoy the show and forgive those rare problems that do drop out of the blue.

While this story provides an interesting example of Potential Problem Analysis, the same event could have benefited from Potential Opportunity Analysis.

If the purpose of the event was to build goodwill and acknowledge contributors, what might have been seen as particularly beneficial?

Perhaps additional stakeholders and influential people could have been invited. These would be people who otherwise would not have an opportunity to visit the facility and witness its capabilities. Special personal invitations could have been made to coax them to attend the event. Once there, interesting and unique capabilities of the facility could have been demonstrated. These demonstrations could have been selected specifically to match the VIPs' interests.

It would be important to aggressively seek out ways to capitalize on the benefits of a favorable impression. The executive could have monitored the news media for positive coverage of the inauguration and for favorable quotes from the VIPs who attended. These endorsements could then be shared with other VIPs and other news organizations. These actions might generate still more coverage and further deepen the goodwill he sought to build.

There can be no promise or possibility of complete security from surprise. The purpose of Potential Problem (Opportunity) Analysis is not to guarantee an error-free or blissful future for plans, projects, and events. The cost of such attention would probably exceed its benefits. The purpose of Potential Problem (Opportunity) Analysis is, rather, to reduce the uncertainty of the future to manageable proportions and to eliminate the kinds of events about which people say too late: "Why didn't somebody think of that?"

A DIFFERENT KIND OF PROCESS

Potential Problem (Opportunity) Analysis has one characteristic that makes it essentially different from the Rational Processes of Problem Analysis and Decision Analysis. Within both Problem Analysis and Decision Analysis, one step leads inexorably to the next, and the steps are followed in orderly and thorough fashion to arrive at a logical conclusion. That is not always the case in Potential Problem (Opportunity) Analysis.

Potential Problem (Opportunity) Analysis comprises logically consecutive steps. However, it is possible to identify potential problems and likely causes for which there are no preventive actions; there are also times when, try as we might, we can't come up with any way to promote the cause of a potential opportunity. When that happens, we must jump the preventive (or promoting) action step and go on to devise contingent (or capitalizing) actions to minimize (or maximize) the effects of the potential deviation.

It is also possible to identify serious potential problems for which there are no feasible preventive *or* contingent actions. When that happens, there are only two paths to take. First, we can accept the identified risk and hope for the best. Second, we can move back from Potential Problem Analysis into a decision-making mode in order to identify a more manageable course of action.

Our first example of Potential Problem Analysis illustrated all its basic activities. In the following example, the result of the Potential Problem Analysis process will be quite different.

CASE HISTORY: CLOSING SAYERS POINT MILL

If ever an announced decision called for meticulous use of Potential Problem Analysis, this one did. The economic facts of life forced the top management of one of our clients in the chemical industry to order the closing of a facility we will call the Sayers Point Mill. It was obsolete, isolated, too costly to maintain, and located in an area where raw materials were becoming increasingly scarce. Its managers were not surprised at the decision.

However, there was more to consider, much more.

The workforce of nine hundred eighty-four people from the local area averaged fifty-three years in age. Many had worked for the company for at least twenty years. Educational levels were generally low. Other local job opportunities were nil. Sayers Point Mill managers were faced with implementing a decision that was both professionally and personally unpleasant.

It was a situation in which any action would have far-reaching effects. Many of these effects would, in turn, create new problems. For these managers, vulnerability—a key subject in Potential Problem Analysis—included neglect and disregard of corporate responsibility. If we bring change into the lives of others, society holds us responsible for the effects of that change. If we disavow the responsibility and refuse to discharge it, society can bring powerful sanctions against us. In this case, the exact nature of that responsibility could only be grasped if management understood exactly what the effects of closing the mill would be.

There could, in fact, be countless effects, but no one can deal with all the possibilities. Management needed to discover where the greatest specific vulnerabilities—in other words, potential problems—lay. Yet it appeared that there would be first, second, and third orders of effects. The managers began by asking, "In what way will this action of closing the mill have the *greatest* impact on us and on others? Where will this action hurt *most?*" These and other similar questions help us identify future threats and opportunities.

For practical reasons, we will limit ourselves to the top five effects identified by management. See Figure 14 for the list of effects. The complexity of the situation makes even this partial list formidable. To reduce the effects of closing a mill to a few simple terms would be to distort reality.

FIGURE 14   **PRIMARY EFFECTS OF CLOSING SAYERS POINT MILL**

These primary effects are still too general and diffuse to be dealt with. Before the mill's managers can begin to consider possible actions, they first have to understand the secondary effects. To do this they change the questions slightly, asking of each primary effect, "Where will this effect have its greatest impact on us or on others? Where are we or others most vulnerable and most likely to suffer because of it?" These clarifying questions lead to working out the most important secondary effects for each primary effect. Figure 15 lists the secondary effects for two of the five primary effects listed in Figure 14.

FIGURE 15   SECONDARY EFFECTS OF CLOSING SAYERS POINT MILL

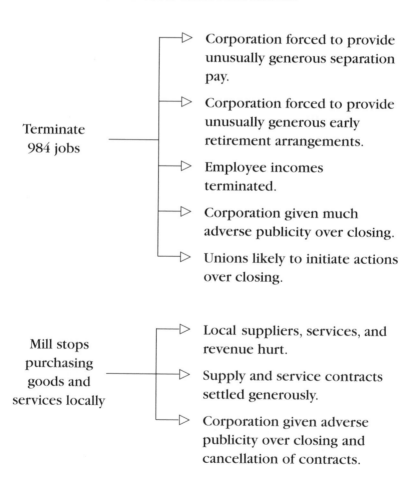

Terminate 984 jobs
▷ Corporation forced to provide unusually generous separation pay.
▷ Corporation forced to provide unusually generous early retirement arrangements.
▷ Employee incomes terminated.
▷ Corporation given much adverse publicity over closing.
▷ Unions likely to initiate actions over closing.

Mill stops purchasing goods and services locally
▷ Local suppliers, services, and revenue hurt.
▷ Supply and service contracts settled generously.
▷ Corporation given adverse publicity over closing and cancellation of contracts.

THE NEW RATIONAL MANAGER

With the secondary effects made visible, the managers now can identify *specific potential problems*. To complete the picture, they need only their past experience and imagination. The results of these changes can be listed as a series of concise statements of outcome:

▷ Heavy cash demands will be placed on the corporation—on the order of X hundred thousand dollars.

▷ The precedent of unusually generous separation payment for early retirement will cause future trouble.

▷ Many mill employees who are terminated will go on unemployment rolls, some for years to come.

▷ Many will become virtually unemployable.

▷ Local merchants and services will be hurt by reduced purchasing power.

▷ The debt structure of the community will have to increase.

▷ The impact on local government will be severe, tax revenue will be reduced, demand on services will increase.

▷ Unemployment will bring social and family disintegration.

▷ Adverse publicity will put the corporation in a bad light and will force it to take a defensive posture.

▷ Closing will create employee distrust and dissatisfaction elsewhere in the corporation.

▷ Class-action suits will be initiated by unions.

▷ Closing will create union bargaining problems elsewhere.

▷ There will be some local business failures, causing hard times for many others.

▷ Services and businesses will reduce their activity, increasing unemployment.

▷ Suppliers will reduce their activity, increasing unemployment.

▷ Suppliers elsewhere will tend to distrust the corporation and might demand cancellation clauses more favorable to them.

▷ The precedent of supplier contract settlements will cause future problems.

▷ Damage suits against the corporation may be brought by suppliers.

The managers saw immediately that most of these effects lay beyond their control. These potential problems could not be prevented, for the very nature of the action they were about to take would cause the effects. They could prepare certain contingent actions. They could provide a large fund for settling claims. They could attempt to transfer more people to other activities. They could phase out the closing over a longer period.

There followed days of heated debate. The company felt it couldn't close the mill, yet couldn't afford to keep it open—and there seemed to be no half-way measure. Then someone suggested that a new process, originally scheduled as a major expansion project for a mill nearly a thousand miles away, might be installed in the Sayers Point Mill instead. There would be disadvantages. There would be some sacrifice in efficiency due to the logistics of the Sayers Point operation. Existing personnel would have to be completely retrained. Totally new equipment would have to be introduced. There would be a host of problems, but the solutions to these problems lay within the organization's control. By replacing the original plan, "Close Sayers Point Mill," with "Convert Sayers Point Mill to the New Process," all the gut-wrenching effects could be prevented. The decision was made to put the new process into the old mill.

There were some problems associated with doing this, but most of the people there responded enthusiastically to the new opportunity. Mill conversion was completed ahead of schedule, and start-up of the new process ran decidedly ahead of schedule. The mill achieved full design production capacity before anyone had believed possible and went on to operate at an average of 115 percent of capacity. The loyalty of the Sayers Point people was totally to the corporation that had taken an action to discharge its responsibility to them.

The result of Potential Problem Analysis, in this case, was the recognition of an alternative superior to the one originally proposed. The contingent actions meticulously devised by the management team never had to be used, but the exercise was hardly a waste of time. The process had given them a picture of their situation that was more comprehensive and precise than they could have gained otherwise. There is no better way to see that a decision is a poor one than to examine in detail the probable effects of its implementation. The "walk into the future to see what it may hold" was worth the trip for the managers at Sayers Point and for the corporation.

WHEN TO USE POTENTIAL PROBLEM (OPPORTUNITY) ANALYSIS

When should we use Potential Problem (Opportunity) Analysis? Whenever experience and intuition tell us something could go wrong in the future and the cost of its going wrong could be great. Potential Problem Analysis is essential for any major project or event. When should we use Potential Opportunity Analysis? When we are confident of success—because of the nature of the action or as a result of a Potential Problem Analysis—but experience or intuition tells us that there would be value in exceeding expectations. NASA, in its space programs, has been a heavy user of Potential Problem Analysis. Dr. Kurt Debus, one-time head of the Cape Kennedy launch complex, told his people, "We can't afford to have *any* problems. We must find them *before* they happen." At every turn he and his people asked: "What could go wrong? What can we do about it now to prevent it?"

Potential Problem Analysis is a technique that enables the manager to make full use of his or her experience. Over the years any manager has seen hundreds of problems and opportunities crop up that should have been anticipated, and has heard of thousands more. This is the body of experience that Potential Problem (Opportunity) Analysis taps and puts to good use. Merely being able to remember a thousand horror stories is of no use unless that body of information can be used to prevent more.

CASE HISTORY: THE LIKELY EMERGENCY

The case described below shows how one manager used his experience and judgment, in a potentially life-threatening situation, to identify the most important likely problems from a host of superficial ones. Observe how the manager and staff systematically examined and evaluated an uncertain future and how judgments were used to set the guidelines. They were successful precisely because they set tight priorities on the most critical of forecasted problems.

The managing director of an overseas branch of a multinational corporation described how he had evacuated his people because street fighting had broken out: "The crisis point arrived suddenly, with scarcely any warning. But we had our evacuation plan ready and everything was rolling in a matter of minutes. Nearly four hundred employees and dependents were involved. We brought them in by private vehicles to a central gathering point, then proceeded in convoy to the airport. Everything went off without a hitch. We sat in the airport until things cooled down twenty-four hours later and then took everyone back to their homes. But if we'd had to leave, we could have done so without incident.

"I'd been in that country more than a year before the riots started. I watched the political situation worsen. My experience told me that things could deteriorate overnight and that we could be targets of hostility and violence. I brought my staff together and shared my concern with them. I asked them to consider what would happen if there were a violent overthrow of the government and we had to get out. My greatest concern was how we would protect our people and their dependents. I told my staff: 'Find out where we would be most vulnerable, where events could hurt our people most.'

"One of the key exposure points they identified was the trip from the security of our buildings to the airport. They showed me an evacuation plan drawn up by my predecessor, with a convoy route clearly marked out. The voice of experience inside me fairly shouted on that one. 'Is it up to date?' I asked them. 'How good is it?' At my urging, a couple of my staff drove the route one noon hour. One of the streets indicated in the plan as safe and quiet, along which the entire convoy was supposed to move, turned out to be a narrow dead end. One bridge they were to use on the way to the airport would have been perfectly adequate—if it had ever been built. Only the approach had been completed. As a result of that analysis, identifying potential problems and correcting them, we had a plan that would work when and if the whistle finally blew."

This manager could very well have asked his people to make a list of *all* the things that could go wrong, writing down potential problems in slavish detail to make sure "we don't miss any." The list would have grown to fearsome length, for hundreds of things could go wrong in such a situation. Some would have been vexatious, some disturbing, some moderately dangerous. While there is benefit in "casting a wide net," the sheer mass of all the things that could have gone wrong cannot be allowed to obscure the potential few that would have been fatal.

Even more likely, the mass of possibilities can be so overwhelming that the group might have said, "We give up! Let's just wait and see what happens!" That attitude might have led one day to a convoy of the corporation's employees and dependents being caught in a narrow, dead-end street during a full-scale riot. The manager instead used common sense and good judgment, coupled with experience, to conduct a systematic Potential Problem Analysis on the few most serious potential problems the team could foresee.

CASE HISTORY: A CRISIS AVERTED

When something has already gone wrong, and it is due to our own actions, we are well aware of whose responsibility it is. But suppose we look ahead and see the potential failure of something for which no one has *direct* responsibility. Whose responsibility is it to raise unpopular questions and suggest possibly needless actions? Unless responsibility has been pinpointed by the organization, our conclusion may be to leave well enough alone.

Serious potential problems are usually broad, affecting many different aspects of an enterprise. It is easy for a manager to say "That's not in my area" and pass responsibility to someone else. Nothing can be more dangerous. A problem that might have been dealt with successfully in its early stages may be difficult or impossible to handle later on. Ideally, organizations should welcome constructive criticism of decisions and policies, but few actually do. This raises a major barrier to effective use of Potential Problem Analysis. Looking ahead and recognizing trouble, then doing something about it, is too often a case of individual managerial courage.

In the spring of 1966, a senior Foreign Service officer assigned to the United States Embassy in Bonn looked into the immediate future and recognized a serious potential problem.

The war in Vietnam was not going well for the United States, despite major commitment of advisory personnel. The officer felt that President Lyndon Johnson would have to decide within the next two to three weeks whether to escalate that commitment or initiate a withdrawal.

Drawing on his knowledge of Johnson's past decisions, he believed that the President would escalate the commitment of personnel. His scenario included the following. Fifty thousand of our best troops would be sent in. They would be taken from Germany, where they were part of our NATO commitment. President Johnson would give the order suddenly, without fully consulting our NATO partners. This would hurt our alliances, upset the balance of power, create confusion, and erode confidence throughout Europe. Especially in Germany. Our allies would see the replacement troops as untrained and unprepared. Hostile nations would be sure to exploit the situation, and our relations would be badly damaged.

The Foreign Service officer carried out a Potential Problem Analysis of the situation, listing the major points of vulnerability that occurred to him. He drew some of his colleagues into the study and got additional points of vulnerability from them. They then explored the preventive and contingent actions that might be taken. They created a plan from these elements for dealing with a sudden withdrawal, and they alerted others who would be involved. In the end, they had enlisted the support of their counterparts in a dozen United States embassies across Europe. The plan of action complete, they waited.

Exactly ten days later, President Johnson gave the order for fifty thousand troops to be airlifted out of Germany, beginning within twenty-four hours. There was little warning to anyone and no consultation with the other NATO nations. The officer's prepared plan was brought swiftly into action. Within minutes Foreign Service officers over a quarter of the world were calling on their foreign counterparts, explaining the move, giving assurances, dealing with problems, and answering questions.

There was a minimum of confusion and no appearance of a void in the NATO forces in Europe. By the time hostile nations heard about it, all questions had been answered and there were no embarrassments to exploit. There had been no frantic scramble, no one making contradictory off-the-cuff statements, no duplication or omission, no chaos. It all went off as planned.

The easiest and most economical time to solve a problem is before the problem has a chance to occur. This means that people must feel free to look into the future and suggest actions for improving it or take the initiative to move ahead out of personal dedication and commitment. How easy it would have been for the Foreign Service officer to have deferred to "those who have official responsibility for things like that!" He didn't. Instead, he organized an effort that turned out to be supremely successful and a service to his country. In a quiet way, his use of Potential Problem Analysis may have averted a diplomatic crisis.

CASE HISTORY: OPENING THE QUICK-SERVICE AIRCRAFT FACILITY

If the people of an organization care about the future and wish to make it better, and the organization itself is open enough to consider suggestions for improvement, Potential Problem (Opportunity) Analysis can contribute to the benefit of everyone. Potential problems and opportunities are not all of the earthshaking variety. Many uses of Potential Problem (Opportunity) Analysis are commonplace. But still they make a difference. The operation runs more smoothly, there is less waste and confusion, and fewer things have to be done over.

> An engineering manager and chief technician were describing a proposed installation to their boss, head of operations for a major airline. They had designed a quick-service facility to be built in an existing hangar. In the new facility, a jet would be brought in, all seats would be removed and stacked on one side, and a crew would work around the clock on inspections and repairs to have the plane ready to fly again in thirty-six hours. Discussion had turned to the storage rack for the seats, a small part of the overall plan. It seemed quite simple, yet the manager of operations said from habit: "What could go wrong? Let's list some things."

A quick Potential Problem Analysis was carried out. The first few items were of no consequence. Then the technician said, "Suppose the deluge system releases accidentally?" The deluge system in an airplane hangar is an oversized version of a commercial sprinkler system used for protection against fire. Modern jets are highly inflammable. They carry huge quantities of fuel and no chance of fire is taken around them. Deluge systems are triggered by sensitive smoke-and-heat sensors and sometimes turn on even when there is no fire. Aircraft workers consider it better to be drenched once in a while than incinerated. But a deluge on two hundred nicely upholstered seats would be another matter. It would put a plane out of commission for days—no trifling concern in a business in which hours of utilization translate directly into return on investment.

What else could go wrong? "We have pigeons in the hangar during the summer." (Something like a deluge system, only smaller.) "What about spray painting?" Overspray drifting onto the upholstery would be catastrophic. Within minutes the original design had been modified to give covered protection to the seats while in storage. Of course, the need for coverings for the seats would ultimately have been discovered the hard way. With Potential Problem Analysis, the operations manager moved directly to the optimal design.

CASE HISTORY: SEARCHING FOR ALASKAN OIL

Potential Problem (Opportunity) Analysis is an attitude, an orientation toward the future. It is positive, not negative. It is a way of thinking that says, "We can foresee the future to some extent, and we can change it in some degree to make it better." In a competitive world, the balance between success and failure is often narrow. The winning margin is often no more than that which is gained by foreseeing the future and changing it, in some degree.

Imperial Oil of Canada, a long-time user of Potential Problem (Opportunity) Analysis, had an ambitious program of exploration mapped out for the Mackenzie River delta. The Mackenzie empties into the Beaufort Sea and the Arctic Ocean. As soon as the ice broke up in spring, a task force of ships, planes, and people would converge on the area to search for oil. Their mission would be to set off seismic charges and plot the underlying strata. Several hundred people had been assigned to the project; plans had been worked out in meticulous detail; schedules had been made; and supplies had been dropped and cached along the way. Everything was ready. Then the plan was subjected to a thorough Potential Problem Analysis. "What could go wrong? What negative effects could our actions have?"

At that point the company recognized that vast schools of beluga whales would be coming into the Mackenzie River delta for three weeks. There they would have their calves, make new liaisons, and mate before returning to the sea. The Imperial Oil crews would be working in the area at the same time, and the noise and disruption would frighten the whales out of their traditional ceremonies of courtship and reproduction. The plans were changed, at substantial cost, and the delta was left quiet and peaceful. The whales arrived, sported in the clear waters, had their progeny and their love affairs, and swam out to sea again, undisturbed.

CHAPTER SUMMARY

Potential Problem (Opportunity) Analysis is, first of all, an orientation, an attitude. It is based on the conviction that one can walk into the future, see what it may hold, then return to the present to take action now—when it can do the most good. Potential Problem (Opportunity) Analysis is the pattern of thinking that enables us to change and improve future events. It is a systematic thinking process for uncovering and dealing with potential problems and opportunities that are reasonably likely to occur and will be injurious (or beneficial) if they do occur.

Potential Problem (Opportunity) Analysis asks two basic questions: "What might happen? What can we do about it now?" The framework for Potential Problem (Opportunity) Analysis includes:

▷ State the action: What specific action and end result are we concerned about?

▷ List potential problems (or opportunities): What might happen that was not planned?

▷ Consider causes for the potential problem (or opportunity): What is likely to create the potential problem (or opportunity)?

▷ Take actions to address likely causes: What can be done to prevent (or promote) the likely cause?

▷ Prepare actions to reduce (or enhance) likely effects: What will be done if the potential problem (opportunity) happens?

▷ Set triggers for contingent (or capitalizing) actions: What will begin the contingent (or capitalizing) action?

Potential Problem Analysis is not simply a search for trouble. Rather, it is a constructive method for identifying ways to avoid and lessen trouble that is likely to occur. Potential Opportunity Analysis is not simply a search for improvement. Rather, it is a deliberate method for identifying ways to find additional value and benefit. As such, Potential Problem (Opportunity) Analysis is one of the most rewarding activities in which a manager or an organizational team can participate. It provides individuals and organizations with their best chance to build the future according to their visions and desires. Potential Problem (Opportunity) Analysis is one of the most practical tools available for bringing into focus today the best thinking of an informed management team that is properly concerned with the future.

SEVEN

SITUATION APPRAISAL

IN THIS CHAPTER
Situation Appraisal, Tool for Evaluation
Situation Appraisal Techniques
Situation Appraisal in Practice

SITUATION APPRAISAL, TOOL FOR EVALUATION

In the preceding chapters we have spoken of Problem Analysis, Decision Analysis, and Potential Problem (Opportunity) Analysis as discrete processes to be used one at a time, each sufficient unto itself. While this is accurate, the use of the processes from day to day does not consist of a blithe stroll from one to another as circumstances dictate. In actual practice, when faced with any situation, we may experience confusion and uncertainty over where to begin. We may struggle to recognize and break apart actions that overlap and are required to address the situation. At best, we may not be clear on which issues to address first or on how to manage a number of simultaneous activities efficiently.

Nearly every manager has entertained the fantasy of starting fresh. Fantasy indeed. Even on the first day in a new job, the manager is beset by issues that were chronic frustrations for the previous incumbent. Lying in wait for the new manager, in addition, are new issues to be understood, problems to be solved, and decisions to be made. All these are part of the job. They do not stand on ceremony. They move right in. Before the week is out, potential problems begin to suggest themselves. The opportunity to start fresh does not exist. Every manager must operate from a middle ground, surrounded by the accumulated problems of the past, a profusion of demands of the

167

moment, and the certainty that future threats and opportunities await and must not be ignored.

The three Rational Processes we have already described consist of *analytical techniques*. Their purpose is to resolve situations and issues. Situation Appraisal, by contrast, consists of *evaluative techniques* that lead to the proper selection and use of the analytical techniques. Situation Appraisal builds the framework for the daily use of Rational Process ideas. It enables managers to make the best possible use of the techniques of Problem Analysis, Decision Analysis, and Potential Problem (Opportunity) Analysis by showing them:

▷   Where to begin.

▷   How to recognize situations that require action.

▷   How to break apart issues that are overlapping and confusing.

▷   How to set priorities.

▷   How to manage a number of simultaneous activities efficiently.

A manager who is skilled in the three basic Rational Processes works more efficiently than one who is unskilled in handling information about specific problems, decisions, and potential problems or opportunities. To be effective in the overall job of managing the daily disorderly flow of information, however, a manager must also be skilled in the process we call Situation Appraisal.

Managers lacking this skill cannot make frequent or productive use of the analytical Rational Processes because they are uncertain of how, when, or to what end the processes can be used. These managers tend to await the arrival of ready-made problems, decisions, and future-oriented concerns that fit the techniques they have learned. When that doesn't happen, they become frustrated. The situations that actually do land on their desks are invariably confusing, multifaceted, overlapping, and fragmentary. As a result, the managers fail to recognize the situations as subjects for Problem Analysis, Decision Analysis, or Potential Problem (Opportunity) Analysis. Frustration sets in, and the managers are apt to say, "I thought those ideas were great when I learned them, but I haven't used them nearly as much as I thought I would...."

There is nothing wrong with the spontaneous use of the individual Rational Processes. But the degree to which they are used on a continuing, systematic basis depends on the degree and frequency with which the manager uses the evaluative management techniques that are about to be presented.

SITUATION APPRAISAL TECHNIQUES

Situation Appraisal techniques enable the manager to increase competence in these activities:

▷ List threats and opportunities.

▷ Separate and clarify concerns.

▷ Consider seriousness, urgency, and growth.

▷ Determine analysis needed.

▷ Determine help needed.

FIGURE 16   **SITUATION APPRAISAL ACTIVITIES**

List Threats and Opportunities
Current or future
concerns that need action

Separate and Clarify Concerns
Specific actions to
meet a need

Determine Help Needed
Necessary information
and commitment

Consider Seriousness, Urgency, and Growth
Relative priority
among concerns

Determine Analysis Needed
Appropriate type and
amount of analysis

These activities, as shown in Figure 16, do not form a lockstep sequence. If we had all the information about every concern as soon as we recognized it, and no new concerns came up until we had resolved all of those on our list, this would be the logical sequence to follow. In reality, however, new information is constantly coming to light. No sooner do we start the analysis of our highest-priority concern, than someone rushes in to tell us that the problem has been solved or that someone has discovered that it is really two or three smaller problems. When this happens, a new list of concerns must be made, more separating questions asked, priorities reset. Each situation may demand a different order and combination of Situation Appraisal techniques.

The basic techniques for each activity are described below. Following the descriptions are examples of the techniques in practice. They show how skillful managers use the techniques under everyday conditions.

LIST THREATS AND OPPORTUNITIES

A concern is any situation that causes an individual to feel a need to act. A perceived threat or opportunity tells the individual to do something within his or her responsibilities and sphere of influence.

Where do these concerns come from? Sometimes both the source and the mandate for action are very clear. Managers may have been assigned specific tasks. A routine report is due at the end of the month. An employee's performance has become unsatisfactory. A project is going to miss its deadline.

Such concerns are straightforward; something needs to be done and they are the people responsible for doing it. But the most efficient managers do not spend their days responding only to obvious mandates. They search out situations that require action and for which they can take some degree of responsibility. They do this not because they have time on their hands and enjoy troubleshooting for its own sake, but because they have no time to waste on troublesome situations that need never have occurred.

We realize that surveying the work environment for all the concerns that require action is no small task. Many managers have found that it helps to break the search into four activities:

▷ List current deviations, threats, and opportunities.

▷ Review progress against goals.

▷ Look ahead for surprises (within the organization and in the external environment).

▷ Search for improvement.

Although it is most effective to focus a Situation Appraisal on a single subject or time frame, one or more of the activities might still be applied. For example, rather than survey the entire work environment, the manager might limit the appraisal to an important client or to production on a single shift.

At times, we will want to go through all four activities—at an annual planning session, for example. At other times, we might find it more appropriate to limit ourselves to one or two of them (for example, to plan the week's work on Monday morning, we would only go through the first activity; the second activity, reviewing progress against goals, might happen monthly).

In some organizations, Situation Appraisal techniques serve as an outline for routine meetings, helping to coordinate the team's resources and efforts to resolve important matters. Each kind of issue is considered in turn: chronic situations, inadequately handled situations, and unexplored situations.

To help us identify concerns, we list threats and opportunities by asking specific questions, such as:

▷ Where are we not meeting standards?

▷ What problems from the last six months remain unsolved?

▷ What recommendations are we currently working on or will be coming up in the near future?

▷ What decisions need to be made now?

▷ What decisions are being made now and will have to be implemented when a choice is made?

▷ What major projects, systems, or plans are about to be implemented?

▷ What changes are anticipated?

▷ What opportunities exist?

▷ What bothers us about…?

These questions are starting points for discussion. Their eventual product will be a list of problems, decisions, and future-oriented concerns that deserve consideration.

When a manager uses Situation Appraisal on an individual basis, this step may consist only of a mental review of current concerns. A few notes or a list of concerns may be jotted down. But whether one manager is making a quick mental tally, or a team is listing concerns on an easel, the process is the same. By beginning this way, we move toward eventual identification and assignment of concerns that can be resolved through partial or full use of one of the three analytical Rational Processes. At this point, we make no identification of which analytical process applies. Before we can make such identifications, we must examine each concern to determine whether it is, in fact, a single concern or a composite of two or more concerns. If it is a composite, we must isolate and examine each concern on its own merits. Once we have made all these determinations, the next step is to arrange the complete list of concerns in a realistic and useful order of priority.

SEPARATE AND CLARIFY CONCERNS

A combination of *concerns* presenting themselves as one *situation* cannot be dealt with effectively. Most issues and concerns that have earned our attention are more complex than they first appear to be. But even if the concern turns out to be simple, it is still useful to examine whether it should be broken down. This exploratory process ensures that we take the information-gathering steps necessary for the evaluation of all concerns, simple or complex. At the same time, the status of a concern will be understood in the same way by everyone involved. It is unlikely that employing the separation step of Situation Appraisal will be a waste of time.

We asked questions in the initial identification stage of the process to list situations that require action. We now ask more questions in order to break apart any situation that consists of two or more components:

▷ Do we think one action will really resolve this concern?

▷ Are we talking about one thing or several things?

▷ Do we agree on the reason for our concern?

▷ What evidence do we have that says this is a concern?

▷ What do we mean by...?

▷ What is actually happening in this situation? Anything else?

▷ What do we see, hear, feel, smell, or taste that tells us we must take action?

▷ What actions are suggested by this concern?

▷ What is there about the way we handled this situation that should be improved?

▷ What is really troubling us about this situation?

Like the identifying questions, these separating questions are starting points for thinking about and discussing our concerns. Some of the questions may seem to overlap, but each represents a slightly different angle for viewing a concern. Taken together, these questions get beneath the superficial description of a situation to elicit hard data. They shift the emphasis from opinion to verifiable information.

While attempting to separate concerns, individuals may pick up the phone to check facts or verify assumptions. When a team is using these separating questions, we often find that two or three people discover that they have different information and, therefore, different viewpoints about the same situation. Without the separating questions it is entirely possible for people to sit through a meeting in the mistaken certainty that their individual, disparate assessments of a situation represent the understanding of the group at large.

Spend some time ensuring that a concern which appears to be singular is really singular and that everyone participating in its evaluation and eventual resolution understands it in the same way. We have found this exercise always saves time and produces better results.

CONSIDER SERIOUSNESS, URGENCY, AND GROWTH

Only after we have separated complex concerns into their components can we set useful, sensible priorities. In the expanded list of concerns that results from separation, each discrete issue we extract from undifferentiated "basket concerns" can be seen to have its own unique features and claims to priority. For example, a concern is originally phrased as: "Need to hire additional account managers in the Midwestern and Western regions." It is subsequently separated into its components: "Need to hire additional account managers in the Midwestern region" and "Need to hire additional account managers in the Western region." Now we may see whether the priority of one may be significantly different from the priority of the other. This is an important point because it represents one of the recurring pitfalls of priority setting. Concerns must be broken down into their component parts in order to set sensible priorities.

We must also have an organized, systematic way of determining what those priorities ought to be. As managers, we may agree on the wisdom of organized, systematic setting of priorities, but, in practice, this activity remains frustrating and difficult for a great many of us.

"What is the most important thing to do first?" is not a useful question to ask when setting priority. When you ask ten managers to define "important," you learn why. One will laugh and say, "My manager said do *that*... so *that* is most important!" Another will think about it for a while and then say, "The situation that will have the most serious impact on operations if you *don't* deal with it—that's the most important, the one you deal with first." Both answers are fair enough in their way, since they represent disparate but perfectly valid objectives.

A practical and systematic process for determining importance is to consider each concern in terms of the three dimensions listed below. This process can be used in any situation, against any content, and by an individual or a group in pursuit of a common goal:

▷ How *serious* is the current impact on people, safety, cost, productivity, customers, reputation, etc.?

▷ How *urgent* is it to keep the concern from becoming difficult, expensive, or impossible to resolve?

▷ What evidence is there that the seriousness will *grow*?

On the basis of one or all of these dimensions, we can judge that one concern is *relatively* more important than another and should therefore be considered first. Or, we can judge that one concern is *relatively* less important and should be considered later.

When a manager works alone to set priorities, the concerns are usually limited enough in number to be bounced off one another rather quickly in terms of these three dimensions. But when a team sets priorities based on an extensive list of concerns, they should *cut away the concerns that rank low in all three dimensions and designate them for further consideration at an appropriate time in the future.*

A typical large-scale use of Situation Appraisal occurs when a team of managers is considering a great many issues. In such a case, it is essential for the team to identify the few *critical concerns* first. It is within this critical minority that the team must initially determine what the priorities are. When numerous concerns have emerged following separation, we do *not* ask, "How do all the concerns stand, each compared with the others, on the basis of their relative seriousness, urgency, and probable future growth?" This process would be a gigantic waste of time. Anyone who tried to tackle all the concerns at the same time would have no time left to resolve any of the concerns.

An experienced managerial team making an orderly evaluation of the concerns can usually pick out the top five in a relatively short time. Discussion of the three dimensions of seriousness, urgency, and probable future growth would then be confined to assessing those five critical concerns. This does not mean that the other concerns disappear. They are simply set aside until an appropriate future time. Nothing is missed or lost, but no time is wasted working on concerns that are of low priority in all three dimensions today. They may be dealt with safely next week or next month. Alternatively, individuals or teams can be assigned to resolve groups of related concerns.

Why does the setting of priorities seem so straightforward when we read about it, and become so difficult when we try to do it? Managers usually do an unsatisfactory job of setting priorities because they approach each issue as it comes along, on the merits presented by the narrow context of the issue itself. Even if they sense that priorities should be set on the basis of relative criteria, it doesn't seem to work out that way in practice. Internal rules for determining what is important are very gradually developed over a long period of time. We work on one concern even though we *know* we should be working on something else that may have more serious effects, that may be more urgent, or that may be getting out of hand. Why do we do it?

Because of our backgrounds, abilities, and technical expertise, each of us has certain *kinds* of concerns that give off high-priority signals regardless of their relative fit in our daily roster of concerns. Management activities *we enjoy most* make stronger bids for our attention than they may deserve. Concerns that reflect the demands of *demanding people* carry weight that may be totally out of proportion to their importance. They assume high priority because of the annoyance inherent in dealing with demanding people. Everyone's ability to set and abide by reasonable, rational priorities is eroded by these and many other natural human factors.

In the midst of so many demands on our time, it requires real discipline to set priorities on the basis of relative seriousness, urgency, and probable future growth. It requires even more discipline to abide by these priorities, given the eroding influence of the many issues around us. But the results are worth the discipline. Nothing brings home the wisdom of setting rational priorities better than the effects of its absence: *What is more obvious than the order in which things should have been done?*

DETERMINE ANALYSIS NEEDED

While listing threats and opportunities, separating and clarifying concerns, and setting priorities, we focused on *what* needs to be dealt with. In this step of Situation Appraisal—determining the type and amount of analysis to be used—we focus on *how* these concerns may best be resolved, who will handle them, and the *kinds* of answers we need.

We asked questions that would isolate situations of concern that are causing us to feel a need for action. In the separation step we clarified these concerns, breaking them down into components as

THE NEW RATIONAL MANAGER

necessary. In setting priorities we focused on concerns that had the greatest seriousness, urgency, and probable future growth viewed from the perspective of the overall number of situations requiring action.

Of these remaining high-priority concerns, some are easy to identify as subjects for partial or full Problem Analysis, Decision Analysis, or Potential Problem (Opportunity) Analysis. But it is not always so cut and dried. To ensure that we choose the correct technique or combination of techniques, we must ask a few questions about each of these concerns:

▷ Does the situation require explanation? Is there a deviation between expected and actual performance? Is the deviation of unknown cause? Would knowing the true cause help us take more effective action? If there is a deviation *and* it is of unknown cause *and* we need to know cause, we can use the techniques of *Problem Analysis*.

▷ Does a choice have to be made? Is there a dilemma around the best action to take? Do objectives need to be set in order to undertake some activity? If so, we can use the techniques of *Decision Analysis*.

▷ Has a decision been made that has not yet been implemented, and is it necessary to act now to avoid possible future trouble? Does a plan need to be made to safeguard some decision or future activity? Would we see value if a plan or decision was implemented better than expected? If so, we can use the techniques of *Potential Problem (Opportunity) Analysis*.

The *kind* of answer we need determines the choice of Rational Process. *How much* of an answer we need determines whether we will use all of a process or only part of it. We may, for example, understand the cause of superior performance in one sales district of a manufacturing company. Yet it may be useful to draw up a specification, comparing that sales district with all others. In this way, we may gain a more precise understanding of the factors that set that district apart. This situation requires only a partial use of Problem Analysis.

The partial use of Decision Analysis is extremely common. Suppose that the need to hire a manager for a new position has been identified as a high-priority concern. At this time, weeks before candidates have been selected for interview, the company sets precise objectives for the new position. Later, when candidates are available for interview, those objectives will be ready to use as criteria in the selection process. This sequence provides time for review and refinement of objectives by those most concerned with the new position and with the new manager, as well as the impact of both on the operation. It is far more efficient to undertake this partial use of Decision Analysis early in the hiring process than to postpone full-scale Decision Analysis until the need to make a choice has become imminent.

Partial use of Potential Problem (Opportunity) Analysis techniques is called for when it is suspected that a competitor may be about to launch a new product. Responding to a faint rumor with full use of the process, complete with preventive and contingent actions, may amount to overkill. In the event that the possibility becomes a probability, however, a review of potential problems becomes very useful. If, or when, it seems worthwhile to complete the process, the groundwork will already have been laid, and all necessary information will be available.

Time pressure can also cause us to shorten the process. Problems that are urgent are best handled by quickly comparing a few IS and IS NOTs to search for distinctions. Decisions that must be made quickly will benefit from identifying a few key objectives and obvious risks.

What is important is that we have identified and initiated specific Rational Process techniques that are relevant to resolving concerns. The point is not to divide concerns among three boxes for subsequent full application of Problem Analysis, Decision Analysis, or Potential Problem (Opportunity) Analysis. The point is to use those *ideas* from each technique that are most suitable and time efficient for resolving concerns.

Once we have identified the techniques we will use to resolve each concern, we may well have the ultimate in TO DO lists! We will have identified the situations that require action, broken them down into components as necessary, established priorities, and identified the techniques we will use to resolve them.

THE NEW RATIONAL MANAGER

The usefulness of Situation Appraisal, however, does not rest entirely on making all information visible. More often than not, the greatest benefits of the process accrue from the simple habit of stopping to assess the situation. *First,* consciously adhere to the discipline of listing threats and opportunities. *Second,* separate the concerns into manageable components. *Third,* set priorities. *Fourth,* and finally, plan for resolution of concerns that have the highest relative priority.

DETERMINE HELP NEEDED

Most concerns require help from others to be resolved successfully. Rarely will a manager have all the information, experience, judgment, or knowledge needed to carry out the resolution process. And, even if others aren't needed during the process, their commitment may be critical during the implementation phase. Commitment is often difficult to obtain without some degree of involvement, so it may be wise to involve them from the beginning. Finally, resolution of priority concerns may be so urgent that it cannot possibly be accomplished by a single person. Often, responsibility for resolving concerns must be shared or assigned to others. Often, this is an opportunity to expose people to new situations and effective use of Rational Process. To ensure that resolution will be timely and successful, we ask the following questions:

▷ Who needs to be involved for:
      Information?
      Commitment?
      Implementation?
      Analysis?
      Approval?
      Development?
      Creativity?

▷ What needs to be done and when?

▷ Who will do it?

▷ Who will document our process and results?

At the conclusion of a formal Situation Appraisal session, or of any meeting in which the techniques are used as an outline for coordinated discussion of concerns, the end result is that people leave with vital information. They know what concerns exist and what individual components make up these concerns. They know what the priority concerns are and why. They know what their own specific responsibilities will be. They know exactly what techniques they are going to use to attempt to resolve the concerns that have been delegated to them. They know the kinds of questions they need to ask to get started. They know how much time is considered adequate for the tasks they have been assigned. They know how and when to report their progress. They will get the greatest possible benefit from their use of the analytical Rational Processes because they have participated in the best possible use of the evaluative Rational Process.

SITUATION APPRAISAL IN PRACTICE

Knowing everything we need to know about a process is of little use if we do not put the process to use. The following discussion illustrates how some managers have used Situation Appraisal.

CASE HISTORY: "SUE'S REPORTS ARE LATE AGAIN"

We have said that every manager occupies a middle ground within the accumulated concerns of the past, the demands of the moment, and the problems of the future. Let us see how one manager used the techniques of Situation Appraisal to deal with a Pandora's box of complex and overlapping concerns.

A complaint reached the manager of the Data Processing Department for one of the largest banks in the United States: "Sue's reports are late again!" Along with the complaint came a cryptic suggestion: "Put some pressure on. We're getting tired of this."

"I asked Sue a few questions," said the manager. "She agreed that her reports were late, and increasingly so. So we began to break down the situation, going through all the kinds of reports for which she was responsible. That's when I found out that information for a certain customer was nearly always late in getting to her. The delay, in turn, slowed up her output across the board. Now we were looking at a problem that was slightly different from the one presented to me."

Did Sue know why this information was slow?

"Sure, because of the high volume of transactions and errors in that account each week."

Why so many errors in that account?

"That was the next interesting discovery. She didn't know and felt it was none of her business, even though those errors were damaging her own reputation on the job."

What happened next?

"I dropped the 'Sue's reports are late again' problem to investigate the problems in that one account. My assistant and I called on everyone involved. We found twenty-seven separate concerns, including unclear instructions, equipment that couldn't read all the mark-sensing digits, and interference in the optical reader from a black border printed around the customer's checks. Each had to be dealt with on its own merits, and we had to set priorities on their resolution very carefully. Some concerns had to be resolved before others could be understood well enough to work on. A few were self-explanatory, but two problems required full use of Problem Analysis over a period of two weeks before they were understood. Several required Decision Analysis, or at least parts of the process. We did a lot of objective setting in order to come up with better procedures for some of the tasks on that account. If I had accepted the initial complaint, reacted immediately, and done what was asked—'Put some pressure on'— the situation would have been twice as bad in another month."

Today's complaint is often the last visible effect in a long chain of cause-and-effect events. When we use Situation Appraisal and ask specific questions, we can identify actions that appropriately address each of the many conditions that lead to that final visible link.

CASE HISTORY: CRUSHED CARTONS

It sounds obvious, even elementary, to say that anyone who is going to deal effectively with a complex situation must stop and think, not strike out immediately to set things right.

But people are inclined to want to do something decisive and dramatic. "Don't just stand there, *do* something!" expresses a mode of action that sounds better than it works. People also tend to panic, as the manager in the following example might well have done—but did not.

One of our clients manufactures cardboard containers for high-quality food packaging. One day, the sales manager received an urgent call from an angry customer, drove immediately to the customer's plant to investigate the complaint firsthand, and walked right into a blast of invective.

"Your cartons are no damn good!" came first out of the customer's mouth. "We're through doing business with you as of right now. My lines are held up because your cartons are bent and crushed. I've got three rush deliveries I can't make, and those customers have been on our phones yelling all morning. Get your truck over here and take this junk back!"

Is that enough to ruin a person's day? The sales manager counted to ten, took a deep breath, and began asking a few questions mentally:

- What actions will resolve this concern?

- What's going on?

- What is actually happening?

- What evidence tells us we must take action?

The questions yielded the following clarification:

- The customer is frustrated and mad. He's dumping a lot of emotion because he feels I'm the person who will listen to him and give him any real help.

- I must help him get some good cartons as soon as possible to get those rush deliveries out.

- He's losing money and reputation and needs assurance that he'll be protected.

- Something's wrong with those cartons, and the cause has to be found quickly.

- Whatever's causing the trouble must be corrected to the customer's satisfaction so that it doesn't happen again—or it's good-bye, contract.

- If the cause of the crushed cartons is in our plant, this is only the beginning of a major problem.

The sales manager told the customer he understood how serious the situation was and promised to straighten it out to the customer's satisfaction as quickly as possible. He got on the phone and got another truckload of carefully inspected cartons on the way—rush. He got clearance from his head office to cover the customer's losses if the cartons really were at fault. He reported these actions to the customer to assure him that something useful was being done.

Then the sales manager began to ask questions about the nature of the damage: what it looked like, where it had been recognized first, when it had appeared first, and so on. He learned that there had been no trouble until that very morning, and he knew that no other customer had reported any problems with the same carton.

He asked the customer whether there had been any change in material handling in his plant. Yes, as a matter of fact, they were using a new side-gripping forklift out on the loading dock.

The sales manager and his customer got to the dock just as the replacement cartons arrived. They saw that the lifters on the forklift were not aligned for handling the pallets on which the cartons were stacked. The lifters were crushing some of the cartons while unloading them. The customer was satisfied that the cause of his trouble had been identified and that it lay in his own shop, not with the container company. The forklift was adjusted and further damage was avoided. No cancellation of business, no return of goods. The sales manager and the customer parted good friends, the customer somewhat sheepishly affirming that he had received excellent service.

Before the sales manager took any action, he broke the situation into components and sorted it out. He identified six major concerns: customer frustration and anger, need for good cartons, need for protection against loss, need to find the cause of the damage, need to correct the problem to the customer's satisfaction, and need to ensure that the problem was not affecting other customers.

The sales manager quickly assigned priorities: First, do what is necessary to calm the customer's fears. A calm customer will help us resolve the other issues. Second, get good cartons to the customer so he can make immediate shipments. Third, assure the customer that he is protected against wider losses. Fourth, find out what is causing the trouble and how to fix it.

The sales manager decided what kind of questions he needed to ask for each sub-concern *before* he started to resolve the overall concern.

He had saved himself and everyone else a lot of time by taking a little time to think through the situation, instead of jumping to cause for a lower priority concern. Imagine what might have happened if he had set out to find the cause of crushed cartons being sent out from his plant, or if he had stayed in his office while he dispatched an immediate replacement into the destructive arms of the new forklift on his customer's dock.

Case History: A Difference of Opinion

Confusion about the nature of a situation is always a prompt that more separation is imperative before the situation can be dealt with effectively. That is why, during the separation step, we ask whether there is disagreement over the cause or the nature of each situation under discussion. We want to avoid, for example, getting all the way to the point of specifying a deviation, only to find that there is a considerable difference of opinion as to exactly what information belongs in the specification. The following case demonstrates how such separation can lead us toward resolution.

A team of technical people at a tire company was attempting to specify what had been termed "The Sidewall Separation Problem." Rubber had separated from tire sidewalls during use, and now the team was trying to find out why.

"But it's also on the foot of the tire," one person said. "To my knowledge, it isn't," countered someone else. Rather than wrangle over differences, two specifications were begun—one on the sidewall, the other on the foot.

"It isn't separation of rubber **that has adhered**. It is failure to adhere properly in the first place," someone offered by way of clarification. "Not so!" was the immediate rejoinder. "It's torn away from the sidewall!" Non-adherence was a new factor, so it became a third deviation to be specified.

It became obvious within twenty minutes that the reason the sidewall separation problem had never been explained was that three separate deviations, each with its own distinct cause, had been woven together. Separated and individually described, the three deviations began to make sense. The introduction of a new, fast-acting solvent was correlated with the non-adherence complaints—a cause that was checked out and confirmed the next day. The other two deviations were explained within the week. None of the three deviations had been open to explanation as long as they remained locked together.

This example points out the usefulness of thinking through a situation before taking action. But if this team knew how to use Problem Analysis, why didn't they also know how and when to use the techniques of Situation Appraisal?

"We never even thought of it," said one member of the team. "We felt that this was one problem, and there was considerable pressure to get it resolved quickly. We didn't stop to think that people on the team might have differences of opinion as to what the problem actually consisted of, much less that we were dealing with three separate problems. Since then we have made it standard procedure to go quickly through separating questions at the outset of any discussion about a problem. Facts, evidence, effects, disagreements, actions already taken. All those questions. It only takes about five minutes, and it's worth it. It is not all that uncommon to hear more than one version of the same problem. I'd say, in fact, that the sidewall separation problem was fairly typical."

CASE HISTORY: "THE MADGE PROBLEM"

When we determine the analysis needed, we make judgments of the kinds of actions that should be taken to resolve high-priority concerns. The questions we ask lead to partial or full use of Problem Analysis, Decision Analysis, or Potential Problem (Opportunity) Analysis. It is important to remember that two equally critical factors must be considered in making this judgment: *the nature of the concern and the kind of answer that is required.*

Human resources first learned about "The Madge Problem" when her supervisor came to them and said that Madge was upset and unable to work. Why? She felt that people were staring at her. This was so disturbing that she "couldn't stand it anymore." A visit to her workspace showed her to be no more exposed to public view than any of the other ten people in her section. What could be done next?

Was this a deviation from the expected? Yes. Was this a matter to be explained? Should Problem Analysis be used? Probably not. A personal or even psychological cause was possible, one beyond the competence of anyone in the organization (and certainly beyond any legal right of inquiry). Madge had been a good employee. Until the "staring problem," she had never given anyone cause for concern. Could some positive adaptive action be taken? Yes, easily. File cabinets were rearranged to give her more privacy. Feeling less visible, she was happy. The human resource specialist went on to other matters, matters requiring more time and effort than the moving of a few file cabinets.

Not all problem situations demand a precise explanation. Another example of a problem that *does* represent a deviation between expected and actual performance but *does not* require a search for cause in order to take appropriate action would be another rise in the price of gas. "*Why* the rise?" is irrelevant for most of us however irritating the fact may be. The questions that do matter for us are: "What do we do now? What choices do we have? What actions can we take?" In problem situations such as this, the sensible question is not "Why did this happen?" but "What can I do?"

It is also true that there are times when Decision Analysis techniques are not required in order to make a decision. A drive motor has just overloaded and burned out. Cause is known: An operator misused it out of ignorance. The only action to take is replace the motor with one that will work. No Decision Analysis or part thereof is needed. As for Potential Problem Analysis, that's another matter—preventive action has to be taken so another burnout doesn't occur.

Nearly every action has implications for the future. These implications should be explored. After using Potential Problem (Opportunity) Analysis, we may find that there are no serious threats or opportunities around the corner. This certainly is important for the manager to know. However, if something new is recognized, we are forewarned and forearmed. We have an opportunity to take control of the situation rather than have it control us.

It is a rare manager indeed who uses Potential Problem (Opportunity) Analysis to the point of overkill. On the other hand, our experience tells us it is extremely unwise to assume that everything has been fixed once and for all by the most recent corrective action or the most recent decision. Just because Problem Analysis or Decision Analysis has been used skillfully to resolve a high-priority concern does not mean that nothing bad will ever happen again.

Two basic functions are served when focusing on a given situation. First, we clarify in our own mind where we are going. This enables us to allocate our time and energy most efficiently. Second, we know immediately the kinds of questions we need to ask and the kinds of information we need to gather. Everyone reading this book has sat in meetings where the discussion went round and round—now touching on why something happened last week, then on what to expect next, then on what to do about it this week, then back to speculations on the "something" that happened last week. This type of meandering may be expected when people have no pattern to follow, no process for gathering, handling, and directing information toward specific purposes.

Once we have determined we need to know why something has happened, then for the present we are concerned only with questions that will lead us to cause. These will be Problem Analysis questions: WHAT, WHERE, WHEN, and EXTENT, to begin with. All other kinds of questions, speculations, and general commentary should come later, in the proper place and time.

If the answer we require is *which* alternative should be chosen, or *which* course of action adopted, then for the present we are concerned only with questions that will lead to a balanced choice: What are the objectives for the decision? Which are MUSTs? Which are WANTs? What alternatives are available? And so on through the Decision Analysis line of questioning.

If the concern represents some possible future threat, then we need to discover what specific potential problems exist, and we need to identify actions that can be taken in the present to avoid or minimize trouble in the future. The questions we ask will focus entirely on the nature of any potential problems and on the actions we can take to preclude them or lessen their effects should they occur. Only Potential Problem Analysis will be used as long as this future-oriented concern is being addressed.

If the future concern revolves around an opportunity, then only Potential Opportunity Analysis will be used.

When a team agrees that this is the most efficient and productive way to handle the concerns for which it is jointly responsible, everyone—using the same process—respects and contributes to the line of questioning that suits the subject at hand. It is a far more efficient and productive way to proceed than the usual ad hoc approach. This is how one executive in a pharmaceutical company put it: "Some of our groups use a Rational Process format for their meetings, some don't. The difference between the approaches is clear. When I walk into a meeting where people are discussing something in that format, I can tell within a very short time where they've been so far and where they're going next. I do not need a twenty-minute rehash of the meeting in order to figure out what's going on."

CASE HISTORY: REPLACING OBSOLETE EQUIPMENT

Sometimes, as a last resort, a forbiddingly complex situation that has resisted resolution for months or years becomes the subject of Situation Appraisal. This is what happened in a mining company located in the Philippines.

This open-pit mine depended upon a great many vital pieces of equipment that were obsolete, badly worn, and in need of replacement. Yet the company's top managers, 350 miles away in Manila, had failed repeatedly to appreciate this situation. They had never produced a long-term plan for updating equipment. Because the company recently had embarked on an extremely, and increasingly, expensive new mineral development in another location, corporate attention was focused on the new venture. What was desired of the old open-pit operation was a minimum number of problems and an uninterrupted flow of profits. This defined which pieces of equipment had top priority for replacement: those which, if lost, would directly interrupt the generation of revenue.

The operations people at the mine felt that their backs were up against a wall. A formal Situation Appraisal session was convened. Its purpose was to address the overall concern of "convincing top management in Manila to set up a program for phasing out and replacing equipment that is obsolete and no longer economical."

This "basket concern" was separated into three components:

• What equipment are we talking about?

• Why hasn't this problem been solved before?

• What does the head office really want from this mine?

Priorities were established. The top-priority question was the second: "Why hasn't this (to us, overwhelmingly obvious and important) problem been solved before?" What has gone wrong with previous requests? Why doesn't top management see the situation the way we do? Since cause was unknown, this called for a Problem Analysis. In short order, several contributing causes were developed:

• Top management had never been given any coherent, overall picture of the situation that could have led to appreciation of its true importance.

• Top management had always been given **lists** of complaints, but never a sound **plan** for replacement of specific equipment in a specific sequence. Managers at the mine had waited, instead, for corporate staff to turn the lists into a plan and then act. This expectation, it was decided, had not been realistic.

• A documented cost justification specific to the units to be replaced had never been presented to management.

• No credible Potential Problem Analysis had ever been presented to management to show the predictable costs of **not** instituting an equipment replacement program.

Put differently, no comprehensive recommendation for specific action had ever gone to Manila. The real, and serious, issues the mine faced, as a result, might well be interpreted in Manila as a collection of ill-defined and endless complaints—an assumption that was subsequently verified.

The third priority—"What does the head office really want from this mine?" —led to a discussion of the needs and objectives of the corporation. The subject of the new mineral development was discussed fully. Top management clearly was not going to be deflected from that project to react in any major way to the plight of the old mine—unless that plight were presented in an organized, accurate, and credible report. The report not only would have to describe the mine's problem but it would also have to offer a sound, persuasive, organized plan for meeting its needs.

Thought was given to what should be communicated to the head office and how it should be presented. Through a Decision Analysis, it was decided that a written report of the situation at the mine should be drawn up immediately. This report would contain the following:

- A thorough Potential Problem Analysis of present vital equipment, indicating the effect of breakdown on productivity, profit generation, and administrative attention.

- A proposal for establishing standards and measures of obsolescence.

- A listing of equipment to be replaced, with order and priority of replacement indicated.

- A plan and schedule for orderly replacement of equipment, including lead times, production requirements, labor, and other pertinent factors.

- Documented cost justification for each piece or type of equipment to be replaced.

- A Potential Problem Analysis of the proposed replacement plan, with actions indicated to ensure that it would be carried out as stated.

The report was forwarded to Manila. Top management gave it plenty of attention. While they did not agree to every single element of the plan, and not all recommendations were accepted, a positive, orderly phase-out and replacement policy was established.

The mine's managers did not get everything they wanted, but they did get what they wanted most. In a situation in which operating managers had felt powerless, a way of achieving progress had been found. Little or no progress could have been made until they were willing to give up their old definition of the situation—"Top management will not support us"—and replace it with the factual, specific, separated components of the situation. Phrasing the components as questions helped them to clarify the situation further. Priorities were set. They then compiled factual answers to *why* the problem hadn't been solved

THE NEW RATIONAL MANAGER

before, *what* the head office really wanted from the mine, and *what* equipment was of concern. The answers were not entirely palatable in that they pointed directly to deficiencies in the mine managers' previous handling of the situation. But they also pointed to productive actions that could be taken to resolve the situation. These actions produced the top-management response sought unsuccessfully for so long.

Chapter Summary

Far too much time and effort are wasted in trying to make sense of concerns that are unactionable *collections* of concerns, each with its own unique features and requirements. Far too many fruitless attempts are made to resolve these concerns, either because of poorly set priorities or because no one asked questions that would have surfaced both the need to act and the type of action required.

The formal and informal use of Situation Appraisal techniques can significantly cut down the amount of time and energy wasted on misunderstanding and misusing information. By using these techniques, managers set priorities more rationally, even under pressure, and work more effectively because they pay greater attention to the most appropriate answers. As a result, they work more productively in every situation they face. Finally, these techniques enable managers to make the best possible use of the analytical Rational Processes on a continuing and systematic basis.

Situation Appraisal is the starting point for any effective team action. For how can a team of well-intentioned people function if they have not reached agreement about where they are going and which concern to deal with first? Using Situation Appraisal techniques can weld a group of disparate people into a concerted team, with the efforts of all its members focused on a common cause. It brings together the best thinking of all its members and organizes their actions so there is minimum duplication and misunderstanding and maximum effectiveness in dealing with priority matters.

The benefit of Situation Appraisal is preparing an individual or team to take rational action. It results in an enhanced understanding of concerns and an accurate identification of time-efficient, appropriate actions for resolving those concerns. Such results can bring a manager as close to starting fresh each day as reality permits and, over time, can help keep efforts focused on priority issues.

EIGHT

MANAGING HUMAN PERFORMANCE PROBLEMS

IN THIS CHAPTER
A Real Challenge for the Manager
The Most Common Human Performance Problems
Manage or Solve
Trying to Answer "Why Did it Happen?"
Deciding What to Do
Performance Problems: Challenge and Response
Honesty in Dealing with People

A REAL CHALLENGE FOR THE MANAGER

Sooner or later, in talking about daily concerns, a manager will say something like this: "What really gives me trouble are *people problems*." Pressed further the manager defines people problems in terms of performance: *People do not do what is expected of them*. Since the manager's job is to accomplish company goals through and with people, resolution of human performance problems is a key to success.

It is one thing to try to find out why an oil filter leaks, why a paint sprayer clogs up, or why a chemical process unit underproduces. It is another thing to search for the cause of a valued employee's poor or declining performance, and yet another to define appropriate corrective action.

The objective of this chapter is to demonstrate the application of Rational Process (Problem Analysis, Decision Analysis, and Potential Problem [Opportunity] Analysis) to human performance problems. In 1979, Kepner-Tregoe acquired the Praxis Corporation, a firm specializing in a rational approach to improving human performance systems within an organization. The Performance System process developed by Praxis complements the approach we discuss in this chapter.

A piece of equipment has no self-esteem, but the kind of person you want working for you has plenty. Identifying the shortcomings of a machine or a system can have only a positive effect on its future performance. Not so with people! You can successfully use Rational Process techniques to investigate and resolve a wide variety of human performance problems, but you will need far more deftness in questioning, flexibility in approach, and plain tact than you will ever need in handling a hardware problem.

The full Problem Analysis process is as appropriate for human performance problems as it is for all other kinds of problems. *Problem Analysis is a systematic method for understanding the true nature and, therefore, the true cause of off-standard performance.* Problem Analysis focuses the search for relevant and factual information pertaining to a problem. The demand for verifiable facts is as great when dealing with human performance as when solving hardware problems.

During an analysis of unacceptable human performance, there rarely is a "Eureka!" discovery of one difference or change that leads to cause. Cause nearly always points to the work environment, not to the person. Sometimes the cause is complex, involving matters that are private to the individual and beyond the expertise or responsibility of the manager.

In dealing with a human performance problem, then, experienced managers know that identification of a reasonable adaptive action is both a sensible and attractive expectation. The reasonable adaptive action improves the situation and avoids the painful, and sometimes destructive, confrontation no manager likes to think about. Is this taking the easy way out? Hardly. It is the manager's job to get things done. Making adjustments in someone's job and work environment is often the best and only way to help that person become more productive.

Decision Analysis plays an important role in choosing how to change the performance environment. The cause of the problem may lie in the past, but it is what lies *ahead* that concerns the manager. How best to use the individual's strengths and resources to accomplish the goals of the organization? Answering this question requires choosing those components in the performance environment that can be modified, with acceptable effort and reasonable risk, to bring about the desired behavior.

Potential Problem Analysis also contributes to the management of human performance problems in the sense that giving a person a fair chance to perform well is an important aspect of handling human performance problems. If the manager anticipates job difficulties and takes actions now to prevent or minimize them, those actions may spell the difference between success and failure in working with people. Much of what is implied in the phrase "consideration for others" is embraced in Potential Problem Analysis. With both Decision Analysis and Potential Problem Analysis, action taken now will mean fewer problems in the future.

It is inaccurate to speak of "solving people problems." It is more to the point to discuss "managing human performance problems." Unfortunately, we seldom explore the many ways that exist to deal with human performance problems. Too often, we prefer to coast along in the hope that the problem will go away magically. The most creative and humane way to deal with people lies elsewhere. We must *manage* a human performance situation, perhaps by adjusting the environment to arrive at the best resolution for both the individual and the organization.

THE MOST COMMON HUMAN PERFORMANCE PROBLEMS

We once asked a number of managers to give us "the first example of a typical human performance problem that comes to mind." As expected, we received quite an array of responses, some bearing the brush marks of bitter experience. These were the most common themes:

▷ A new employee, who is supposed to be just great, is a complete disappointment.

▷ A person who once performed well no longer does—at least not all of the time or on all aspects of the job.

▷ Performance in one whole department declines steadily over a period of months. There is no obvious reason for the decline.

▷ The same errors are repeated needlessly.

▷ An employee is antagonistic.

▷ An employee is unwilling to take responsibility.

▷ An employee insists on taking more responsibility than is appropriate.

▷ An employee is frequently absent or late.

▷ Employees play politics instead of doing the job.

▷ Employees have a poor attitude.

We will explore most of these themes in this chapter. All lend themselves to various Problem Analysis, Decision Analysis, or Potential Problem Analysis techniques. All imply some performance ACTUAL that is below a stated or understood SHOULD. In each case, some choice of action must be made. Since the management of human performance begins in the past, continues through the present, and extends into the future, Potential Problem Analysis will be appropriate in some form.

MANAGE OR SOLVE

To manage or to solve human performance problems is not an either/or choice. We would like to resolve such problems insofar as we can. At the very least, we want to be able to manage them effectively. Within the body of Problem Analysis, Decision Analysis, and Potential Problem Analysis techniques, we can find a number of contributions to the management of performance problems—and therefore to the management of human resources in general. These techniques help us to understand cause-and-effect relationships. They set guidelines for making important choices. They provide a mechanism for anticipating and avoiding future trouble. And they provide techniques for breaking down complex, tangled matters into simple, manageable elements.

Trying to Answer "Why Did It Happen?"

Defining and Communicating a SHOULD

If a performance SHOULD is to be achieved, it must be clearly communicated to and fully understood by the person who is to perform. A surprising number of apparent performance problems vanish overnight when a manager merely defines and communicates the SHOULD to the person whose performance has been unacceptable. People cannot be expected to meet standards that have not been explained fully.

Describing the Problem Situation

When a problem situation is made visible, we can begin to see the difference between fact and opinion, between reality and speculation. This visibility is brought about by a factual, comparative specification in the four dimensions of WHAT, WHERE, WHEN, and EXTENT. This process requires disciplined questioning and gives us a basis for challenging information that may be biased or untrue. It helps us sort out individual concerns and break apart the unwieldy amounts of information that typify most human performance problems. A tight specification provides the basis for a fair hearing for the individual, regardless of what the situation may be.

In Chapter Two, we presented the questions to be used in specifying a problem. The questions used to analyze human performance problems are similar to those used in Problem Analysis except for some of the wording. The earlier OBJECT and DEVIATION now become WHO/WHAT and BEHAVIOR OBSERVED. There is also greater flexibility in the specifying questions as they are used for performance problems. See Figure 17.

The goal of these questions is a four-dimensional view of the situation. This includes *everything seen and heard* that answers a specifying question and appears to have a bearing on the situation. Any speculations that must be made for a time along the way should be acknowledged as such ("temporary and speculative") until they can be checked out, verified, or discarded.

FIGURE 17   **SPECIFYING QUESTIONS FOR HUMAN PERFORMANCE PROBLEMS**

WHAT	WHO is the person (or group) about whose behavior we are concerned? WHAT, *specifically*, is that behavior? (Include actions taken and remarks made by the individual.)
WHERE	WHERE is the behavior observed?
WHEN	WHEN did this behavior first become apparent? and WHEN since that time did we observe this behavior? (If there is a recognizable pattern in the timing of the behavior's occurrence, note it.)
EXTENT	What is the EXTENT of the behavior? (For example: How many complaints? How great is the effect on the operation? How widespread is the effect of this behavior?)

On the other side of the specification—the areas of close logical comparison in the problem's four dimensions—we follow exactly the same procedure as solving hardware problems. We want to know about the person who *could* be exhibiting the undesirable behavior, but *is not*; the task that *might* be performed poorly, but *is not*; and so on throughout the specification. We will then have a comparative analysis on which to build our subsequent evaluation of the total problem.

CASE HISTORY: "BOB IS NOT MOTIVATED"

The following human performance problem, which we have adapted from a real-life situation, illustrates how this process works. It concerns the high error rate of Bob, an accounts payable clerk in a small manufacturing company.

> "Bob is not motivated to do the job" is the problem statement (and heartfelt opinion) of the manager. He is fed up with Bob's performance. Although motivation may eventually turn out to be a factor in this situation, the term really provides very little information at this point. "Bob IS unmotivated, but others ARE NOT unmotivated."

THE NEW RATIONAL MANAGER

What do we do with that? We need *facts* in order to construct either a problem statement or a specification; opinions and negative feelings are not enough. What is really behind the manager's negative feelings? Two separating and clarifying questions from Situation Appraisal often help a manager spring out of this deadlock: "WHAT specifically makes you say that?" and "WHAT do you mean by that?"

"Why do you say Bob is unmotivated to do the job?"

"Because he obviously doesn't care. He has been able to do error-free work in the past. Now he's content to turn in a sloppy job. His error rate averages 3 percent."

"What exactly do you mean by 'error-free work'?"

"Before I brought him into my shop six months ago, he worked in marketing at the same kind of job and didn't make any errors. And he filled in for Jim, handling expense accounts, and didn't make any errors at all. Now he's inputting the wrong data."

Now we are getting somewhere. We rarely find someone whose performance is poor across the board. Some aspects of performance are bound to be acceptable or even excellent. There is nearly always a considerable range. If Bob's performance had been totally unacceptable in every conceivable aspect of the job, the manager would have fired him long ago and would not now be carrying out a Problem Analysis. But it is sometimes tough to enumerate those parts of the job that are *not* a problem. There is a tendency to ignore what is going well and concentrate only on what is going badly. That, after all, is what needs to be explained. But if the situation merits analysis, then it deserves all the explicitness and objectivity we can give it. To accomplish this, we ask questions designed to get *behind* the feelings, to get to the facts that have produced them.

In specifying human performance problems, comparative information is particularly important because it provides us with insights that may otherwise be unobtainable. If a person does well on one part of a job but not on another, there must be a reason. Whatever the reason may be, comparative information is essential. You develop it from the answers to IS and IS NOT questions: WHO/WHAT? WHERE? WHEN? EXTENT?

"Bob, accounts payable, IS inputting wrong data; Jim, expense accounts, and Betty, accounts receivable, ARE NOT making errors."

"Bob IS making errors now; WAS NOT for over a year when he worked in marketing."

"Bob DOES input wrong data on the accounts payable workstation; DOES NOT make any errors at all on other work, as when he filled in for Jim on expense accounts."

IDENTIFICATION OF DISTINCTIONS FROM THE SPECIFICATION

As managers we provide an analytical approach that focuses on the *total* environment when we identify *all* components of a situation: the sharp factual contrast between the performance of one person and another, or between one task and another for the same person, or between performance in one workplace and another. This approach is far more efficient and significant than one that settles on an individual's shortcomings, as though he or she were isolated from everyone and everything else. Something is obviously different about that one part compared with the other.

What is the implication of such a difference? Does the person lack skill for one part of the job and not for the other? Are the expectations and instructions clearer for one than for the other? Are conditions for doing all parts of the job equally favorable? Does the person dislike something about one part that gets in the way of good performance? If you ask such specific questions, perhaps the person can tell you. Perhaps the person isn't even aware that there *are* differences. Your pointing them out may unlock new information for everyone. Perhaps you can only interpret the distinctions by drawing in other information from your own experience and from the experience of others.

When you have discovered a body of IS and IS NOT information about a performance problem, you have struck paydirt. IS and IS NOT facts seldom appear as coincidence alone. *Bob is making too many errors. Jim and Betty, on relatively similar work, are not.* This rules out factors common to the three employees and points us toward Bob and his unique characteristics. He is younger than the other two, has more education, is ambitious and aggressive. He *is making errors now but wasn't while in marketing*—which was also accounts payable work. But he did other things besides accounts payable, and he worked with another kind of machine. For Bob, coming to his present position was a change to a more mechanical, less varied job. *He makes errors on the workstation, but not on what little other work comes his way*—as when he filled in for Jim.

DISTINCTIONS CHARACTERIZED BY CHANGE

When we identify changes in the work environment, we are providing more than just clues to the cause of current difficulties. Once we recognize that a specific change produces negative behavior or a decline in performance, we can use this information to improve the implementation of similar kinds of changes in the future.

GENERATION OF POSSIBLE CAUSES

Distinctions, changes, and a tight specification suggest possible causes. All causes we generate from these sources emerge from known facts about the problem situation in all its dimensions. They do *not* emerge from speculation about the person's behavior. A tight specification also helps us use our experience as managers. We can tap the insight and understanding we have gained from years of working with people and dealing with other performance problems.

We saw before that Bob makes errors when inputting data on a workstation but not when doing other kinds of work. What is different about inputting data on a workstation compared with the other work Bob is doing? What does this suggest as a possible cause? *Bob is bored out of his mind, entering data on the workstation all day long.* He's young, ambitious, and aggressive. Perhaps he's being underutilized in his present spot. His strengths—as they appear on the IS NOT side of the specification—are that he is cooperative, a good worker (although not accurate with entering data on the workstation), and does a fine job on expense accounts, as he did on his other work in marketing.

TESTING OF POSSIBLE CAUSES

We must remember that bias and guesswork are with us during every workday. A manager may be convinced that the true cause of John's slipshod performance on Project B is that "he's just plain lazy." But if John worked day and night on Project A, and turned in an outstanding report, and this fact is reflected in the specification ("Deviation IS poor performance on Project B… could be but IS NOT poor performance on Project A"), then "just plain lazy" simply will not survive the test against the facts. That possible cause cannot convincingly support and explain all the facts recorded on *both* sides of the comparative specification.

CONFIRMING THE MOST PROBABLE CAUSE

When we formally confirm a problem's most probable cause, we are protecting everyone concerned. Without confirmation we may be tempted to build a case for a particular theory about someone's unacceptable performance. Every bit of evidence seems to fit perfectly, and a lax test of the cause does not give enough grounds for rejection. Only upon verification of the possible cause, when additional confirming information is gathered, does it become apparent that the theory is wrong.

> Bob's manager had him in for a chat. Bob said he liked his job but didn't feel much enthusiasm for it. He said he'd enjoyed the expense account work that he'd done while Jim was away. He was sorry about his error rate and said he'd try to do better. Bob improved slightly in the days that followed, but, as the manager could now see, Bob's heart just wasn't in it.
>
> A month or so later Bob was assigned Jim's job on expense accounts. Jim was promoted to a job he had wanted for some time. The new arrangement worked out extremely well. Much later Bob said he was glad to be rid of the workstation. Asked why he hadn't said something about it earlier, he replied that he hadn't any other choices open to him. He had wanted to keep his job until something better turned up—either with his present employer or somewhere else.

Was the problem solved or managed? The answer is not very clear, but, in this case, it also doesn't make much difference. When specific questions were asked, information became available. This information resulted in actions. The actions improved the situation for everyone. The whole matter began with the manager claiming that Bob was unmotivated; it ended with the department retaining a good worker in a job he really liked and performed well. In another case, asking the same questions might have turned up a fault in equipment, inadequate working instructions, or some other true cause. Here the fault lay in the job placement of the person.

In another case, an underwriter in an insurance company was accused of slipshod work, low productivity, and a negative attitude toward her job. Everything fitted that cause *until* the assumed cause was confirmed. The company found that the underwriter had a case load nearly 50 percent heavier than had been supposed. Neither she nor her superiors were aware of the discrepancy. The case load was adjusted and the problem disappeared. As this case illustrates, managers dealing with performance problems have an obligation to take particular pains in the confirmation of the most probable cause. It is all too easy and too human to see only those facts that fit a preconceived, but incorrect, theory.

Confirmation of a problem's most probable cause as the true cause serves another vital function: It provides documentation in support of a personnel action. It is important to have visible evidence of the entire process by which a performance problem was evaluated. It is equally important to have the reasons for the final conclusion about cause and a record of subsequent actions on file. When an employee is dismissed on the basis of a confirmed cause, many managers file a copy of the related Problem Analysis and subsequent Decision Analysis in the event the dismissal is challenged. This kind of record has been accepted in courts of law as legal evidence that a factual, objective analysis was carried out in arriving at the decision to dismiss the employee.

Hunch and intuition enter into the analysis of human performance problems. All of us have years of experience in dealing with other people, and it is important that we make full use of this wealth of information. It is a priceless resource, bought and paid for the hard way. During careful Problem Analysis we can tap that resource in the most productive manner.

Our research into the management of performance problems tells us that most errors come about as a result of *lack of solid data* rather than through misinterpretation of the data and reliance on rumor and supposition. Given enough solid information, most managers can draw on their experience to good effect. Given fragmentary information or unfounded speculation about a person's motives, the same managers are likely to commit an error.

The key to successful management of human performance problems lies in the *quality* of available information. Problem Analysis, Decision Analysis, and Potential Problem (Opportunity) Analysis demand disciplined, systematic collection and organization of data; reliance on fact; and constant questioning of information. In every problem situation, these procedures for handling and visibly arranging data can only improve our use of experience to interpret information. Intuition and judgment work best from a base of good information.

DECIDING WHAT TO DO

SETTING CLEAR PERFORMANCE OBJECTIVES

In dealing with human performance problems, we must set clear objectives because of the danger that bias and emotion may enter, perhaps unconsciously, to sway our judgments. Objectives state *explicitly*, in visible terms, what we are trying to do. They provide a valuable check on our motivations. In addition, they are useful in communicating our position to other people. Objectives can be commonly understood by a group of people, so the sharing of information and experience becomes more efficient. This is important in managing human performance problems.

Setting clear objectives is also vital in matters of human resource selection and performance evaluation. In human resource selection, objectives form a visible set of criteria against which a choice will be made. They provide all candidates with the fairest possible basis for consideration. In performance evaluation, objectives form a visible set of measures against which an assessment can be made. Objectives constitute the SHOULD for the employee—a set of guidelines against which to model his or her own performance. Setting clear objectives takes the mystery out of working with others and ensures the possibility of satisfactory performance.

Nobody likes to fire anyone. Moreover, by the time a manager decides to fire someone, the investment in that person may already be sizable. There is a certain loss of face, not to mention money, when we have recruited, hired, trained, and managed an employee over a period of time and then have to admit we were wrong: "He just didn't work out the way I had hoped." "She doesn't seem to be right for the job." One attribute effective managers share and respect is the ability to find, effectively manage, and keep the best people.

One of the best ways to avoid having to fire people is to give everybody adequate guidance from the outset, telling them what is expected on the job. Most of the time, unfortunately, no one is quite sure about what ought to be happening: The manager has one set of standards in mind, the employee another. Each has a different SHOULD against which to assess ACTUAL performance. Under these conditions nobody can be completely satisfied with what gets done. One sees a deviation where the other has no inkling that a deviation exists. If both manager and employee understand the same set of standards for a job, they have a basis for communicating about it, for evaluating performance, for discussing changes that need to be made, and for handling problems that arise. *Each person is proceeding from a known, visible, measured framework for behavior.*

Making the ground rules clear at the outset prevents a host of future problems. The more explicit the objectives, the better. Weights need to be assigned to the various dimensions, for all are not equally significant. Although manager and employee may initially see the objectives in common, they may have widely differing views on how much emphasis each should receive. Job objectives are often separated into MUSTs and WANTs: the former are *mandatory* performance criteria, the latter *desirable* criteria. All performance standards should be measurable and realistic.

Some of our clients speak of "emphasis areas"—that is, performance objectives that designate a specific percentage of the total effort.

"Customer service, 40 percent," for instance, means that the employee is expected to devote nearly half of all energy toward this target. It also means that the employee should not go overboard, doing nothing but customer service. The degree of guidance a manager can give an employee depends on the explicitness and quantity of these objectives. Performance objectives are especially helpful for low performers. Such people often have the greatest difficulty in figuring out what the manager has in mind.

One major benefit of clear performance objectives is the hiring of fewer average performers. Once a 50 percent performer is on board and part of the organization, the manager is assured of a constant source of headaches and frustration. However, when the manager has developed job performance objectives for use as selection criteria, he or she has taken a big step in the right direction. The more closely the hired person fits the demands of the job, the more likely will be his or her success on the job. What do you really want this person to do? Equally important, what do you want the person *not* to do?

When a job calls for tact in dealing with peers and clients, recognize this requirement as an important characteristic. Don't hire an abrasive, insensitive person. If such a person is hired, the ultimate fault lies in the organization's failure to do its homework adequately.

Systematically Evaluating ALTERNATIVES

When our alternatives consist of people or of actions that affect people, our evaluation must be especially careful and systematic. How much more palatable it must be to a person to know that he or she has been assessed openly against stated objectives, than to have the feeling that the future has been decided by a mysterious lottery. People deserve the best treatment they can get, and honest evaluation of their efforts goes a long way toward meeting that need. When we manage human performance problems, the communicative advantages of a visible, systematic evaluation of alternatives are enormous. In any selection situation, someone wins and someone else loses. The fact that a *systematic* evaluation has been made brings credit to the organization.

The trick lies in getting pertinent information. Only then do we have a sound basis for making a judgment. Take, for example, hiring decisions. People being interviewed for jobs are on their best behavior. Their responses are slanted in what they judge to be the most acceptable manner. Their abrasiveness (if they are usually abrasive) is carefully controlled. Their insensitivity (if they are usually insensitive) is carefully hidden. Job candidates wish to sell themselves. Consciously or unconsciously, they will do everything in their power to appear as if they are the answer to the organization's prayers.

Past performance can be the best source of valid information—provided that the right questions are asked. Unfortunately, prospective employers hesitate to ask straight, hard questions about a candidate. To make a choice, you need to know how the candidate did behave, or would behave, in typical job situations.

Assessing CONSEQUENCES Good and Bad

In dealing with human performance problems, assessing consequences is an attempt to protect an employee's future against unintended harm. For example, where travel constitutes an adverse consequence, a hardship, and an intolerable strain on a particular employee's family, it would be wrong for an organization to promote that employee to a position requiring a great deal of travel.

All factors must be taken into consideration. Actions affecting human beings have multiple consequences—some good, some harmful. Fairness requires, at the least, that any unintended effects be assessed. The organization should not decide for the employee how he or she should live in the future; rather, it must be aware of how the decisions it makes today may affect the employee tomorrow.

Consequences are not always adverse. Some of our clients have begun to provide affordable, on-site day-care service for their employees' children. The positive consequences of this action—less time away from work, increased employee commitment to the organization, and reduced turnover—have been significant. The search for positive consequences can be a source of added productivity and satisfaction for everyone concerned.

PREVENTING POTENTIAL PROBLEMS

The best kind of performance problem is one that we have anticipated and prevented: The employee is spared unnecessary harm, and
the organization has avoided confusion and disruption. Everything
continues as it should, and everyone's energies are focused on the job
to be done.

Potential Problem Analysis is the prime tool of the manager of human performance. It is usually done implicitly, informally. When a manager must take an action that will affect someone in the organization,
the manager reviews the potential problems: "I won't put those two
together—the chemistry won't be right." "Stratton is relatively new to
the job. He'll need more supervision than the others at first. I'd better
assign Linda to keep an eye on him, help him out." This is the kind of
thinking that pays big dividends. If ever the maxim "Look before you
leap" makes sense, it is in the area of human performance problems.
In all matters of human resource management, the best time to recognize trouble is *before* the fact—not when feelings have already been
hurt, when people are angry and frustrated, and when productivity
has fallen.

PERFORMANCE PROBLEMS: CHALLENGE AND RESPONSE

CASE HISTORY: INPUT ERRORS

Often, in dealing with a performance problem, good management
of the problem requires that the manager pinpoint the true cause of
the deviation; adaptive action is simply not good enough. Such a case
calls for the use of the entire Problem Analysis process. In the following example, what begins as an apparently typical human resource
problem ultimately produces an unexpected explanation. Note the
inadequacy of any action taken, as long as cause remains unknown.

> An insurance company was heavily involved in trusts and retirement funds.
> The investments section in its main office updated client accounts on a
> daily basis. Operators would query the computer record, read the desired
> information from the monitor, enter the new information into the computer,

and send the modified data back into memory. Although this critical function was protected by error-checking devices, operator accuracy was paramount. All transactions were handled on three monitors, and the expected error rate was about 1 percent.

In April of one year, a number of changes were made in the investments section. The entire area was redecorated and made more pleasant for the operators. Dingy walls were repainted in bright, light colors, and new draperies were hung. Equipment was relocated in a more informal arrangement. Many employees commented favorably on the changes, and morale seemed to improve substantially. When one of the operators was promoted, a young woman was moved from a position in another department to take the operator's place on the Number Two Monitor.

By mid-May, it was apparent that the section had a problem with the new transfer. She was a loner. She ate lunch by herself, usually with a book as a companion, and was unwilling to join in office small talk. This irritated several of her co-workers. The young woman was pleasant enough but never initiated a conversation. She did not show much enthusiasm for her job.

Yet she did an adequate job—until about the first of June. At that time her error rate climbed from the normal 1 percent to nearly 10 percent. Her supervisor had a talk with her, and the error rate dropped to normal for a couple of days. But then it climbed back to 10 percent. The supervisor talked with her again. This time the woman responded poorly, complaining sullenly about the work and about headaches. There was no improvement.

By mid-June, the situation had become intolerable. The woman was transferred to another department and a less demanding job. The operator of the Number One Monitor was shifted to Number Two, and a new person, recently trained, was put on Number One. The error rate promptly dropped to normal.

Two days later, the error rate on the Number Two Monitor jumped to 10 percent—although it was now in the hands of a seasoned operator. The error rate remained stable at 1 percent on the other two monitors, one of which was operated by the new, recently trained employee. The situation made no sense at all to the supervisor.

A team was formed to look into the matter and find an explanation for the high error rate on the Number Two Monitor. A meticulous examination of the monitor was completed; nothing was wrong with the monitor. Then a comparative specification was drawn up. The Number Two Monitor was compared with the other two monitors. Its operator was compared with the other two operators. Days of high error were identified and compared with days of good performance. The analysis produced no reasonable explanations for the sporadically high error rate.

The computer manufacturer sent in representatives to examine all the monitors, but they couldn't account for the trouble. The study team returned to its initial specification and asked, in each dimension of the specification, "What could explain this comparative information?" When they considered the dimension of timing, comparing days of high error with days of normal error, someone said, "How about sunspots? We've tried everything else!" Everyone laughed and then someone remarked: "Sunspots... sun... weather... what about weather?"

It was spring. Some days were bright and sunny, a few were overcast and rainy. "So what? It rains every spring, and this is the spring we have the trouble!" But then they looked at the monitors. They saw that the Number Two Monitor was located near a large window in the south wall of the building. And they noticed that the new draperies were of a light color and loose weave. Sunlight! Obviously, on bright days enough light could come in through those draperies to make it difficult to read the display. This could easily cause errors (and headaches). But on overcast days, with less outside light, the display would be clearer and easier to read accurately.

Weather statistics were checked out, and the cause was verified: overcast days were the days that had the 1 percent error rate.

The loner who had preferred to eat lunch by herself, who complained of headaches, continued to hold the less demanding job. For various reasons, the company felt it was "too embarrassing" to return the woman to her old job at the Number Two Monitor.

This can only suggest that more thorough testing of cause should have been carried out *before* the adaptive action (transferring the woman) was taken. Even at that time there was enough information to show that cause lay in another direction. Management of human performance problems demands that we be as accurate as possible in our conclusions. When mistakes are made, the losers are usually innocent bystanders.

Case History: "Our Boy Genius"

No one argues the point that there is great diversity among human beings. Yet when we are investigating a human performance problem, we seldom focus on one aspect of this diversity: the effects of past work experiences on current performance. Even when this information is available, we may be too late in understanding its implications. This mistake is illustrated in the following example.

The space industry expands and contracts in response to the flow of appropriations from Congress. It was in a period of cutback that a highly touted young engineer was transferred from one organization to another. Despite his youth, Roy came with a solid gold record of achievement. His new manager considered the transfer a great coup.

But Roy just couldn't seem to settle down and get things done. When you put him on a project, before you knew it he'd be off on some nutty tangent that had little or nothing to do with his assignment. He seemed totally undisciplined and continually overreached his authority. On top of everything, when his manager finally criticized him for his behavior, Roy was totally surprised—and then he got mad: "I don't get to make any decisions anymore!" His boss replied that was preposterous—Roy had shown no decision-making ability at all since the day he joined the organization. Roy replied heatedly that he had been "knocking himself out" and "doing a great job." The meeting ended on a bitter note.

In the wake of Roy's stormy exit, the manager sat and wondered: What was really going on? Roy's youth? Excessive enthusiasm? Or was he simply a bright nut who had had a couple of lucky breaks in his past job? The manager decided to try Problem Analysis techniques in order to get a better understanding of the "Roy problem."

He carefully specified the situation in terms of WHAT, WHERE, WHEN, and EXTENT. In the dimension of WHERE, he wrote "IS in this organization." He looked across at the space on the page under "Where else could Roy be but IS NOT…" and then stopped short. He had always assumed that Roy's work in his previous job had gone fine. The recommendations certainly indicated that. He needed to get detailed, factual information on exactly what Roy had done before. Setting aside the analysis, he picked up the phone and began to do some research.

He talked to a number of people who had worked with Roy in the past. They all thought he was just great. The manager asked: What had Roy done? Why, he'd held a sort of roving assignment. He was the hotshot who did anything and everything, who probed into whatever interested and challenged him. How had he gotten away with that? Well, at the time, there had been so much work, so many potentially useful projects in sight, so many directions in need of exploration, that Roy's mode of operation was not only tolerated but welcomed. There were always plenty of workers available... Roy was what you might call a minor chief nicknamed "our boy genius" by his colleagues, whom he didn't see very often. He had been the individual contributor par excellence.

Would he be likely to do well in a more routine job? "Roy? Hell, no!" said one of his old friends. "He'd be like a meteoric square peg in a slow round hole...."

Before the manager had time to resolve the problem, Roy decided to quit. He gave the reason that "this place doesn't suit me." (It didn't.) But the manager suspected that he might have salvaged an extremely bright engineer for his organization if he had not waited so long to start a systematic analysis of the problem.

This story illustrates two important elements common to many performance problems. The first element is that the *unacceptable behavior was a result of the positive effect such behavior had had in the past*. In his earlier job, the man had been rewarded for doing exactly the thing that would get him into trouble in a job with very different requirements. No wonder that Roy was surprised and angry when his new boss criticized him for doing what he had always done and been praised for doing. Roy had been unaware that the rules of the game had changed.

Such a cause for unacceptable performance, especially in a new or transferred employee, is so common that it deserves serious consideration. Comparing past and present jobs may bring out the fact that previous rules and expectations are at the core of the problem. As long as such a fundamental misunderstanding exists between manager and employee, any attempt at communication will be fruitless.

The second element common to human performance problems is *inadvertent lack of attention by those involved to what is being said*.

THE NEW RATIONAL MANAGER

When we asked this manager, a year after the incident, "What did Roy have to say about his work situation?" he recounted the bitter conversation in his office. In his Problem Analysis, the manager had carefully listed Roy's faults—unreliability, overreaching of authority, and so on—but he had not included anything Roy had actually *said*. Had he considered Roy's statements as behavior, he might well have followed up on the critical remark "I don't get to make decisions *anymore*" to learn exactly what Roy meant.

The sheer visibility of such a remark can help a manager consider its implications. Then, he or she can decide how best to discuss the problem with the employee. The uncommunicative meeting between these two men (the manager missed the import of Roy's complaint) could hardly provide valuable insights into the nature of the problem, much less its cause. Had the manager used a complete specification of the problem (including words and deeds) as the basis for the second meeting, differences might have been resolved and a mutually acceptable performance SHOULD established.

It is not always easy to determine the relevance of a particular remark. It is essential, however, that we make an effort to understand both its meaning and its source. There is something distasteful about including angry remarks or gripes as part of an analytical process. To many people, such information smacks of gossip. But if the gripe is part of the problem situation, rather than hearsay or secondhand information, then it ought to be included. Someone's remark may contain clues to the cause of the problem. We have to be alert to that possibility and we have to *listen*. A remark such as "I don't get to make decisions *anymore*" clearly deserves attention. It should have been considered as part of the problem's *WHAT* dimension, along with all the other descriptive information on Roy's behavior.

CASE HISTORY: "NOBODY CAN STAND CARL"

Almost anyone can manage great performers—people who always do more than is expected, who initiate ideas, who are blessed with impeccable judgment, who are well liked by everyone. It is the ability to get the best performance from the *average* person that is the mark of excellence.

Carl was a bright young Ph.D., newly assigned to a staff position in a United States Government agency. His competence and enthusiasm were unquestionable, he loved his work, and he worked harder than anyone on the staff. After six months on the job, his manager was about to fire him. Why? Because Carl could not get along with people. Carl had approached the agency with a superb résumé; during his interviews he had impressed everyone. In fact, when Carl first agreed to come to work for him, the manager had been absolutely delighted.

But things had not worked out delightfully. Carl was arrogant with the administrative staff, abrasive with peers, and rude to the agency's clients. Every meeting he attended turned into a shouting match. His behavior had become a grim joke throughout the agency, but his boss wasn't laughing. "I finally checked back with the guy he used to report to, and he said Carl had always been that way. 'Sure, he **produced**, but nobody could **stand** him.' And he had written such a glowing letter about Carl…. Well, that's typical. People just don't like to write negative comments in those letters, do they?"

The manager wanted to find the least painful way to get rid of Carl. As a first step, he specified Carl's performance, listing all unacceptable features in the IS column, and all good features in the IS NOT column. He was using only the WHAT dimension of the Problem Analysis process to make the nature of Carl's performance visible. In this way, he could see how to deal with the problem. It was not a cause-finding effort; the problem's cause was perfectly apparent. The more the manager wrote, the more he thought through the situation and the more convinced he became that Carl—whatever his personality shortcomings—was a valuable employee who should not be fired or transferred!

The information under "IS NOT a problem" consumed far more space than did the information on the other side. For all his faults, Carl was reliable, punctual, flexible, and willing to take on unpopular assignments. He showed great originality of thought and unflagging initiative. As a matter of fact, not only did Carl shine in these areas, he outshone most of his peers.

The manager realized that he had lost his sense of proportion in his obsession with Carl's personality flaws. If he fired Carl, he would lose much-needed skills, with no adequate replacement in sight. For a week or two the rest of the staff would be grateful… and then? The manager estimated that within two months the department would be unable to keep up with its workload and would have far worse problems than those caused by Carl's bad temper and insensitivity. The chances of quickly finding a new employee with Carl's training and ability were virtually nil.

The manager then began a tentative restructuring of Carl's job. It would severely limit Carl's contacts with agency staff and with client representatives while actually increasing Carl's level of autonomy and responsibility. How did he achieve that? Origination of proposals within the department was currently split among five staff members, each one spending about 10 percent of his or her time in this function. Henceforth, the majority of such work would be Carl's. The manager found that plan acceptable to nearly everyone. Besides, Carl preferred that kind of work, viewing it as more creative than the endless paperwork that was second nature to other people on the staff. Carl was also given a variety of responsibilities for other work that was unpopular with his peers but acceptable to Carl. While this was neither a perfect solution nor a perfect plan, the manager now had a workable course of action.

Two months later, the manager reassessed the actions he had taken. The job restructuring, he said, had been successful "to a degree of about 6 on a scale of 1 to 10." Although he was quietly on the lookout for a possible replacement for Carl, the manager emphasized that firing Carl in a moment of anger and frustration would have been a terrible mistake.

We are seldom able to turn the Carls of this world into likable people. As managers we have to work with and through all kinds of people, some disliked by their peers, some by us. But people with unpleasant personalities may possess valuable skills. To use these skilled people properly, we must assess them rationally and dispassionately. By specifying the IS characteristics from the IS NOT characteristics, we begin to put human performance problems more clearly into perspective.

HONESTY IN DEALING WITH PEOPLE

How better to conclude this chapter than to say that one should be fair and decent in dealing with people? And how better to *behave in that manner* than by making full and objective use of the information available, whether it be for Situation Appraisal, Problem Analysis, Decision Analysis, or Potential Problem (Opportunity) Analysis?

Few things hurt people's productivity more than their feeling they have been dealt with unfairly, arbitrarily, and that they have been misunderstood. Asked with skill and courtesy, the kinds of questions used in Situation Appraisal, Problem Analysis, Decision Analysis, and Potential Problem (Opportunity) Analysis cannot help but improve matters for everyone concerned.

CASE HISTORY: PICKING THE NEW CONTROLLER

One of the best examples of such use was shared with us by a president of Automatic Timing and Controls Company. It represents the *management of human performance problems* in an almost ideal way.

The company was in the process of hiring a new controller. Key people in the Finance Department were asked to develop a list of objectives. These were people who, in fact, would be working for the new controller and would be his or her peers. The list of objectives—MUSTs and WANTs, along with the weighting—was developed with some input and massaging from the Management Committee. Therefore, everyone who had a stake in the outcome had a voice in developing the criteria.

Elaborating on the process that was used, the president shared the following story with us.

"We gave the list of objectives to each of the candidates when they came in. They spent the entire first day with the key people in the Finance Department who would be working for them, asking questions and finding out how our system worked. Ostensibly, they were gathering information to enable them to make a presentation to our Management Committee of their qualifications against our objectives, and in light of the job as they understood it. Actually, at the end of the first day, I held a meeting with all of the key people in the Finance Department who had spent time with the candidates, and there followed a free and open discussion evaluating their experiences with them.

"Although I had not promised them the right to blackball any candidate, at least 60 percent of the candidates did not get invited back for good and sufficient reasons that came out of those discussions. All of the candidates who did get invited back had the willing approval of the people who would be working for them. I considered this to be a very valuable attribute of this method, since to a large measure, a person's ability to be successful in an organization depends on the willingness of people to accept his or her leadership.

"Each candidate invited back was asked to make a presentation to the assembled Management Committee, with whom he or she would be working as a colleague. This presentation was to give their educational history, work experience, and other background that would enable us to evaluate and score the candidate on each objective.

"It worked out very well. In my opinion, the most important element was involving the people who would be working for the candidate in the selection process."

CHAPTER SUMMARY

To manage or solve human performance problems? It doesn't really make much difference. The important thing is to treat people fairly and honestly, making full use of all relevant information. This means knowing and communicating the objectives of a job so that everyone understands the rules of the game in the same way. It means asking for, getting, and using accurate information on which to base decisions. A large share of human performance problems is handled by managers who can control and change the work environment in order to help people adapt to the requirements of the job.

Managing human performance problems calls for a compassionate, considerate approach. Potential Problem Analysis, used as a thinking tool to identify and avoid future problems, is of the greatest importance. Bits and pieces of all thinking processes can be used as the situation warrants, to give people the benefit of every doubt. In this way, the rational use of information does indeed allow managers to deploy employees, the organization's prime resource, more effectively.

NINE

Installing Rational Process Within an Organization

ENSURING THAT THE PROCESS WORKS

The examples of Rational Process used in the preceding chapters are representative, not unique. More than three thousand clients have similar examples in their files. Of course, some have more and better examples than others. The near-tragedy of *Apollo XIII*, mentioned earlier in Chapter Three, fascinated audiences when it was depicted in an Oscar-winning film starring Tom Hanks. In reality, Rational Process skills had a great deal to do with averting the tragedy aboard the spacecraft.

Since writing *The Rational Manager* in 1965, we have learned a great deal about the conditions under which Rational Process takes hold within an organization, keeps its momentum, and continues to pay off year after year. Through thousands of discussions with managers, we have learned what they *do* to achieve success with the ideas. And we have observed what organizations do—a month, a year, and five years after the initial decision to install Rational Process ideas—to keep Rational Process alive and working.

There is nothing mysterious about the seven conditions for success with Rational Process that are described in this chapter. Nor can there be much controversy about them. Clients who provide all seven conditions invariably report that they gain substantial, lasting benefits. Those who seriously neglect one or more of these conditions find that the use of the ideas dwindles away. The results that were initially projected or hoped for never materialize fully, or the ideas are used once in a while by a few enthusiasts. No organization wants that to happen, but it is the most likely consequence of the failure to provide one or more of the conditions that are described below.

SEVEN BASIC CONDITIONS FOR SUCCESS

1. *The objectives to be achieved and the results to be obtained through the use of Rational Process ideas have been clearly defined and are understood and accepted by top management and contributors alike. All personnel are committed to their use within the organization—at all levels and in all kinds of situations.*

The installation of Rational Process is likely to succeed when people know what it is they are expected to learn, know how these ideas are to be used, believe that the ideas are useful, and are committed to putting them to work on behalf of the organization. Success is ensured when people know that top management understands, accepts, and uses the ideas and is fully committed to their application throughout the organization. Employees watch their managers. They know that what managers *do* can be more important than what managers *say*. The validity of Rational Process is confirmed when top management shows by its own use of the ideas that the ideas work and have been accepted as part of the organization's way of life.

2. *The Rational Process ideas are presented to those who will use them in such a way that they are, first, immediately recognized as practical and beneficial; second, relevant to their specific jobs; and, third, easy to transfer to the real, everyday situations with which they must deal.*

People do not resist practical and useful ideas that promise to be supportive of their own best interests. People do resist obscure theorizing that has no apparent helpful reference to their lives, threatens them because of its strangeness, and must be taken solely on faith. They accept those ideas that prompt the immediate reaction "I can *use* that…," especially if their second reaction is "I can benefit from using that…." People use ideas that make sense to them and can be applied to their own areas of responsibility. The kind and quality of teaching through which the ideas are imparted are critical to people's success in using the ideas later in their jobs.

3. *The application of Rational Process ideas to real concerns is not left to chance. Rather, it is guided and guaranteed by using real problems and choices as teaching vehicles. Successful use of the ideas on the job is most likely if the ideas are applied at the time they are learned.*

People who learn new ideas or techniques in a classroom or from a book are always faced with the question: "But will it work for me when I really need it?" No matter how great the idea or technique may seem to be, it remains great only in theory until it is used and found workable. If not applied immediately, the ideas that once seemed so clear may be hard to recall and harder to put into practice. That is why the ideas of Rational Process are best learned through demonstration. Relevance—to the needs of the individual and of the organization—should be built into the learning process from the beginning.

4. *Systems and procedures within the organization are modified and redesigned to fit with, and capitalize on, the Rational Process ideas, thus institutionalizing their use. The four patterns of thinking become a fundamental part of how the organization conducts business.*

When the ideas people have learned are unrelated to the way things are done in their organization, they must struggle to find opportunities to use their new knowledge. If their organization acts as a deterrent, a barrier to change, the struggle will be short-lived. When the systems and procedures of the organization have been modified to accommodate the use of new ideas, opportunities abound.

The individual is pulled forward into new experiences, not restrained by the status quo.

5. *Rewards and personal satisfaction are provided to those who use Rational Process ideas to deal with the organization's concerns and decisions, and to those who supervise and manage the use of those ideas. Rational Process thus becomes first the preferred, and eventually the automatic, way of thinking and working.*

People do those things that produce good results for them. When the use of Rational Process is rewarded by the organization, its use will be greater than it would be if there were no reward, no notice taken. When those who manage the use of Rational Process by others are rewarded for doing so, they will plan more uses for the future. Success in using the ideas perpetuates success only when specific, successful applications are made visible and are rewarded.

6. *There is continued follow-on activity to reinforce and sharpen capabilities already acquired, to extend application to new areas of organizational concern, and to reaffirm top management's commitment to the use of Rational Process.*

No attempt at change and improvement that is introduced as a one-shot effort, or that is perceived as such by the people expected to do the changing and improving, can be expected to have any lasting positive effects. The Rational Process ideas represent basic patterns of thinking, not "the latest approach" to problem solving or decision making. Yet use of the techniques derived from these basic patterns depends on follow-on activities. A carefully planned program of extension and augmentation ensures that use of the ideas and their effectiveness will grow with time.

7. *There is continued monitoring and evaluation of the use of Rational Process, assessment of progress against initial objectives, and feedback about results to all concerned.*

Evaluation of results is vital. Beyond demonstrating to management how much of a return is being realized from the investment of resources, evaluation of results provides the basis for further decisions about the use of Rational Process. Feedback of information about successes motivates users, since everyone likes to be on the winning team. A special application of the ideas developed in one sector of an organization, properly communicated, may be equally useful in another sector. Making such results visible throughout the organization does much to enhance success.

THE MEANING OF "INSTALL"

We say that we *install* the ideas of Rational Process. This word has a special meaning for our clients and for us. Acquisition of Rational Process skills is not unlike the acquisition of a major piece of capital equipment. Once it is acquired, you can expect it to work and produce as predicted only if it is properly installed and integrated into the functioning of the rest of the organization.

Rational Process is a set of tools for getting things done, for handling information productively so that problems are solved and successful decisions made. It can and should pay for itself many times over through increased productivity and money saved. Its results can and should be tangible, measurable, visible, and verifiable. Yet, as with most other things of value, what the user gets out of Rational Process is a function of what the organization puts into it, both at the outset and as the months and years go by.

What is implied in installation of Rational Process goes far beyond what we ordinarily understand as training. Training comprises bringing together a number of people, presenting them with a set of material to be learned, then releasing them back into the environment from which they came. Training is too often superficial and short-term in its results. It does some good, but rarely leads to positive, permanent changes within the organization.

Successful installation of Rational Process comes about through careful planning and preparation. The objectives to be accomplished are *identified and actively embraced by top management.* The target population—those who ultimately will use the ideas—is designated, and the sequence and schedule of exposure to the ideas are determined. Internal instructors—those who will teach the ideas to this target population—are selected and prepared. Systems and procedures are redesigned to support continuing use of the ideas on everyday tasks and assignments. Follow-on activities are selected and scheduled. Reward systems are put in place and measurement procedures are developed. These are actions that ensure success.

As surely as a piece of complex capital equipment is installed within a manufacturing system, Rational Process is installed within the system of relationships, roles, and responsibilities that make an organization what it is. Installation, in these terms, constitutes the framework within which the seven conditions for success can be provided.

Two Methods of Installing Rational Process

There are two distinct methods of installing Rational Process. A client organization may choose to follow one or the other, depending on which is more convenient and more compatible with the way the organization customarily operates. The first is the *Organizational Focus* method, in which Rational Process is introduced initially to deal with *specific organizational concerns*. With this method, the ideas are seen as a top management organizational tool for achieving predetermined results.

The other is the *Individual Focus* method. A significant number of users are equipped to work with Rational Process ideas and then are directed toward targets of opportunity—that is, *concerns that lie within their areas of responsibility.*

ORGANIZATIONAL FOCUS

The Organizational Focus method begins when someone at the very top level of management identifies a set of concerns that requires analysis and correction. These concerns are of significant importance to the organization, rather than routine operational concerns. They are persistent, undesirable situations that have grown over time and have never been adequately addressed. It is clear that a major effort is required to solve them and that new skills and approaches have to be developed if the effort is to be successful.

The entire project is planned as an attack on situations identified *before* the introduction of Rational Process ideas within the organization. Objectives are defined. These are: analysis and correction of the target situations, and simultaneous installation of Rational Process as a way of life within the organization. This planning cannot be delegated. It is done by top management, since responsibility for the project must reside with those who initiate it. By actively directing the project, top management makes its support of the ideas evident to everyone. By participating in the project throughout its duration, top management retains control and ensures success.

Working with Kepner-Tregoe representatives, management draws up a comprehensive plan and schedule. The population that can contribute to solving the target situations is identified. Workshops are scheduled. It is in the workshops that the participants will learn to use Rational Process. Later, they will apply their skills to analysis of their assigned concerns. Top management is included in this population. *All* who can contribute share in the learning experience. Teams of individuals who will work together on particular concerns attend workshops together.

Line managers are selected as internal instructors for the workshops. They are taught by Kepner-Tregoe to introduce and install the ideas and to act as process consultants, or resident experts, for the organization. Work is assigned to the participants. This consists of research into the backgrounds of designated organizational concerns, enabling the participants to bring current data to the workshop sessions. Then the workshops are held in rapid succession, preparing a critical mass of participants for effective action. As results are obtained and documented, this information is fed back to top management to guide further direction of the project and serve as a basis for evaluation.

Systems and procedures are redesigned concurrently to support and take advantage of Rational Process. Meetings, repetitive activities, and organizational communications are streamlined to fit in with the ideas. Informal reward systems of recognition and appreciation are set up to motivate participants who have made good use of the ideas. Formal rewards are instituted for outstanding achievers. Follow-on activities are established to sharpen and extend skills.

As the project moves forward and selected organizational problems are solved and corrected, the ideas of Rational Process become institutionalized within the organization.These ideas become the standard way of operating.The individuals involved internalize the ideas which then become second nature to them. They share a common language and a common orientation toward problems, choices, and concerns about the future. Next, other populations are drawn in, exposed to the ideas, and assigned new problem situations for analysis and correction. Eventually, everyone who can use Rational Process productively is exposed to its ideas.

With the expansion of the number of people using the ideas, more daily operational problems are attacked. New targets of opportunity are addressed. Use of the ideas becomes a fundamental part of the way the organization conducts its business at all levels.The measurement of results continues, as does feedback to management and participants. It is important that everyone understands what has been accomplished. In any organization that installs Rational Process, there is no day on which the effort is complete, no end to the program.

INDIVIDUAL FOCUS

The Individual Focus method of installing Rational Process begins when someone at an upper management level realizes that problem-solving and decision-making skills in the organization need improvement.The focus is on the individual users—people whose skills are to be upgraded through the introduction of Rational Process.It is accepted that if those involved in significant matters in the organization deal with those matters in a more efficient and thorough manner, the productivity of the entire organization will increase.

The project is conceived as a human resource development program.The objectives to be set have to do with improving the capabilities of significant personnel. Plans for putting such a program into effect are usually, but not always, delegated to an appropriate staff function.Top management may participate in the program, often to the extent of attending an appropriate version of the Rational Process workshop. But this participation does not entail the deep personal involvement of top management that characterizes the organizationally focused program. Commitment to the usefulness of the ideas may be just as great, but the resolve to use the ideas personally on a day-to-day basis may fall short.

Working with Kepner-Tregoe representatives, those assigned by their organization to plan and organize the program draw up a schedule of events. Individuals to be included are identified by name and position. Workshops are scheduled. Functional, or *family*, groups—people who customarily work together or share information—are formed as workshop teams. Line managers are selected as internal instructors for the workshops and are taught by Kepner-Tregoe to introduce and install the ideas and to act as process consultants.

To this extent, the individually focused program is identical with the organizationally focused program. A major difference between them is the nature of the work that participants are required to do before attending a workshop. In the individually focused program, each participant researches and brings in problems and "choice situations" *from his or her own job.* The participant's manager may become involved in the selection of these situations. An important problem or decision that requires the inputs of several people may suggest that these people should attend the same workshop. In this way, it is possible to mount task forces to deal with specific situations within an individually focused program.

The workshops are then held according to schedule. The participants apply their new skills to their own problem situations, continue to work on them back on the job, and sometimes share their skills with co-workers. The initiative to use the ideas generally comes from the individual user, who is encouraged by the workshop leader acting as a process consultant to push individual or team applications to successful completion. As results are obtained and documented, they are fed back to management. These results assist in evaluating the program's impact and in revising or expanding its direction and purpose.

Systems and procedures may be redesigned to support and take advantage of Rational Process. In the individually focused program, these steps are usually taken in response to individual user demand. They cannot be taken at all, however, until enough people have been exposed to Rational Process to make the steps worthwhile. Since the formation of a critical mass of people able to use and share the ideas is not a keystone of the individually focused program, revision of systems and procedures to fit with Rational Process methods often takes place on an ad hoc basis.

Informal and formal reward systems are set up as additional motivation for those who have made good use of the ideas. Such systems usually have lower visibility than they do in the organizationally focused program. Like the original workshops, follow-on activities reflect the specific needs of individual users.

As more and more people within the organization become users, the ideas of Rational Process gradually become institutionalized as the preferred way of operating. Users internalize the ideas and draw on them as needed. They also share the ideas of Rational Process with others who have been exposed to them. In the individually focused approach, Rational Process tends to be "catching." In one very common situation, we find six people assigned to formulate a decision. Four of them are able to use Decision Analysis, and the other two will be assigned to a Rational Process workshop. In this way, the entire team can use a common approach in arriving at decisions.

Application of the ideas spreads to all levels of the organization until the use of Rational Process occurs routinely in daily situations. At this point, people will be bringing the ideas to bear on organizational concerns faced both by units and the corporation as a whole. Feedback to management and individual users continues. The measurement of results continues.

A COMPARISON AND A RECOMMENDATION

Neither the Organizational Focus nor the Individual Focus method is inherently superior. Those of our clients who have achieved substantial increases in productivity through the use of Rational Process are found in each camp in about equal numbers. Success lies not in how the ideas are introduced, but in the degree to which the seven essential conditions are provided to support and perpetuate Rational Process within the organization.

The Organizational Focus method requires a greater commitment of time and effort on the part of top management, as well as its active participation in the project from the start. That participation must be maintained indefinitely. It implies a higher degree of urgency. It aims at achieving specific organizational results at the outset, rather than later on as the program matures. It provides top management with more control over the investment. Introduction of the ideas of Rational Process usually is rapid and pervasive because it is important to build a critical mass of users as soon as possible.

The Individual Focus method, on the other hand, places more reliance on such staff functions as human resource planning or personnel development. It places more reliance on the individual user to find opportunities for application and to carry these forward to successful conclusion. It provides unit managers, rather than top management, with the desired degree of control over the use of Rational Process. The Individual Focus method is usually a long-term, continuing effort conducted on many fronts.

The choice of method must be made by the individual client organization. Which fits better? Which accomplishes the objectives of the organization better? Which is more compatible with the way the organization chooses to operate? As long as the seven conditions for success are understood and provided, either method produces tangible, substantial benefits for the organization.

Nevertheless, all things being equal, when we are asked to recommend one method over the other, we recommend the Organizational Focus. Our experience has shown that *active involvement of top management* in planning and executing any activity gives that effort a higher probability of success. So it is when installing Rational Process. When top management adopts a new way of doing things, people take note and guide their actions accordingly.

Management involvement, however, is a double-edged sword. If top management appears insincere about the commitment, everyone will perceive that lack of wholehearted interest. Presuming that the Organizational Focus is wholeheartedly embraced and that the seven conditions are met, the expectation for a successful program is excellent. Greater benefits will be experienced, in a shorter period of time, through the Organizational Focus method rather than through the Individual Focus method.

There are hybrid approaches that lie somewhere between the two methods. Some of our clients have begun with an Individual Focus and then moved to an Organizational Focus as top management became involved. In some cases, middle managers were exposed to Rational Process ten or fifteen years ago, within an individually focused program. Now, they are top management, and they control and maintain a Rational Process program that is clearly focused on organizational problems and concerns.

One thing is clear. If an individually focused program never moves to the point at which significant organizational concerns are approached and resolved through Rational Process ideas, the organization's investment has realized only a fraction of its potential. Upgrading of management skills is a worthwhile objective, but we are eager to see organizations realize every possible benefit from their relationship with us. We are equally concerned with upgrading Rational Process programs that have lagged or that have failed to produce results as rapidly and dramatically as expected. Our business is only tangentially concerned with *programs*. It is centered on producing *results*.

RATIONAL MANAGEMENT

The goal of Rational Management is to make full use of the thinking ability of the people of the organization and to direct that ability toward meeting the organization's problems and concerns.

This goal is achieved by giving people the conceptual tools they need to do the job: a set of methods and techniques they can share as they gather and handle information to resolve problems, make choices, anticipate future concerns, and break complex situations into manageable components. In addition, the organization must provide its people with a supportive framework within which coordinated use of these ideas by the team can flourish.

Rational Management cannot just happen. Rational Management must be planned and managed into being as a planned intervention. It represents a major change in the way the organization operates, so it must be introduced by top management. If Rational Management is to succeed fully, a major commitment must be made and particular conditions must be met.

The four patterns of thinking most widely used in the day-to-day work of an organization—finding cause, choosing the best course of action, foreseeing future problems or opportunities, and rendering a complex situation manageable—can be sharpened and made more productive through the installation of Rational Process. When this is carefully done, the productivity of the entire organization increases. Responsibility for quality moves in ever-widening circles from the organization's center. More people contribute in a significant way because they have learned how to coordinate their thinking with the thinking of others for the good of all.

Rational Management presides over no miracles. It releases intellectual resources that have been hidden, unused, or underused. It opens channels of communication among people by giving them common approaches and a common language for dealing with the ordinary and extraordinary situations they face in their jobs. Installation of Rational Process makes it possible for the organization to be closer to what every manager always believed it could be, but too seldom was—an effective, efficient, and dynamic entity.

INDEX

Page numbers in italics refer to figures.

productive use of, 99
purpose/benefits of, 80, 99, 137-38
quick and continuing use of, 137-38
required use of, 128-29
and risks, 79, 94-97, 98, 101
and routine decisions, 102, 128-29
as standard procedure, 129-31, 138
and subdivided evaluations, 121-22
sugar cane processing, 122-23, *123,*
124-25, 126-27
and teams, 138
technique of, 85-98
as transferable skill, 4-5
and types of decisions, 101-2
uses of, 101-38
and yes and no decisions, 102, 109-16
Decision making. *See also* Decision
Analysis; Decisions and team building
Decision statement, 80-81, 85, 86, 123,
130, 131
Decisions
complex, 102-3, *104-7,* 108-9
requiring action, 74-75, 170-72
routine, 102, 128-29
and team building, 4-8
types of, 101-2
yes and no, 102, 109-16
Departmental performance decline, 196
Desirable performance criteria, 204-6
Deviation, performance, 22, 24, 25, 29,
30, *33, 36,* 45, 65, 67, 70, 75, 177,
184-86, 197, 208.
See also Distinctions
Differing opinion, 184-85
Distinctions
and human performance, 200-201
and Problem Analysis, 26, 34-35, *36-37,*
38, *39,* 40, 45, 56, 59, 61-62, 65,
66-67, 70-71
separating from specification, 200-201
Documentation, process and results, 179
$27 solution, 65-67

Effect, primary/secondary, 155-57, *155, 156*
Effectiveness, organizational, 1-8
8:30 arrival, 63-64
Emergencies, likely, 160-61, 181-84
Emphasis areas, 205
Employees
average performer, 206
firing of, 205
hiring of, 129-30, 206, 207, 216-17
new, 195
SHOULD, 205
Error, repetition of, 196
Evaluation
and choices, 79, 116-21
comparative, 91, 108
results, 222
Situation Appraisal as tool for, 167-69
subdivided, 121-22
Expectations
employer, 193-95
and Problem Analysis, 63-67
Expensive question (orange crystals),
135-36

Failure, in Problem Analysis, 44
Failing pumps, 69-72
Feeding the cattle, 61-63
Firing employees, 205
Florida Power and Light Co., 121-22,
132-34
Food packaging, 181-84
Future events. *See also* Potential Problem
(Opportunity) Analysis
and their consequences, 139-42
Situation Appraisal and, 171, 176
thinking about, 10, 13

Goals
and Potential Problem (Opportunity)
Analysis, 142

review of, 171
and team building, 3
and thinking patterns, 9
Government
case histories about, 70-72, 109-13
and Decision Analysis as standard
procedure, 129-30
inauguration planning (government
laboratory), 145-53
irrigation project of, 69-72
and water quality management, 109-13
and yes/no decisions, 109-13
Groups, and teams, 2-3, 227

Help needed, determining necessary, 169,
179-80
Hiring
controller, 216-17
employees, 129-30, 206, 207, 216-17
objectives, 129-30
R&D director, 79-80, 81
Honesty with people, 215-16
Human performance problems
Automatic Timing and Controls Company,
216-17
case histories
controller, hiring of, 216-17
input errors (computer operator),
208-10
insurance underwriter caseload, 203
obnoxious personality (Carl),
213-15
unacceptable behavior (Roy),
211-13
unmotivated clerk (Bob), 198-203
common, 195-196
computer operator as loner, 208-10
data entry error rate, 198-203
manage or solve, 196
managing, 215-17
specifying, 197-98, 199

Human resources, development of, 226-27,
229
Hunches, 27-28, 203-4

Ideal, and Decision Analysis, 108, *119*, 121-
22
distribution system, 116-18, *119*, 120-
121
Ideas
and conditions for workable change, 8
introducing new, 7
of Problem Analysis process, 51
support for new, 8
Identical unit output, 65-67
Imminent strike, 72-74
Impact, preparing for, 143, 155
Imperial Oil of Canada, 164-65
Importance, definition of, 174-75
Improvement, search for, 171
Inadequately handled situations, 171
Inauguration planning (government
laboratory), 145-53
Individual focus, of Rational Process, 226-
28
Information quality, 204
Input errors (computer errors), 208-10
Installing Rational Process, 5-8
Insurance underwriter caseload, 203
Intention versus process, 149
Intervention, planned, 7, 8
Intuition, 203-4
Involvement, identifying other, 169, 179-80
Irrigation project, 69-72
IS and IS NOT comparisons
and human performance, 199, 200-201
and Problem Analysis, 31-32, *33*, 34, 35,
36-37, 38, 45, 53, 59, 62, 65, 67, 68
and Situation Appraisal, 178
Issues
overlapping, 168
separation and clarification of, 172-73

Panic, 59
Paper manufacturing company, 140-41, 143
Paper and wood products company, 116-18,
    119, 120-21
Performance deviations. *See* Deviations,
    performance
Performance objectives. *See* Objectives
Performance standards, 24. *See also* Ideal
Personnel. *See* Employees; Human
    performance problems
    personnel information system, purchas-
    ing best, 86-98
Planning, annual team, 171
Politics versus work, 196
Potential Problem (Opportunity) Analysis
    and actions, 142, 143, 144, 149-50,
        151-53
    and adverse consequence thinking, 144
    and alternatives, 144
    basic activities of, 142-53
    basic questions in, 142, 165
    case histories,
        aircraft service facility opening,
            163-64
        Alaskan oil searching, 164-65
        cost of complacency, 140-41, 143
        crisis averted, diplomatic, 161-63
        inauguration planning (government
            laboratory), 145-53
        likely emergency, 160-61
        Sayers Point Mill closing, 154-59
    and change, 144-45
    chemical mill closing, 154-59
    and causes, 142, 148-50
    and consequences of future events,
        139-42
    and Decision Analysis, 144, 153
    focus of, 143-45
    and goals, 142
    human performance and, 208
    Imperial Oil of Canada, 164-65
    and listing of potential problems or
        opportunities, 142, 146-48, 161

North Atlantic Treaty Organization
    (NATO), 162-63
    overview of, 15
    paper manufacturing company, 140-41,
        143
    and Problem Analysis, 153
    and risks, 144
    and stating the action, 145-46
    and vulnerabilities, 146-48
    as different kind of process, 153-59
    partial use of, 178, 185
    purpose/benefits of, 140, 141, 152-53,
        159, 165-66
    responsibility for, 154-59, 161-63
    street riots, 160-61
    Vietnam War, 162-63
    whale habitat, 164-65
    when to use, 159-65
Priorities
    human factors in, 176
    setting, 168, 174-76, 188-91
    and thinking patterns, 10
Problem Analysis. *See also* Potential
    Problem (Opportunity) Analysis
    abbreviated use of, 56-63
    Bank in Hawthorne, 52-54
    benefits of, 22, 44-47, 75
    case histories,
        Apollo XIII, 57-60
        bank accounts shrinking, 52-54
        circuits rejected, 55-56
        $27 solution, 65-67
        imminent strike, 72-74
        leaking soybean oil filter, 26-43
        NASA contract dispute, 74-75
        on-time misunderstanding, 63-64
        pumps failing, 69-72
        sewing machine sales (Model A),
            67-69
        spoiled cattle feed, 61-63
        spray nozzles, plugged, 60
    and causes of problems, 22-23, 26,
        34-43, 45-47

and change, 35, 38, *39,* 40, 45, 52-54,
  62-63
and choices, 26
and comparison data, 31-32, *33*
and conditions and skills of problem
  solving, 21-24
Day one deviation, 25, *25,* 65, 67
and defining the problem, 23-24, 26
determining and verifying most probable
  cause in, 26, 43-44
and distinctions, 26, 34-35, *36-37,* 38,
  39, 40, 45, 56, 59, 61-62, 65, 71
8:30 arrival, 63-64
and expectations, 63-67
experience and, 27-28, 34, 45
failure in, 44
feeding the cattle, 61-63
and habit of problem solving, 49-51
human performance and, 194
identical unit output, 65-67
irrigation project, 69-72
and IS and IS NOT comparisons, 31-32,
  33, 34, 35, *36-37,* 38, 45, 53, 59, 62,
  65, 67, 68
as legal evidence, 203
and managerial questioning, 51-56
overview of, 14
partial use of, 177, 185
and performance standards, 24
and Potential Problem (Opportunity)
  Analysis, 153-54
process of, 26-47
proper use of techniques of, 54-56
skills for, 21-24
and specifying the problem, 30-32, 33
speculation and, 51, 54, 57-60, 73, 197
and stating the problem, 29, *33, 36-37,*
  39, 45
strike imminent, 72-74
and structure of problems, 24-25, *25,* 35,
  44
and testing of possible causes, 26, 41-42,
  46, 51, 202

uses of, 49-75
Problems. *See also* Potential Problem
  (Opportunity) Analysis; Problem
  Analysis
defining, 23-24, 26
describing, 197-200
identification of, 14
listing potential, 142, 146-48, 161
specifying, 30-32, *33, 36-37,* 197
stating, 29, *33, 36-37, 39,* 45
structure of, 24-25, *25,* 35, 44
Procedures
  and installing Rational Process, 224-25,
    228
  intention versus, 147
  Potential Problem (Opportunity) Analysis
    and, 149,153-59
  systematic, 78-79
Process questions, 137
Process trinkets, 54

Questions
  answers versus, 55
  basic Potential Problem (Opportunity)
    Analysis, 142, 165
  of managers, 51-56
  and Problem Analysis, 30-32, *33, 36-37*
  process, 137
  specifying, 30-32, *33, 36-37,* 197

R&D director, hiring of, 79-80, 81
Rational management. *See also* Decision
    Analysis; Potential Problem
    (Opportunity) Analysis; Problem
    Analysis; Situation Appraisal
  application of, 18-19
  overview of, 19-20
  premises of, 1-20
  summary about, 230-31
The Rational Manager (Kepner and Tregoe,
    1965), 2, 96, 219

performance, 24
Street riots, 160-61
Strike imminent, 72-74
Sugar cane processing, 122-23, *123, 124-25,* 126-27

Tact, dealing with, 206
Teams
    application of model to, 18-20
    and benefits of good teamwork, 8-9
    building, 3-8, 15-20
    case history about, 5-8
    and change, 7
    coordination of, 4
    and Decision Analysis, 138
    and decision making, 4-8
    definition of, 2-3
    goals of, 3
    and groups, 2-3, 227
    meetings, 188
    and models of superior teamwork, 16-18
    and Problem Analysis, 67-75
    rise and fall of, 15-18
    and thinking patterns, 9-13, 16
Thinking. *See also* Thinking patterns
    adverse consequence, 102, 134-38, 144
    cause-and-effect, 9, 11, 14, 22-23,
        34-41, 75, 180-81
    clarification of, 9, 10
    coordinated, 8
    level of skill in, 16
Thinking patterns
    and anticipating the future, 10, 12-13
    basic, 9-13
    cause-and-effect, 9, 11-12, 14, 22-23,
        34-41, 75, 180-81
    and change, 10, 11
    and choices, 9, 12-13, 78-79
    and goals, 9
    Potential Problem (Opportunity) Analysis
        as, 165
    Problem Analysis and, 22-23

and teams, 9-13, 16
Threats, listing of, 169, 170-72
Time-line, 147
Time pressure, 178
Timing, performance deviation, 55-56
Tire separation problem, 184-85
TO DO list, 178

Unacceptable behavior (Roy), 211-13
Unexplored situations, 171
Unmotivated clerk (Bob), 198-203
Unsolved problems, 171
Urgency consideration, 169, 174-76, 233

Vietnam War, 162-63
vulnerability, 146-48, 155

WANT objectives
    alternatives and, 89-93, *92-93, 94-95,
        104-5, 106-7,* 123, *124-25*
    complex decision, 104, 106
    evaluating distribution system merit and,
        119
    and techniques of Decision Analysis,
        82-83, 85, 86, 87-88, 89-93, *92-93,
        94-95,* 110-13, 117-18, *119,* 123,
        124-25, 130, 131, 132-33, 137
Water quality management, 109-13
Weighted scores. *See also* MUST objectives;
    WANT objectives; *specific case
    history*
    alternative development and, 124-25
    and complex decision, 104-7
    hiring and, 130
    measured against model, 119-20
    total, 92-93
Whale habitat, 164-65

Yes/No decisions, 102, 109-16

ABOUT THE AUTHORS

Charles H, Kepner, Ph. D., cofounded Kepner-Tregoe, Inc. in 1958 along with Benjamin B. Tregoe. Based in Princeton, New Jersey, the organization specializes in strategic and operational decision making. Dr. Kepner served as vice chairman of Kepner-Tregoe until his retirement in 1983. He is coauthor of *The Rational Manager,* a landmark book of management methodology.

Benjamin B. Tregoe, Ph. D., is chairman emeritus of Kepner-Tregoe, Inc. Dr. Tregoe has helped executives in the United States, Canada, Latin America, and the Far East set strategy and install Rational Processes in their organizations. He is a leading lecturer whose articles have appeared in business journals throughout the world. Dr. Tregoe is coauthor of *The Rational Manager; Top Management Strategy;* and *Vision in Action.*